MILTON STUDIES

XLI

MILTON STUDIES

XLI *Edited by*
Albert C. Labriola

UNIVERSITY OF PITTSBURGH PRESS

MILTON STUDIES

is published annually by the University of Pittsburgh Press as a forum for Milton scholarship and criticism. Articles submitted for publication may be biographical; they may interpret some aspect of Milton's writings; or they may define literary, intellectual, or historical contexts—by studying the work of his contemporaries, the traditions which affected his thought and art, contemporary political and religious movements, his influence on other writers, or the history of critical response to his work.

Manuscripts should be upwards of 3,000 words in length and should conform to *The Chicago Manual of Style*. Manuscripts and editorial correspondence should be addressed to Albert C. Labriola, Department of English, Duquesne University, Pittsburgh, Pa., 15282–1703. Manuscripts should be accompanied by a self-addressed envelope and sufficient unattached postage.

Milton Studies does not review books.

Within the United States, *Milton Studies* may be ordered from the University of Pittsburgh Press, c/o CUP Services, Box 6525, Ithaca, N.Y., 14851, 607–277–2211.

Published by the University of Pittsburgh Press, Pittsburgh, Pa. 15260

Copyright © 2002 by the University of Pittsburgh Press

Manufactured in the United States of America

Printed on acid-free paper

10 9 8 7 6 5 4 3 2 1

ISBN 0-8229-4189-9

ISSN 0076-8820

CONTENTS

MILTON STUDIES
XLI

RECONSIDERING CHRONOLOGY IN *PARADISE LOST*

Anthony Welch

I

STRUGGLING TO PIECE together a time scheme for *Paradise Lost*, Thomas Newton finally threw up his hands on the matter: "It is not easy to state and define the time exactly," he complained in 1749, "since our author himself seems not to have been very exact in this particular."[1] Although Newton settled for an eleven-day chronology of events in *Paradise Lost*, he found several passages in the poem that threatened to scuttle his efforts at a day-for-day timeline. Milton's structural and numerological interventions in *Paradise Lost* have since received intense scholarly attention. On the question of chronology alone, a number of efforts have followed Newton's: a thirty-one-day chronology by Grant McColley, a twenty-eight-day time scheme by Galbraith Miller Crump, and other tallies by Douglas Northrop, Sherry Lutz Zivley, Gunnar Qvarnström, and Alastair Fowler.[2] All of these have taught us about the structural ordering of Renaissance epic. They have also tended to downplay the chronological roadblocks that so preoccupied Newton and other early readers of *Paradise Lost*. The most comprehensive and most influential of the chronologies is Alastair Fowler's thirty-three-day timeline from the exaltation of Christ in heaven to the exile of Adam and Eve from paradise. This essay glances at the other timelines mentioned, but focuses on teasing out the few stray threads in Fowler's grand chronological weave. I suggest that each of the chronologies quietly struggles with its intractable materials, moments of lapse and confusion that cannot be explained away. Rather than simply propose another overarching chronology, I join Newton in arguing that the idea of chronology itself needs rethinking. Ironically, it is the telling gaps in the poem's timeline that I think can best help us to establish how time and chronology function in *Paradise Lost*.

Writing some decades before Newton, Joseph Addison shows that his generation was also alert to the organization of time in epic poetry. Nevertheless, Addison dismisses out of hand a chronology of Milton's poem:

The modern Criticks have collected from several Hints in the *Iliad* and *Aeneid* the Space of Time, which is taken up by the Action of each of those Poems; but as a great

1

Part of *Milton's* Story was transacted in Regions that lie out of the Reach of the Sun and the Sphere of Day, it is impossible to gratifie the Reader with such a Calculation, which indeed would be more curious than instructive; None of the Criticks, either Antient or Modern, having laid down Rules to circumscribe the Action of an Epic Poem with any Determined Number of Years, Days, or Hours.[3]

While Dryden, Rymer, and others bickered about the precise application of the Aristotelian unities to English drama, the rules for how epic poets should dispose of time benefited from no ancient authority. Addison is responding most directly to René Le Bossu, the French neoclassicist who had famously declared that Homer "has made an exact journal of the time he allows in his two Poems," the action of the *Iliad* and *Odyssey* taking forty-seven days and fifty-eight days respectively.[4] Le Bossu's pronouncements heavily influenced the English neoclassicists' speculations on the proper length of the epic plot. But Le Bossu had trouble with his own literary authorities. In his famous treatise, he concedes that Aristotle set down no clear rules for the duration of epic action; furthermore, even if Homer's chronologies can be worked out with some precision, those of Virgil's *Aeneid* cannot. Because classical theory was silent on the issue and classical practice was inconsistent, Le Bossu is forced to conclude that "the precise time of the *Epopéa* admits of dispute."[5] Epic poets of the sixteenth and seventeenth centuries need have felt little obligation to concern themselves with strict chronology so long as their story comprised a unified action, beginning dutifully in medias res and bulwarked by pleasing digressive episodes. Even some of those obligations were perhaps more honored in the breach than the observance; Le Bossu's English translator singles out his countrymen for their "notorious neglect of following the Rules which *Aristotle* and *Horace* have prescrib'd."[6]

Milton himself, some decades before the English critics had begun reading their Le Bossu, had looked instead to "the *Italian* Commentaries of *Castelvetro, Tasso, Mazzoni*, and others" to learn "what the laws are of a true *Epic* poem, what of a *Dramatic*, what of a *Lyric*, what decorum is, which is the grand master peece to observe."[7] The Italian critics do touch on the proper duration of the epic plot, if only in passing. Tasso maintains that a complex plot is limited only by the time it takes to work out the story's full arc (for example, performing a full reversal of fortune from end to end). In a simple plot, the time frame should correspond to the amount of action that can reasonably be retained in the reader's memory as the story unfolds.[8] For his part, Castelvetro explicitly contrasts the unities of drama with the looser structures of epic. A tragedy, he explains, spans no more than "one whole day, that is, twelve hours," while an epic poem can extend anywhere from a few hours to "an indeterminate number of days" ("più giornate senza certezza d'alcun numero").[9] The Italian theorists celebrated the epic's capacity to range over unfamiliar regions of space and time, unaffected by the mimetic constraints of the theatre. In practice as well as in theory, Milton's immediate epic predecessors—Ariosto, Tasso, Marino, Spenser, Davenant—preferred the loose *entrelacement* of plot episodes to the step-by-step forward motion of Homer's *Iliad*. The *Divine Weeks* of Du Bartas openly flouts lockstep readings of chronology. After the six divine days of creation are described, each subsequent 'day' figuratively incorporates whole centuries of Old Testament history.

II

As we turn to Book One of *Paradise Lost*, we find ourselves in a region as strange as any in Homer's epics—and, as we shall see, a region where time itself becomes dauntingly unfamiliar. But in these famous first moments it seems that the narrator will at least give us a chronological signpost to cling to:

> Nine times the Space that measures Day and Night
> To mortal men, hee with his horrid crew
> Lay vanquisht, rolling in the fiery Gulf
> Confounded though immortal; But his doom
> Reserv'd him to more wrath; for now the thought
> Both of lost happiness and lasting pain
> Torments him; round he throws his baleful eyes
> That witness'd huge affliction and dismay
> Mixt with obdurate pride and steadfast hate[.]   (PL 1.50–58)[10]

The obvious chronological point is that the devils lie on the burning lake for nine days. This and other signals invite Milton's chronologists to stitch these first hellish moments into a single, continuous timeline that spans hell, heaven, chaos, and Paradise. The underlying assumption is so straightforward that it seems hardly worth making explicit: that Milton measures time equally across these varied landscapes. But even as we learn that the devils have been lying vanquished for "nine days" as mortals measure time, the remarkable circumlocution reminds us that hell itself has no day or night to measure by. For the fallen angels, their temporal disorientation signaled by the passage's restlessly swiveling verb tenses, time here plays out as a shifting landscape akin to "space." This *spatium*, pivoting between space and time, registers the devils' spatial distance from heaven, the temporal gap between the 'now' of their lasting torment and the 'then' of their lost happiness, and most especially the physical barriers of time and space that thwart the ability of "mortal men" to appreciate the magnitude of either distance.[11]

This nearly self-defeating chronological moment encapsulates the rebel

angels' experience of time in hell. Milton imagines time here as movement
without change, duration without sequence. As the devils "roll" on the burning lake, they also roll backward and forward through time, tossed between
remembered happiness and present torment. Like the unceasing pain meted
out by Sin's hellhounds, "hourly conceiv'd / And hourly born" (2.796–97), the
devils' suffering spans untold revolutions of "irksome hours" (527). Any possibility of change here is indefinitely deferred. Dryden picks up this sense of
time as stagnant, rolling repetition in *The State of Innocence*, when his Lucifer groans, "Before yon' Brimstone-Lake thrice ebb and flow, / (Alas, that we
must measure Time by woe!)."[12] The narrator's distancing language in Books
One and Two describes time in hell by the only means possible: a gesture at
mortal measurement that only demonstrates the futility of attempting that
same measurement. If even angels cannot find their bearings in this new
landscape, we humans cannot expect to do so.

Does the foreignness of Milton's hell really matter to his chronology of
events? For Fowler (as well as McColley, Crump, and Qvarnström), hell and
paradise and heaven may differ profoundly in many respects, but Milton is
practical-minded enough to make heavenly days and hellish days functionally
equivalent to earthly days in order to make his plot unfold along a continuous
timeline. Convenient though it is, this assumption inadvertently elides Milton's systematic distinctions between the universe of Adam and Eve and the
poem's other settings—such as chaos, "where length, breadth, and highth, /
And time and place are lost" (2.893–94). This is the problem that Addison
intuits when he refers to the far-flung "Regions that lie out of the Reach of
the Sun" that somehow resist chronology. As we shall see, only in paradise
before the Fall does a conventional chronology operate, free of the temporal
lapses and lacunae that intrude on the action everywhere else. Those important gaps in time grow out of the distinct character of 'day' in each place,
which a global chronology effectively collapses. Sherry Lutz Zivley acknowledges that there are moments in *Paradise Lost* when "the story time is not
obvious." "Nevertheless," she continues, "Milton specifies exactly when all
events occur."[13] But when our local *experience* of time strains against the
numbers, we should consider whether smaller-scale readings of chronology
would better serve Milton's purposes and our own.

Another moment in hell provides an extreme example of this problem.
Here, literal and figurative time measurement strain against each other:

> And here let those
> Who boast in mortal things, and wond'ring tell
> Of *Babel*, and the works of *Memphian* Kings,
> Learn how thir greatest Monuments of Fame,
> And Strength and Art are easily outdone

> By Spirits reprobate, and in an hour
> What in an age they with incessant toil
> And hands innumerable scarce perform.   (1.692–99)

On this evidence, both Fowler and Qvarnström clock the building of Pandemonium at one hour.[14] Yet it seems clear that "in an hour," with its indefinite article, contrasts the little time of this angelic engineering marvel with its puny human analogue, the construction of the pyramids for a whole "age" of "incessant" work by "innumerable" hands. This sense of "hour" is "used somewhat indefinitely for a short space of time, more or less than an hour" (*OED* "hour" 2a). The same usage appears in *Samson Agonistes*, when Manoa laments over Samson: "Select, and Sacred, Glorious for a while, / The miracle of men: then in an hour / Ensnar'd, assaulted, overcome, led bound" (363–65). In the Pandemonium passage, Milton sets the reader's own moment against the remote historical age of the Pharaohs, itself difficult enough to conceive, and then scorns to compare even that lost age with a prehistoric "hour" that is categorically irrecoverable. It is precisely the tension between this highly figurative "hour" of angelic labor and our very human conception of a sixty-minute interval that structures the rhetorical coup. By citing this figurative instance as a marking of mundane clock-time, Fowler and Qvarnström only highlight the determined way in which Milton's hell parries our efforts to exploit such chronological clues.

III

Time in Milton's heaven operates according to different principles. Unusually, Milton insists that time passes and has always passed in some recognizable sense in heaven: a position in conflict with the majority view, both classical and ecclesiastical, that time began only with the creation of our universe. Defiantly facing down authorities from Plato to Augustine, the *De Doctrina Christiana* states that "there is certainly no reason why we should conform to the popular belief that motion and time, which is the measure of motion, could not, according to our concepts of 'before' and 'after,' have existed before this world was made."[15] Whether or not the *De Doctrina* should be taken into evidence, this doctrine explicitly makes its way into *Paradise Lost*. As Raphael describes heaven to Adam, he notes in an Aristotelian aside that "Time, though in Eternity, appli'd / To motion, measures all things durable / By present, past, and future" (5.580–82). How does this impact on the poem's chronology? As Fowler, McColley, and others have noted, there are four consecutive days of narrated action in Milton's heaven: the exaltation of the Son on the first day leads to three days of war, ending with the rebels' expulsion and the victors' rejoicing. According to Fowler, "in

spite of the difficult theology involved M[ilton] is bound to continue comput-
ing the days of the action, even when it does not take place on the earth, for
the sake of his numerological structure."[16] Putting the question of numerol-
ogy to one side for the moment, we are repeatedly reminded by Raphael's
narrative that, like so many other aspects of heaven and earth, the days of
heaven relate with terrestrial days analogously, not interchangeably. Hence,
Raphael refers to heaven's "Grateful vicissitude, *like* Day and Night" (6.8, my
emphasis), and has the Father make an otherwise inexplicable caveat to the
Son: "two days are past, / Two days, as we compute the days of Heav'n"
(6.684–85). Unencumbered by the mechanics of sun and stars, the angels
have their days and nights "for change delectable, not need" (5.629), admitting movement and change but elapsing at an unknown rate.

The exaltation of the Son, the chronological point at which the plot of
Paradise Lost begins, takes place "on such day / As Heav'n's great Year brings
forth" (5.582–83). Patrick Hume was among the first to read this as a reference to the Platonic Great Year, the cycle of time completed when all of
the celestial bodies return to their original positions. Plato had estimated
that this cycle would take roughly thirty-six thousand terrestrial years. Some
later commentators supplied more conservative estimates; in John Davies's
Orchestra, the "great long yeare" makes an appearance at a duration of
"threescore hundreths of those yeares in all / Which the Sunne makes with
his course naturall" (35.5–7).[17] Although Milton significantly stops short of
quantifying the "days of Heav'n," the implication is strong that heavenly time
moves inconceivably slowly. This would also have Biblical sanction, as Hume
reminds us in a paraphrase of Milton's line: "On such a Day, as Heav'n's great
unaccountable Year brings forth, where a thousand Years are in (God's) sight
but as yesterday when it is past, and as a Watch in the Night [Psalms 90.4]."[18]
But while the clock of heaven creeps forward, "the speed of Gods / Time
counts not" (10.90). At the very brink of the eternal, the acts of the Father
and Son take place with such swiftness that Raphael can barely capture them
in language: "Immediate are the Acts of God, more swift / Than time or
motion, but to human ears / Cannot without process of speech be told"
(7.176–78). This dizzying juxtaposition of fast and slow motion locates heavenly time well beyond Adam's and Eve's experience, and encourages us to
imagine two conflicting impossibilities at once.

This sketch of time in heaven is troubled further by an event left out of
all of the chronologies: the allegory of Sin and Death. Sin reminds Satan of
her birth "at th' Assembly, and in sight / Of all the Seraphim with thee
combin'd / In bold conspiracy against Heav'n's King" (2.749–51). Having
sprung from Satan's head, "familiar grown, / I pleas'd, and with attractive
graces won / The most averse" (761–63). Sin and her father take their joys "in

secret," leading to the conception of Death. "Meanwhile," Sin continues, "War arose, / And fields were fought in Heav'n" (766–68). This tightly packed narrative prompted William Empson to ask just when Sin would have had time to dally with Satan and conceive Death *during* the rebels' public council. Even if Satan could have found a few private moments with Sin while the council took place, where did Sin find the time to be "familiar grown"?[19] Stephen Fallon, too, puzzles over the fact that "the monstrous birth and copulation do not occur *after* Satan's tempting speech and *before* the War in heaven, but over *the same time.*" His solution to the problem lies in the narrative status of Sin and Death. Sin's story constitutes an "alternative vision of the fall, and not merely an event unfolding within the context of the fall narrated by Raphael."[20] As allegory, Sin and Death inhabit an alternative narrative mode, which allows their story and the rebels' council to overlap in time and space. This is a kind of heavenly double time, whereby events take place simultaneously on different ontological planes. It is worth noting that we do not witness the arrival of Sin and Death on earth. The mystically layered time zone that they inhabit is never grafted onto that of sublunar paradise, and they can make their way to our universe only after the Fall has unsettled the firm foundations of prelapsarian time.

IV

The network of contrast, distortion, and paradox that governs time outside paradise might still be taken as incidental to chronology proper. The importance of remembering how the nature of time differs from place to place becomes clearer when we look at the chronological gaps that open as the narrative shifts from one setting to another. For if these different regions do carry temporal identities distinct enough to interfere with an overarching timeline, then much of the strain will show at those moments when the flow of events carries us from heaven to hell, or from prelapsarian to postlapsarian paradise. The most serious of these gaps yawns forth just when time as we know it begins. How long after the rebel angels' defeat did the creation of our universe begin?

Milton seems to offer a range of possibilities. Raphael explains that the creation took place "after *Lucifer* from Heav'n . . . / Fell with his flaming Legions through the Deep / Into his place" (7.131–35). Fowler, adding the four days of narrated action in heaven to the nine-day fall of the rebel angels through chaos, determines that the creation must begin after day thirteen of his chronology.[21] Meanwhile, in a key moment spotted by Qvarnström and Fowler, Raphael mentions that during the sixth day of creation, when God created man and woman, the angel was on a mission to hell. Arriving there, he had found hell's gates "fast shut / . . . and barricado'd strong" (8.240–41). If this is the case, Adam must be created before Sin opens hell's gates on day twenty-two of Fowler's timeline (following the devils' further nine-day astonishment on the burning lake). These clues provide *termini a quo* and *ad quem*: the creation takes place sometime after Fowler's day thirteen and before day twenty-two. Without this minimal information, the creation could just as well have taken place aeons after the war in heaven. Opting for a tight time scheme, Fowler sets the beginning of the week of creation at day fourteen, one day after the rebels land in hell. Adam and Eve are therefore created on day nineteen.

A closer look at Raphael's journey to hell, though, exposes the slipperiness of Milton's ordering of time. When the angel reaches hell's gates, he hears loud "Noise, other than the sound of Dance or Song, / Torment, and loud lament, and furious rage" (8.243–44). The devils are noisy indeed to be heard above the cacophony of chaos, but this is consistent with Milton's portrayal of the noisy devils *after* they have awakened from their stupor on day twenty-two (e.g., 1.666–69, 2.519–20). For Fowler, these noises are "chronologically irrelevant," since "we would expect the devils to be tormented during their stupor" in any case, groaning and raging before their day twenty-two awakening.[22] But on day nineteen, there is *no noise* in hell. When Satan eventually utters his first words there, he is "breaking the horrid silence" (1.83). This awful silence seized the imaginations of Milton's early commentators; Hume elaborates it into "the dismal, the dreadful silence, which, under the Astonishment and Amazement they were overwhelmed with, till now [i.e., Satan's expostulation] was never broken."[23] Whether or not the devils were in torment before their awakening on day twenty-two, Raphael could not have heard "furious rage" from them on day nineteen.

To accommodate this information on Fowler's timeline, we would have to push the date of Raphael's excursion—and with it, the creation of man— back from day nineteen to day twenty-two. Only then would the devils be free to roam and rage while hell's gates remained barred. In some respects, this alternative works. It would, for example, enable the sinister irony of Satan's awakening in hell on the same day as Adam awakens to explore paradise. Moreover, if the devils were roaming freely in hell, Raphael's mission on that day would make more sense: "to see that none thence issu'd forth a spy, / Or enemy, while God was in his work" (8.233–34), a more genuine possibility after the devils have loosed their chains.

The neatness of this formula, though, unravels before the fraught question of how long Adam and Eve have been alive when we first encounter them. They have inhabited paradise long enough to become comfortable there, but briefly enough that their first memories of the place are still fresh in their minds. According to the brisk schedule of Fowler's chronology, which assumes no unaccounted-for lapses of time in the poem's action, we first see Adam and Eve on day twenty-three. If they were created on the previous day (day six of the week of creation), then day twenty-three would be the Sabbath day. Yet no one seems to attribute unusual significance to the day, and Raphael later describes the first Sabbath as an event firmly in the past. More importantly, this small time chafes against the poem's many hints that Adam and Eve have been alive for a much longer period. For example, awakening from her satanic dream, Eve complains, "Such night till this I never pass'd" (5.31); presumably she has had more than one previous night's dream for comparison.

Similar examples are numerous. Richard Bentley complained about Eve's reference to "All seasons and their change," since "yet in her life of one Week [she] could have no Notion of *seasons*." Bentley equivocates over the exact chronology here; a few pages earlier, he had suggested that Eve "had not yet lived above Three or Two [days]."[24] Laurence Babb draws attention to the prayers that Adam and Eve offer "each Morning . . . / In various style" (5.145–46), and to Eve's knowledge that fruits can become ripe by "frugal storing" (5.324).[25] Then there are the pair's many uses of the word "oft": "that day I oft remember" (4.449), "dream'd, not as I oft am wont, of thee" (5.32), "reasoning I oft admire" (8.25), and so on. Newton remains agnostic over these details, but both he and the Richardsons cite several passages that seem to place Adam and Eve in paradise for "many days" before the Fall.[26] By this process of quiet repetition, Milton builds what Helen Gardner has called "the sense of a long Paradisal time" for Adam and Eve.[27] If he intends us to understand that Adam and Eve are created on either day nineteen or day twenty-two, why does Milton dwell on their elaborate daily routine and rich stores of experience? No matter where we place the day of Adam's and Eve's creation, the resulting numbers do not explain the feeling of long time in Books Four through Nine. While Augustine maintained that Adam and Eve sinned on their very first day of life, Milton makes us feel that they have lived in paradise for weeks or even months. In Raphael's testimony he appears to offer us the tantalizing possibility of dating the creation, but insoluble problems force us to reject each date within the range provided by Raphael's information.

V

When we put these murky flashbacks behind us and turn to the narrative in paradise, the chronological struggles and stumblings that have been bothering us fall away. Our arrival in paradise triggers a straightforward chronology that belongs uniquely to the prelapsarian world. Only in the garden before the Fall—but everywhere there—are we constantly aware of the comforting cyclical movement of time from morning to evening and back to morning. There are four days of narrated action in paradise, observed in every chronology of the poem. Two of the narrated days contain prominent descriptions of morning (5.1–8; 9.192–200), noon (5.300–304, 310–11; 9.739), and evening (8.630–32, 9.48–52; 10.92–99). We also find references to the evening of the first day, after Satan reaches paradise (4.352–55, 539–43, 598–609), and the morning of the fourth day, when Michael arrives to banish Adam and Eve (11.133–36). There is a hiatus in this orderly chronology while Satan orbits the earth for "the space of seven continu'd Nights" (9.63), in partial overlap with the four narrated days in paradise.[28] He slips away early on the morning of the second day (4.1015), orbits for seven nights, and returns on the eighth (9.67). The action resumes when Satan reenters paradise at midnight (9.58) before the day of the fall, that is, day three of the four paradisal days. The cumulative total is ten days, including the partial first and last days in paradise. But Milton seems to stress the four radiantly clear days of action directly narrated, as against Satan's shadowy offstage journeys and the fuzzy retrospective glimpses of the creation week by Adam, Eve, and Raphael. The narrator takes pains to show paradise to us at each time of day, to render up the distinct pleasures offered by its daily cycles. These descriptions are supported by constant references to the circling of the celestial bodies, which "move / Thir Starry dance in numbers that compute / Days, months, and years" (3.579–81). Time is stable, ordered, and measurable for the benefit of humanity—until the Fall begins to crumple the temporal structures of paradise into the inscrutability characteristic of the other timescapes in the poem.

Eve's lovely lyric passage, "Sweet is the breath of morn" (4.641–56), sets forth in miniature the delicate cycle of human time that governs her homeland. Eve maintains a graceful balance between the idea of changing paradisal "seasons" and the sense of equal enjoyment radiating from each one—with human needs and relationships orchestrating the whole. Far from "forget[ting] all time, / All seasons and thir change" (4.639–40), Eve dwells on the moments of transition in a daily cycle from sunrise to dewy morn, through to the return of evening and glittering starlight. The speech itself balances delicately between the onset of evening and the quieter shades of night and starlight that follow it. Newton sets his chronology in motion here, in the process revealing his debt to Addison: "This is the first evening in the poem; for the action of the preceding books lying out of the sphere of the sun, the time could not be computed."[29]

Eve also reminds us that the prelapsarian world parades its pleasures in sympathy with human rhythms. Not only does paradise offer delights for humanity's benefit, but its gracious order finally depends on the central rela-tionships between Adam, Eve, and God. When Eve asks Adam for whose benefit the stars shine all night long, Adam uses astronomy to link the parents of mankind with their future progeny. The heavenly bodies "have thir course to finish . . . though to Nations yet unborn, / Minist'ring light prepar'd, they set and rise" (4.661–64). And as "th' hour / Of night, and all things now retir'd to rest / Mind us of like repose," Adam takes occasion to point out that human "labor and rest" have their parallel in "day and night to men / Successive" (4.610–14), the celestial cycle of time both mirroring and order-ing the human microcosm. Raphael, too, slips easily into analogies between the heavens and human biology, when he speaks of the stars and planets "communicating Male and Female Light, / Which two great Sexes animate the World" (8.150–51). Explicitly created "for Signs, / For Seasons, and for Days, and circling Years" (7.341–42), the planets and fixed stars preside over the middle books of the poem, overseeing the keeping of time so integral to our experience of paradise.

With the Fall, the orderly structures of the created universe begin to lose their footing. Nature registers her grief. The angels tilt the axis of the globe and introduce seasonal change. For the first time, Adam and Eve face a cosmos where the Edenic cycle of time is broken, and their sin, like that of Satan and the devils, has permanently severed their present woe from their past happiness. As Fowler has shown, Adam's and Eve's changing relation-ships with God, from disobedience through repentance to eventual salvation, play out not least in terms of time. Having been warned that eating the fruit would bring death on "the day thou eat'st thereof" (8.329), Adam and Eve come to understand that their "long day's dying" (10.964) will not come about when evening falls on the day of their transgression, but over a lifetime of days.[30] Their literalistic understanding of the cycle of prohibition, disobedi-ence, and punishment modulates into a more complicated picture of provi-dential *kairos*, blurring distinctions between sequence and cycle, temporality and eternity. This revaluation of time comes to a spectacular climax with the angel Michael's account of futurity, but begins almost as soon as Eve eats the fruit.

The hours immediately after the Fall are difficult to keep in order. The first postlapsarian night, for example, posed problems for Thomas Newton that have yet to be satisfactorily resolved. Evening falls at the beginning of Book Ten (10.95). Almost 1,000 lines later, we find Adam seeking warmth and shelter "ere this diurnal Star / Leave cold the Night" (1069–70). Adam has already "lamented loud / Through the still Night" (845–46), and the sun will not rise for another 200 lines (at 11.135), so why does Adam refer to the setting sun, "this diurnal Star," as if it were currently visible?[31] Conversely, if

Adam were perhaps seeing the *rising* sun at this moment, why would he propose making a fire in order to "supply the Sun" (10.1078)? As Newton intuits, the loss of paradise for Adam and Eve also means the loss of the tidy chronology of prelapsarian life, an all-too-brief evocation of the unfallen order of things that the reader must forfeit as well.

Further heightening the confusion during that long night, the narrator abruptly skips back in time to join Sin and Death at hell's gates. Sin feels "new strength within [her] rise, / Wings growing" (10.243–44), just as Adam and Eve felt a sensation of growing wings immediately after eating the fruit.[32] Ashraf H. A. Rushdy explains that this scene effectively constitutes a restaging of the Fall. The two moments take place simultaneously, but we must endure them in sequence, experiencing the triumph of Sin and Death for a second time and reading that new information back into the initial description of the Fall.[33] After this narrative hiccup comes more temporal misdirection for Newton to puzzle over. Somehow, Satan arrives to meet Sin and Death journeying toward earth "while the Sun in *Aries* rose" (10.329), long before the sun rises on paradise in Book Eleven. Fowler resolves this apparent inconsistency:

The information that a point between Scorpio and Sagittarius is at Satan's zenith clearly indicates that the time in Paradise is between 2.00 A.M. and 4.00 A.M. (or, assuming Sol to be in the centre of Aries, 3.00 A.M.) on Day 33, the day after the Fall. . . . Satan . . . is between Scorpio and Sagittarius, i.e., at an aspect of 120°–150° to the sun in Aries; hence the horizon of reference cannot possibly be that of Paradise (where his aspect to a rising sun would be 90°).[34]

Fowler's perceptive reading shows how a sunrise can take place here before it dawns in paradise, but the reasoning required might be beyond even the capacities of Milton's fit readers. On first glance, at least, day and night seem to trip eccentrically across the postlapsarian landscape, leaving us longing for the clear demarcations of time that prevailed before the Fall.

After dawn finally arrives in the garden, the elliptical narrative sequence gives way to the most dramatic distortion of time in *Paradise Lost*, the angel Michael's account of future ages in Books Eleven and Twelve. Michael's arrival shortly after sunrise coincides with yet another ominous interruption of the graceful diurnal cycle, as the sky is "suddenly eclips'd / After short blush of Morn" (11.183–84). The angel's narrative clarifies the relationship between *kairos* and *chronos*, the mingling of God's eternal grace with linear time. The wobbly chronology that has governed the first hours after the fall puts the angel's salvation narrative in context, anticipating the disorderly flow of Old Testament history that Michael will reveal to be ultimately ordered by divine grace. Appropriately, Adam's response to Michael's epic vision focuses on time:

How soon hath thy prediction, Seer blest,
Measur'd this transient World, the Race of time,
Till time stand fixt: beyond is all abyss,
Eternity, whose end no eye can reach.   (12.553–56)

The significant word "measure" reasserts the opposition between "this transient world," with its measurable time, and the foreign climes and times that lie beyond the visible cosmos. Adam and Eve are to parent a "race of time" which will, in fact, run a "race of time," always subject to the inexorable motions of the stars. The end of the world, like its beginning, stands beyond measure, in a vision of eternity that "no [mortal] eye can reach."

VI

It is tempting to conclude that Milton simply nodded from time to time, and that his occasional inattention to detail does not invalidate his whole chronological architecture—although I suspect that few would confidently argue, as a rule, for Milton's inattention to detail. But if this were the case, gaps and inconsistencies should not keep emerging at structurally important moments, and we should not have to perform such acrobatics to accommodate them to Milton's putative timeline. More fundamentally, the global chronologies of Fowler and others achieve their continuity at the expense of the reader's actual experience of time in the poem. When the whole narrative holds its breath over the fabled fall of Mulciber from heaven ("from Morn / To Noon he fell, from Noon to dewy Eve, / A Summer's day" [1.742–44])—while Raphael describes the much longer fall of the real angels in four blunt syllables ("Nine days they fell" [6.871])—Milton is deliberately exploiting the imaginative power of experiential over chronometric time. Perhaps the most obvious point about the chronology of *Paradise Lost* is that the narrative plays out in composite fragments, revealing the past incrementally while events unfold in the present—a construction that actually blunts our awareness of the chronological sequence of events. The forward and backward pull of the narrative extends into recent human history as well as back into prehistory, as our first parents' actions generate consequences that ripple through future ages. Time in *Paradise Lost* is not just out of joint, but "fans its spokes out into a cosmos of reference," carrying what Isabel Gamble MacCaffrey has called a "mythical charge."[35]

Milton's time and space are not fixed quantities, but malleable ones. Indeed, in a region such as chaos, where they are at their most elusive, it becomes more useful to express them in terms of each other—as when Satan falls into a "vast vacuity," drops ten thousand fathoms, and "to this hour / Down had been falling" (2.932–35), had not a timely gust from below restored him to his path. The inconceivable dimensions of this landscape force not only the halfhearted spatial estimate of ten thousand fathoms, nor a mere conceptual swivel to the measurement of time, but a dizzying face-to-face meeting of prehistoric events and the reader's present moment. As W. B. C. Watkins observes, "These few concessions to human literalness only indicate that all creation is as precisely measurable by God as the fragments within our ken by us."[36]

This feeling of human fallibility before cosmic mysteries was a central message of *Paradise Lost* for its eighteenth-century audience. Bentley was unhappy with any reference to the dimensions of a region like chaos, as we see in his gloss on 1.73–74, where hell is said to stand "as far remov'd from God and light of Heav'n / As from the Center thrice to th' utmost Pole." "The Distance is much too little," Bentley complains. "I would express it without any Comparison from things known to Us; which, though never so excessive, must needs fall too short."[37] Adam's desire to know why God chose "through all Eternity so late to build" his world (7.92) makes Patrick Hume even more uneasy:

Why God was not pleased to create the World 100,000 Years before he did, and how he employed his infinite Power, Wisdom, and other unaccountable Perfections, before the Creation; are some of those vain and Atheistical Enquiries of impertinent and daring Men, who, little acquainted with the terms and motions of their own frail and unruly Wills, would pry into the Secrets of the *Eternal Mind*, and ask an account of that *Almighty Will*, which created all things *how* and *when* he pleas'd.[38]

While allowing for the exigencies of postlapsarian storytelling, Milton was anxious to preserve the mysteries that lay outside the purview of right reason. Vignettes such as the nine-day fall of the angels, the three-day war in heaven, and the noon–midnight scheme in paradise (as valuably elaborated by Albert R. Cirillo[39]) all grant chronology a structural and numerological significance. But the confusions and contradictions that stubbornly attend other moments, such as the timing of the creation and the first muddled night after the Fall, discourage efforts to place them on a continuous timeline. In order to balance pragmatism with orthodoxy, Milton rejects a single overarching chronology in favor of several.

Milton does not reject chronology altogether, as some have argued. MacCaffrey maintains that Milton's poem "slights chronology in favor of a folded structure which continually returns upon itself," while Stanley Fish refers to "a conviction of timelessness in the narrative," and Anne Davidson Ferry sees Milton establishing "some nontemporal scheme analogous to the unity of divine vision which encompasses all things simultaneously."[40] But despite the circularity and slipperiness that pervade his portrayal of time,

Milton is nevertheless prepared to compromise, to set out his plot according to a set of small-scale chronological templates. Every moment does not receive equal treatment. Some clearly interest Milton more than others, and he shows his interest not by stressing similarities, but by drawing contrasts.

To widen the distance between our own fallen age and the time of the poem's events, Milton makes available not just one point of contrast, but many. Our experience of time resembles Satan's, which painfully sunders the present from the irrecoverable past; it bears vestigial similarities to the blissful cycle of time in paradise, but remains at best a poignant shadow of prelapsarian day and night; it cannot begin to supply adequate tools for measuring the alien landscape of chaos; and it will someday be subsumed into the grateful vicissitude of Milton's heaven, where the teleological trajectory of all days can be surveyed at a glance. To structure his plot, Milton supplies local timelines that correspond roughly to the poem's several settings: heaven, hell, chaos, and paradise before and after the Fall. Each has a characteristic temporal flavor, and each is juxtaposed loosely with the others. The result is the series of fissures in time from setting to setting that we have been noticing, such as the blurry transition from the end of the war in heaven to the creation of the universe. Although this strategy sacrifices the elegant numerological schemes that have been conjectured by Qvarnström, Fowler, and others (which sometimes appear to have been the basis for their chronological conclusions rather than the consequence of them), it also magnifies the importance of small-scale numerological signals that best reflect Milton's localized attention to time. Newton and Hume, for example, have pondered Milton's uses of the number nine, while Christopher Hill has hinted that events such as the three-day war in heaven may even represent a kind of political number symbolism.[41]

Thus, there are four days of narrated action in heaven, albeit of unknown nature and duration. After the war, the narrative shifts from heavenly days to the rebel angels' nine-day fall and further nine-day stupor in hell, both rendered in human terms but in a context dazzlingly resistant to our modes of measurement. After the rebels awaken, a few scant references to the passage of time in hell help to establish their disorientation and sense of irreversible pain and loss. Satan soon escapes from hell. After a journey of unknowable length through chaos, he arrives in our universe, which has been created at an indeterminate earlier time. The prominent chronology in paradise spans four days of narrated action, overlapping with Satan's week of travel around the earth. After Eve's fall at noon on the third narrated day, the timeline in paradise begins to deteriorate. Michael arrives as the sky unnaturally darkens the next morning, and his epic manipulation of time and space in a vision of futurity confirms the end of the neat chronology that we associate by now with prelapsarian paradise. God's providential plan, as well as Milton's epic, turns on our changing relationship with time. The poem's chronological templates play a part in that process, rendering the tragedy of mortal fallibility after the Fall, the intricate dance of divine *kairos* and human *chronos*, and not least the tenets of Renaissance epic convention. At the same time, they constitute a *concordia discors* that Patrick Hume, referring to the inscrutably wheeling constellations of Milton's heavens, once gruffly described as "a just Reproof to the presuming Sons of *Adam*."[42]

Yale University

NOTES

My grateful thanks to Dr. John Leonard for his guidance and encouragement as this paper took shape, and to the participants of the eighteenth British Milton Seminar in October 1998, where it was presented in an earlier version.

1. John Milton, *Paradise Lost: A Poem in Twelve Books*, ed. Thomas Newton (London, 1749), vol. 2, 314. For brevity, I cite footnoted commentary by Milton's editors by page number alone, and omit footnote or line number.

2. See Grant McColley, *"Paradise Lost": An Account of its Growth and Major Origins* (Chicago, 1940), 16–17; Galbraith Miller Crump, *The Mystical Design of "Paradise Lost"* (Lewisburg, PA, 1975), 163–72; Douglas A. Northrop, "The Double Structure of *Paradise Lost*," in *Milton Studies* 12, ed. James D. Simmonds (Pittsburgh, 1978), 75–90; John Carey and Alastair Fowler, eds., *The Poems of John Milton* (London, 1968), 443–46. Fowler's chronology reappears in his second edition of *Paradise Lost* (London, 1998), 29–33, but is treated there in less detail. References here are to the 1968 edition. Qvarnström's 33-day chronology substantially agrees with Fowler's; see his study, *The Enchanted Palace: Some Structural Aspects of "Paradise Lost"* (Stockholm, 1967), especially 10–54. Sherry Lutz Zivley counts 33 days plus four separately measured days of action in heaven, in "The Thirty-Three Days of *Paradise Lost*," *Milton Quarterly* 34:4 (2000), 117–27. I owe my knowledge of Crump's chronology to Dr. Zivley's essay.

3. Joseph Addison, *Notes Upon the Twelve Books of Paradise Lost* (London, 1719), 8–9.

4. René Le Bossu, *Monsieur Bossu's Treatise of the epick poem*, trans. W. J. (London, 1695), 156.

5. Le Bossu, 154–55.

6. Le Bossu, sig. b2v.

7. *Of Education*, in John Milton, *Complete Prose Works of John Milton*, ed. Don M. Wolfe et al. (New Haven, 1953–82), vol. 2, 404–5; hereafter designated YP and parenthetically cited by volume and page number in the text.

8. Torquato Tasso, *Discorsi del Poema Eroico*, in *Prose*, ed. Ettore Mazzali (Milan, 1959), 571.

9. Ludovico Castelvetro, *Poetica d'Aristotele Vulgarizzata et Sposta*, ed. Werther Romani (Rome, 1978), vol. 2, 151.

10. John Milton, *Complete Poems and Major Prose*, ed. Merritt Y. Hughes (New York, 1957), 212–13. All quotations from *Paradise Lost* are from this edition.

11. Patrick Hume returns to the conflation of "space" as both "place" and "time" when he sees a temporal dimension in Satan's comment, "Space may produce new Worlds" (*PL* 1.650). See Patrick Hume, *Annotations on Milton's "Paradise Lost"* (London, 1695), 42, and my note 28.

12. John Dryden, *The State of Innocence, and Fall of Man*, in *The Works of John Dryden*, gen. ed. H. T. Swedenborg, Jr. (Berkeley, 1956–89), vol. 12, 104.

13. Zivley, 120.

14. Fowler, 444; Qvarnström, 25.

15. *De Doctrina Christiana*, in YP, 6:313–14.

16. Fowler, 759.

17. See Plato, *Timaeus*, 37–38; Sir John Davies, "Orchestra," in *The Poems of Sir John Davies*, ed. Robert Krueger (Oxford, 1975), 99.

18. Hume, 186.

19. William Empson, *Milton's God* (London, 1961), 58–59.

20. Stephen M. Fallon, *Milton Among the Philosophers: Poetry and Materialism in Seventeenth-Century England* (Ithaca, N.Y., 1991), 185.

21. Fowler, 444, 828. Raphael glosses the fall of the angels through Chaos bluntly and unequivocally: "Nine days they fell" (6.871). He is speaking to Adam, and so, presumably, refers to "days" as Adam knows them.

22. Fowler, 445, 828.

23. Hume, 9.

24. Richard Bentley, *Milton's Paradise Lost: A New Edition* (London, 1732), 122, 130.

25. Lawrence Babb, *The Moral Cosmos of "Paradise Lost"* (East Lansing, 1970), 129.

26. Newton, 1:263; Jonathan Richardson, Jr. and Sr., *Explanatory Notes and Remarks on Milton's "Paradise Lost"* (1734; reprint, New York, 1970), 164.

27. Helen Gardner, *A Reading of "Paradise Lost"* (Oxford, 1965), 39.

28. It should be added that the blurry word "space" from 1.50 returns here, even as the narrator appears to map out Satan's orbit around the earth with great precision. But see Crump, 167–68, and Zivley, "Satan in Orbit: *Paradise Lost* IX.48–86," *Milton Quarterly* 31:4 (1997), 130–36, for different chronologies of this journey. It seems that Satan's point of view, and the language associated with it, remains in the blurry landscape of hell even as Satan moves in the easy currents of paradisal time.

29. Newton, 1:275.

30. Fowler, 966.

31. Newton, 2:296–97 and 315–16.

32. Fowler, 937.

33. Ashraf H. A. Rushdy, *The Empty Garden: The Subject of Late Milton* (Pittsburgh, 1992), 130–31.

34. Fowler, 943.

35. Isabel Gamble MacCaffrey, *"Paradise Lost" as "Myth"* (Cambridge, MA, 1959), 82.

36. W. B. C. Watkins, *An Anatomy of Milton's Verse* (Hamden, 1965), 50.

37. Bentley, 5. Bentley alters the offending line to "Distance, which to express all Measure fails."

38. Hume, 214.

39. See Albert R. Cirillo, "Noon–Midnight and the Temporal Structure of *Paradise Lost*," *Journal of English Literary History*, 29 (1962), 372–95.

40. MacCaffrey, 45; Stanley Eugene Fish, *Surprised by Sin: The Reader in "Paradise Lost*,*"* 2nd ed. (London, 1997), 35; Anne Davidson Ferry, *Milton's Epic Voice: The Narrator in "Paradise Lost"* (Cambridge, 1963), 47.

41. Newton, 1:455; Hume, 7; Christopher Hill, *Milton and the English Revolution* (London, 1977), 372–73.

42. Hume, 187.

MILTON, HOMER, AND
THE ANGER OF ADAM

Stella P. Revard

M ILTON CRITICS HAVE most often looked for traces of Homer in the murky darkness visible of Hell in Books One and Two or on the battlefields of Heaven in Book Six of *Paradise Lost*. If we consider Homer's influence on Milton to be largely a matter of Homeric similes or of the proper equipage for spear-bearing angelic warriors, we will not be disappointed in these findings.[1] There is more than a little of Homer's militarism in *Paradise Lost*. Yet is this all that Milton found in his favorite Greek poet? Although the *Iliad*, often dubbed the greatest battle epic ever written, contains endless descriptions of battle carnage, it is also a deeply human conflict. The scenes involving Agamemnon and Achilles, or Hector and Andromache, or Priam and Achilles that most deeply touch us rarely occur on the battlefield. They concern the personal crises that fuel the war—Achilles' turning bitterly to revile Agamemnon, Achilles (in despair) sitting alone on the seashore and calling his mother to him. They involve personal choice—Hector deciding (despite his wife's pleas) to return to the battlefield, Achilles rejecting the embassy of friends sent to him and choosing, rather than to assist them, to nurse his solitary pride. And there are scenes of reconciliation—indeed, the climax of the epic is just such a scene. Priam embraces the knees of his foe and kisses Achilles' hand while Achilles, thinking of his father, raises the old man and yields to his request, finally giving up that heart-eating anger that has consumed him from the very outset of the epic. Milton would have been a very poor reader of Homer if he had not found models for his own epic in the interpersonal conflicts of the *Iliad* that take us beyond the encounters on the battlefield.

In looking at these interpersonal relationships, we rarely find verbal echoes or exact one-to-one parallels between the *Iliad* and *Paradise Lost*. But the question of one poet's influence on another goes beyond mere verbal echoing or ready parallels. We must consider the subtle dynamics of transference and equivalency. Neither to Adam nor indeed to any other character in *Paradise Lost* does Milton directly compare Achilles. Yet critics have frequently pointed out how Milton has ransacked Homer for ready parallels between the *Iliad*'s warriors and his warring superbeings. Because the Son is the supreme charioteer, and because Satan wields a spear in Book One that seems the clone of Achilles' famous spear, critics have often likened the Son and Satan to Achilles. Such images are hard to resist. Assuredly, Satan, whose pride made him think himself impaired, has some affinities with Achilles nursing his injured τιμή. Further, as an army of one, the Son of Book Six outwardly resembles the supreme warrior of the *Iliad*. However, both John Steadman and Francis Blessington have cautioned against such uncritical comparisons.[2] True, Adam neither drives a chariot nor wields a spear. But are the warring Son and battle-ready Satan more perfect realizations of Homer's Achilles than the unarmed Adam? I think not. Neither Satan nor the Son occupies the place in *Paradise Lost* that Adam and Achilles occupy in their respective epics. It is Man's disobedience and Achilles' μῆνις (anger) on which the arguments of the two epics depend. Further, the doomed Achilles who knows that his time is only brief and the unhappy Adam who has forfeited immortality have more in common than would at first appear.

Achilles is one of the classical heroes actually named in Book Nine of *Paradise Lost*. Even though Milton tells us that he is looking for an "argument / Not less but more Heroic than the wrath / Of stern *Achilles* on his Foe pursu'd / Thrice Fugitive about *Troy* Wall" (9.13–16), he neither dismisses the heroic type that Achilles represents nor denies the genre of epic poetry that Homer composed in the *Iliad* and *Odyssey*. Can we fail to remember that blind Maeonides (as he refers to Homer in 3.35) is the epic poet whom Milton wishes to equal? In summoning Achilles at the point when Adam and Eve are about to undergo their greatest trial, Milton may be telling us more about his view of Homer and his epic intents than we at first realize. Even if he is searching for an argument greater than the one Homer posed in the *Iliad*, does he therefore dismiss from his epic its hero and the human choices he faces?

As Aristotle explained in the *Poetics*, the genres epic and tragedy are related. Both contemplate the value and the ultimate meaning of life. Though differing in length, in narrative style, and in meter, as Aristotle goes on to say, epic and tragedy employ many of the same characters from the heroic past and use many of the same poetic devices.[3] *Catharsis, anagnorisis*, and *peripeteia*, as Aristotle notes, are terms that apply to epic as well as tragedy. In the proemium of Book Nine, Milton is aware that he is partaking more than usual of the genre of tragedy, as he turns his "Notes to Tragic" (9.6). Preparing to tell of the fall of Adam and Eve and its aftermath, he is creating in Books Nine and Ten what might very well be called a tragedy in epic form. Like Homer, when he approached the climax of action in Books Sixteen through Twenty-two of the *Iliad* and its aftermath in Twenty-three and Twenty-four, Milton employs many of the techniques of the tragic poet.

Homer therefore becomes a particular model for him as epic poet turned tragic dramatist.[4] Thus, far from dismissing the *Iliad* and its account of the "wrath of stern *Achilles*" as a model for *Paradise Lost*, we should carefully reflect on how the choices that Achilles faces in Homer's epic relate to those that Adam and Eve face in Books Nine and Ten.

In the Renaissance, Achilles was often regarded as the exponent par excellence of the virtue *fortitudo* or *fortezza*—that is, valor. In fact, the three principal qualities that Renaissance critics believed were desirable in the hero were represented by three Homeric types. Achilles was recommended as the prime warrior because of his valor, Odysseus the counselor was admired for his sagacity—prudence and contemplation were his virtues—and Agamemnon was singled out as the *dux*—the leader.[5] When Milton in Book Four describes Adam, he glances at these Homeric paradigms. Like Agamemnon, Adam is our ἄναξ ἀνδρῶν, our lord of men—the first of the human race; like Odysseus he exemplifies intellectual prowess and like Achilles, courage. In the very first description of Adam, Milton tells us that "for contemplation hee and valor form'd" (4.299). Moreover, when Satan in Book Nine considers the opponents he must face in Eden, it is Adam that he wishes to shun, principally because he possesses in combination the qualities of the Homeric heroes Odysseus and Achilles—intellect combined with strength and courage:

> [His] higher intellectual more I shun,
> And strength, of courage haughty, and of limb
> Heroic built, though of terrestrial mould,
> Foe not informidable, exempt from wound,
> I not.　　　　　　　　　　　　　　　　　　　(9.483–87)

At the very point at which he is sallying forth to meet Eve, Satan ironically reminds us that he is avoiding the kind of contest at which Achilles excels, the sort of heroic contest that he himself once undertook and lost, when in the war in Heaven he pitted himself against his angelic superiors and against that super-warrior, the son of God. But, as Francis Blessington has pointed out, Satan never was a very successful Homeric warrior, hardly in the category of an Achilles. Despite his boasting, he is bested by Abdiel, by Michael, and by the Son, who like Achilles in the *Iliad* acts as an army of one.[6]

We need to be often reminded that Satan is not a type but a parody of Achilles. Blessington cogently argues that Satan does not truly embody the classical tradition, but "represents a perversion of the values found in Homer and Vergil" (p. xii).[7] True, there appears to be a parallel between Satan withdrawing from the mount of God and deciding upon desperate revenge for his so-called slighted honor and Achilles withdrawing from battle because of Agamemnon's insult to his τιμή. But on closer examination, it becomes clear that Achilles' situation contrasts with rather than resembles Satan's. Before the whole Achaean army Agamemnon has insulted Achilles, deprived him of his prize of honor, and reviled him as the most hated of all the Zeus-nourished kings who came to Ilium. Jeering at him, Agamemnon tells Achilles to go home; he doesn't need him. What has God done to Satan? Nothing in any way comparable. Satan-Lucifer is among the highest of the angels, if not the highest. It is Satan alone who interprets God's announcement of the kingship of the Son as an injury to his self-esteem. Further, God is Satan's creator and his lord, to whom he owes absolute allegiance. Agamemnon does not stand in comparable relation to Achilles, being merely the leader of the expedition to Troy, which Achilles freely has joined. Prince in his own right, Achilles is faced with a moral dilemma after Agamemnon has insulted him. He has been disgraced before his peers. Should he remain at Troy or go home? It is the gods who send Athene to him, advising him to wait until reparation comes for Agamemnon's insult before he rejoins the conflict. And so he does, asking his mother, Thetis, to intercede with Zeus on his behalf and grant him honor. Zeus agrees—and thereon hangs the action of the first part of the *Iliad*. Zeus himself avenges Agamemnon's insult to Achilles' honor. It is only after he stubbornly refuses in Book Nine to accept Agamemnon's gifts that Achilles places himself in the wrong, scorning the attempted resolution of the quarrel and ultimately bringing tragedy down upon himself and his comrades at Troy.

Disobedience is the theme of *Paradise Lost*; μῆνις (wrath) the theme of the *Iliad*. Yet despite Milton's insistence in Book Nine that his argument is higher than Homer's, the two arguments have a certain relevance one to the other. The famous μῆνις of Achilles comes upon him for very personal motives unrelated to the battlefield. He is first consumed with anger against Agamemnon when Agamemnon threatens to take Briseis from him, to deprive him of the woman he loves, his justly won battle prize. This μῆνις is not purged nor the quarrel with Agamemnon resolved until a greater μῆνις comes upon him, the anger against Hector who has killed his beloved Patroclus. It is this "wrath" that Milton refers to—strategically—at the beginning of Book Nine, just when Adam like Achilles will face a trial of love and honor, a trial that will force him to choose between forsaking a beloved companion—his wife, Eve—or disobeying God and losing Eden and his own life. Adam, like Achilles, chooses love.

Martin Mueller was one of the first critics to insist that Achilles in his human plight resembles Adam, demonstrating how closely related are those choices that Adam and Achilles must make.[8] Two-thirds of the way through the respective epics comes the turning point for each hero that determines the climax of action and the tragic outcome. Moreover, before Achilles and Adam make the crucial decisions, the heroes have unwittingly set up the circumstances that will decide the final tragedy, having acceded to the plea of a beloved companion and permitted him or her to go forth alone into potential danger. Patroclus begs Achilles that he might put on Achilles' armor and assume Achilles' place in battle in order to turn the tide for the Greeks. Achilles yields to Patroclus' request, making him promise to come back and not tempt the gods to oppose him—and Patroclus departs. Intoxicated with battle, he forgets his promise to Achilles, and hoping to win glory for himself, he leads the Achaeans to the very walls of Troy, provoking the god Apollo to oppose him. Apollo urges Hector to seek Patroclus, and Patroclus falls to the superior warrior.

Eve, of course, does not request to go into battle; her plea to be permitted to garden alone seems far removed from the battlefields of Ilium. But, as Adam reminds Eve that their "malicious Foe" is lying in wait, hoping to surprise them "by sly assault" (*PL* 9.256), the language of epic encounter creeps into *Paradise Lost*. Eve denies that Satan intends violence, but Adam, continuing to use the language of battle, tells her, "such affront I labor to avert / From thee alone" (9.302–03). Underestimating perhaps Satan's cunning, he assures her: "first on mee th' assault shall light" (9.305). Eve, who up to now has only been thinking of the advantages of separate gardening, turns her thoughts to glory and honor. What if she, alone, were to encounter Satan and repulse him:

> his foul esteem
> Sticks no dishonor on our Front, but turns
> Foul on himself; then wherefore shunn'd or fear'd
> By us? who rather double honor gain
> From his surmise prov'd false, find peace within,
> Favor from Heav'n   (9.329–34)

Like a warrior entering battle, Eve confidently sallies forth alone, not expecting that "A Foe so proud will first the weaker seek" (9.383). But just as Patroclus underestimates Hector, so Eve does Satan. The Miltonic narrator warns her, "O much deceiv'd, much failing, hapless *Eve*" for whom "ambush hid among sweet Flow'rs" (9.404, 408). The Homeric narrator also comments on Patroclus's folly: "Fool, it was for his own death and evil fate that he was praying" (*Il.* 16.46–47).[9]

While Homer and Milton turn their attention to Patroclus and Eve, describing their heroic encounters and informing the audience of their tragic falls, they keep their respective protagonists uninformed. Achilles and Adam wait in dread and growing apprehension, while the poets delay the moment of epic recognition. For an entire book the Greeks fight over the body of Patroclus while Achilles remains ignorant of the fate of his friend. Book Eighteen opens with him yet unknowing, but suspecting the truth:

ὤ μοι ἐγώ, τί τ᾽ ἄρ᾽ αὖτε κάρη κομόωτες Ἀχαιοὶ
νηυσὶν ἔπι κλονέονται ἀτυζόμενοι πεδίοιο;
μὴ δή μοι τελέσωσι θεοὶ κακὰ κήδεα θυμῷ,
ὥς ποτέ μοι μήτηρ διεπέφραδε, καί μοι ἔειπε
Μυρμιδόνων τὸν ἄριστον ἔτι ζώοντος ἐμεῖο
χερσὶν ὕπο Τρώων λείψειν φάος ἠελίοιο.
ἦ μάλα δὴ τέθνηκε Μενοιτίου ἄλκιμος υἱός,
σχέτλιος. ἦ τ᾽ ἐκέλευον ἀπωσάμενον δήϊον πῦρ
ἂψ ἐπὶ νῆας ἴμεν, μηδ᾽ Ἕκτορι ἶφι μάχεσθαι.

Ay me, why is it that again the long-haired Achaeans
in terror are being driven across the plain to the ships?
May the gods not have brought evil cares to my heart,
Even those that my mother once told me of,
That while I still lived, the best of the Myrmidons
should at the hands of the Trojans leave the light of the sun.
Truly, the brave son of Menoetius is now dead,
the headstrong one, for I bid him to come back,
when he had thrust away the consuming fire from the ships
and not to contend in might with Hector.   (18.6–14)

At the same time, Adam, who had often charged Eve with quick return, waits, "desirous her return," weaving meanwhile a garland of choicest flowers to adorn her tresses, and wondering at her long delay. Yet, "oft his heart, divine of something ill, / Misgave him" (9.845–46). He goes to meet her, passing by the Tree of Knowledge, and finds her just returned from the tree.

Antilochos, Nestor's son, bears the news to Achilles at Menelaus' bidding. Speechless with horror, he sheds tears as Antilochos speaks the message. Homer relates in detail Achilles' reaction. It is not merely grief at the death of a loved one that Achilles is experiencing. True, he tears his hair and lies outstretched in the dust. But immediately he understands the inevitable consequences of Patroclus' death. In the colloquy with his mother that ensues, Achilles reveals his inner thoughts, coming to terms with his own fate:

μῆτερ ἐμή ...
ἀλλὰ τί μοι τῶν ἦδος, ἐπεὶ φίλος ὤλεθ᾽ ἑταῖρος,
Πάτροκλος, τὸν ἐγὼ περὶ πάντων τῖον ἑταίρων,
ἶσον ἐμῇ κεφαλῇ. τὸν ἀπώλεσα ...
νῦν δ᾽ ἵνα καὶ σοὶ πένθος ἐνὶ φρεσὶ μυρίον εἴη
παιδὸς ἀποφθιμένοιο, τὸν οὐχ ὑποδέξεαι αὖτις
οἴκαδε νοστήσαντ᾽, ἐπεὶ οὐδ᾽ ἐμὲ θυμὸς ἄνωγε

ζώειν οὐδ' ἄνδρεσσι μετέμμεναι, αἴ κε μὴ Ἕκτωρ
πρῶτος ἐμῷ ὑπὸ δουρὶ τυπεὶς ἀπὸ θυμὸν ὀλέσσῃ,
Πατρόκλοιο δ' ἕλωρα Μενοιτιάδεω ἀποτίσῃ.

My mother . . . what pleasure remains to me,
now that my dear comrade is dead?
Patroclus, whom I honored above all my comrades,
equal to my own self, him have I lost!

. . . .

Now your heart also will suffer grief without measure
when your own son perishes; never again
will you welcome him home, returning.
Nor does my heart bid me to live nor mingle with men,
unless Hector, felled by my spear,
first lose his life and pay back the price of
the spoil won from Patroclus, the son of Menoetius.
(18.79–82, 88–93)

Thetis replies, "My child, your doom will be swift thereafter . . . for immediately after Hector, your own fate is near" (18.95–96). Achilles, in anguish,
replies, "Straightway may I die, since I was not at hand to help my comrade
when he was struck down!" (18.98–99).

In Book Nine Achilles had weighed the double destiny that his mother
had foretold to him—short life with everlasting glory vs. long life and ingloriousness. In the *Second Defense* Milton, contemplating his own double
destiny, alludes to the choice that confronted Achilles. Comparing himself to
Homer's hero, he deems more noble the sacrifice of his eyesight for a greater
object of esteem than the sacrifice of life for glory or renown.

I called to mind those two destinies, which the oracle of Delphi announced to the son
of Thetis:—

> Two fates may lead me to the realms of night;
> If staying here, around Troy's wall I fight,
> To my dear home no more must I return;
> But lasting glory will adorn my urn.
> But, if I withdraw from martial strife,
> Short is my fame, but long will be my life. (*Il.* 9.410–16)

I considered that many had purchased a less good by a greater evil, the meed of glory
by the loss of life; but that I might procure great good by little suffering; that though I
am blind, I might still discharge the most honorable duties, the performance of which,
as it is something more durable than glory, ought to be the object of superior admiration and esteem; I resolved, therefore, to make the short interval of sight which was
left me to enjoy as beneficial as possible to the public interest.[10]

In Book Nine Achilles faced a clear choice—to remain at Troy and seek glory or to return home to long life and ingloriousness. The dilemma that confronts him in Book Eighteen, however, is yet more complex. Indeed, in one sense the choice has (so to speak) been made for him, for once he has sent his friend to fight in his place, he has forfeited his options. With Patroclus' death Achilles is compelled by a moral responsibility to avenge his friend. If in killing the great Hector, he wins excellent renown—κλέος ἐσθλὸν—so be it. It is certainly true that the entire classical ethos would support such a motive. However, desire for glory no longer moves him as it once had. Further, unlike Satan, Achilles does not seek to vindicate lost self-esteem or merely to pay back an enemy, spite for spite. He goes forth knowing he will die, but committed to encounter the killer of the man he loved. Love for his lost comrade and the moral compulsion to avenge him possess Achilles wholly.

Adam is no less horrified than Achilles when he realizes that his beloved companion is doomed. Like Homer, Milton freezes the moment as he describes Adam's reaction: "while horror chill / Ran through his veins, and all his joints relax'd . . . Speechless he stood and pale" (9.890–91, 894). Adam thinks of his companion in superlatives. If for Achilles Patroclus was "the best of the Myrmidons," Eve is the "last and best / Of all God's Works" (9.896–97). Now she is lost, he finds life insupportable without her: "How can I live without thee, how forgo / The sweet Converse and Love so dearly joined" (9.908–09). In *Paradise Lost*, romantic love joins with the regret of lost companionship. However, unlike Achilles, Adam does not fully acknowledge his failure to protect the woman "to me committed and by me expos'd" (X, 957) until his regeneration has begun.

The resolution to throw in one's lot with a loved one is Homeric. No comparable motive moves the biblical Adam, who merely accepts the apple from his wife. As the words "lot" and "doom" indicate, even Adam's language suggests a Homeric complex: "However, I with thee have fixt my Lot, / Certain to undergo like doom; if Death / Consort with thee, Death is to mee as Life" (9.952–54). But before we blame Adam for a pagan disposition, we must interrogate the ethic of free choice that each poet here poses. However devoted to his beloved, Adam can choose *not* to die with Eve, Achilles *not* to die avenging Patroclus. A complicated web of motive and circumstance makes the choice before each hero *seem* inevitable: Patroclus is Achilles' dearest friend, Eve Adam's wife and other self. Both heroes have been involved in and feel responsible for their companion's plight. Yet neither is in any way compelled by anything other than his own free volition; no ulterior "lot" has been assigned them either by a Homeric or a Christian God. While their choices have far-reaching, even cosmic repercussions, for each this is a personal not a preordained tragedy. Even though the theological underpinnings of the *Iliad* and of *Paradise Lost* are different, remarkably similar is the ethic of free choice that each poet has made an indispensable component of his epic.

At the moment of willing self-sacrifice both Achilles and Adam appear admirable. The unarmed Achilles retrieves the body of his friend from the contending Trojans; Adam accepts Eve's embraces and her tender tribute: "that he his Love / Had so ennobl'd, as of choice to incur / Divine displeasure for her sake, or Death" (9.991–93). However, both Homer and Milton soon make us re-examine their heroes' apparent nobility. At this point Milton places different Homeric contexts before us, ones that we can hardly fail to recognize. Less admirable characters take the place of the heroic Achilles as prototypes for the fallen Adam, who, after he has shared Eve's apple, is inflamed with carnal desire. In the sex play that follows we encounter in the fallen Adam and Eve glimpses of the promiscuous Paris and Helen and the deluded Zeus and deluding Hera.[11] Before the fall, the lovemaking of Adam and Eve had been compared to the fertile love of these very wedded gods; Adam delighted in Eve as "*Jupiter* / On *Juno* smiles, when he impregns the Clouds / That shed *May* Flowers" (4.498–501). The unfallen Adam had wooed Eve with a tender aubade and with "looks of cordial Love" (5.12). Now he "on *Eve* / Began to cast lascivious Eyes, she him / As wantonly repaid; in Lust they burn: / Till *Adam* thus 'gan *Eve* to dalliance move" (9.1013–16). The words that ensue are those of Paris to Helen, or rather a parody of those words. In *Iliad* Three Paris has just returned from the battlefield, dishonored and defeated by Helen's former husband. Eager to solace himself in lovemaking, he reminds Helen of the sexual bliss of their "honeymoon":

> ἀλλ' ἄγε δὴ φιλότητι τραπείομεν εὐνηθέντε·
> οὐ γὰρ πώ ποτέ μ' ὧδέ γ' ἔρως φρένας ἀμφεκάλυψεν,
> οὐδ' ὅτε σε πρῶτον Λακεδαίμονος ἐξ ἐρατεινῆς
> ἔπλεον ἁρπάξας ἐν ποντοπόροισι νέεσσι,
> νήσῳ δ' ἐν Κραναῇ ἐμίγην φιλότητι καὶ εὐνῇ,
> ὥς σέο νῦν ἔραμαι καί με γλυκὺς ἵμερος αἱρεῖ.

> Come now let us lie down and disport ourselves in love-making.
> For never yet did desire so overwhelm my senses,
> Not even when, having snatched you
> from lovely Lacedaemon, I sailed in my seafaring ships
> and on the island of Cranae first made love to you.
> Even now I desire you, as sweet longing seizes me.   (3.441–46)

Similarly, in *Paradise Lost* Adam invites Eve to make love:

> now let us play,
> As meet is, after such delicious Fare;

For never did thy Beauty since the day
I saw thee first and wedded thee, adorn'd
With all perfections, so inflame my sense
With ardor to enjoy thee, fairer now
Than ever, bounty of this virtuous Tree.   (9.1027–33)

Adam seizes Eve's hand and leads her to a shady bank, just as Paris had led Helen to their bed. Homer does not tell us what Helen felt, compelled by the goddess Aphrodite (or perhaps her own inner aphrodite) to submit to her husband's invitation. Eve is a willing accomplice, who well understands Adam's "glance or toy / Of amorous intent," her own eye darting "contagious Fire" (1034–36). Both Paris and Adam are remembering a honeymoon, but the run-away excursion to the isle of Cranae is little like the wedding idyll in Eden. Even as Adam recalls how his bride was brought to him "adorn'd with all perfection," his lust sullies the memory of the innocent pleasure of Eden. Like Paris, he is solacing himself in lovemaking to forget his shame. Once in their bliss the most sublime of prelapsarian lovers, in their guilt Adam and Eve have become—by allusion—merely the most famous of postlapsarian lovers. What a fall!

But Milton is not finished with Homeric reminiscences. As Adam and Eve lie down upon the bed of flowers, Milton evokes the flowery couch that Hera and Zeus once shared when Hera duped her gullible, sexually eager husband.[12] Turning from Paris' delusion, Milton now looks at Zeus's. If Adam lost paradise "fondly overcome with Female charm" (9.999), the king of the gods is not impervious to female allure. He allows himself to be distracted from overseeing the battle at Troy when Hera opportunely arrives, sporting the girdle of Aphrodite that makes her sexually irresistible. He too announces that he has never felt such desire before, the line in the *Iliad* replicating exactly the line Paris had spoken to Helen: "ὥς σέο νῦν ἔραμαι καί με γλυκὺς ἵμερος αἱρεῖ" (So I desire you now, as sweet longing seizes me. [14.328]). Zeus clasps his wife in his arms and beneath them spring fresh grass and flowers: lotus and crocus and hyacinth. Milton also gives Adam and Eve a flowery couch: "Pansies, and Violets, and Asphodel, / And Hyacinth, Earth's freshest softest lap" (9.1040–41), thereby signaling how they enjoy the very couch of the gods. The episode in Book Fourteen of the *Iliad* is slyly ironic, but apart from permitting a temporary reversal in the battle, it changes nothing. Zeus wakes from a postcoital sleep and reprimands Hera for her craftiness, reminding her how he punished her on another occasion when she opposed him. In *Paradise Lost*, however, the scene of lovemaking marks the transition from innocence to experience: the relationship between the human couple is unalterably changed. The innocent Eve who once decked her bridal bower with flowers is now a cunning spouse who accedes to her husband's lust to make him forget that she has led him to sin. Once exemplars of the gods' happiness, Adam and Eve have become tainted with their quarrels and treachery. Adam wakes to accuse Eve, "*Eve*, in evil hour thou didst give ear / To that false Worm" (9.1067–68).

In turning from the paradigm of the tragic Achilles to the less-than-heroic paradigms of Paris and Zeus, Milton has left Adam exposed, naked of the heroic garment of Achillean self-sacrifice that he wore at the fall. Much as we approve his devotion to his companion, less noble motives now become apparent as Zeus's uxoriousness and Paris's wayward passion reveal themselves in Adam. In the aftermath of the fall Adam first indulges his sexual appetite and then reviles Eve for her part in leading him astray. An all-consuming wrath overcomes him.

Wrath, of course, is the defining characteristic of Achilles. It first takes hold of him in Book One, when he responds to Agamemnon's insult; it possesses him when he goes to avenge his friend, tainting the ideal of self-sacrificing love as he gives in to fury. No longer the magnanimous warrior, Achilles rages against the enemy, his excesses spoiling the noble motive of avenging his friend. In abusing the dead body of Hector, he violates all codes of heroic behavior. He no longer grants mercy or honors former codes of battle as he indulges in a bloodbath of killing; he coldly sacrifices innocent victims on Patroclus's tomb. It would take much to defend the μῆνις—or should it be called mania—of the fallen Achilles or, for that matter, of the fallen Adam.

Milton has dealt sparingly with anger in *Paradise Lost*. Most often, as Blessington has pointed out, wrath is a word used by Milton to describe the displeasure of God. True, he shows Satan consumed by "pale ire," but he reserves human anger for the moment that Adam turns his full fury on Eve at the end of Book Nine. His is a destructive rage that fractures the relationship between husband and wife in *Paradise Lost*, just as rage in the *Iliad* divided leader and warrior and finally set Achilles apart from his companions as he wages war alone. Nor is Adam's anger—like Achilles'—in any way easily appeased.

However, at the moment when Adam first rebukes his wife, he less resembles the angry Achilles than the engaged Zeus, the ever-provoked husband of a provoking wife. The quarreling of the Edenic spouses in Book Nine begins with unmistakable overtones of the bickering of the Homeric gods. Waking at the beginning of Book Fifteen and finding that Hera has diverted his attention from the battle in order to assist the Greeks, Zeus blazes forth in anger as his wife, cowering before him, protests her innocence. Just as suddenly, however, Zeus's anger subsides as he repairs the damage done while Hera diverted his attention, and he returns to masterminding the battle.

When Adam wakes in Book Nine after his own postcoital sleep, he assumes the tones of imperious Zeus as he chastises his wife: "Would thou hadst heark'n'd to my words, and stay'd / With me, as I besought thee, when that strange / Desire of wandering . . . possess'd thee" (9.1134–37). "Mov'd with a touch of blame," Eve declares her innocence of ill intention. The words she uses to disarm Adam's attack have a peculiarly Homeric ring: "What words have past thy Lips, *Adam* severe" (9.1144). Indeed they echo a familiar formula in the *Iliad*, used by Hera and others alike to counter an unpleasing speech. Some editors cite Odysseus's rebuke of Agamemnon in Book Fourteen, 83: "ποῖόν σε ἔπος φύγεν ἕρκος ὀδόντων" (What word has escaped the fence of your teeth?). The relevant citation, I believe, should be *Iliad* One, 552: "αἰνότατε Κρονίδη, ποῖον τὸν μῦθον ἔειπες" (Most dread son of Cronos, what kind of a word have you spoken?). In *Paradise Lost*, as in the *Iliad*, we are dealing with the mutual accusations of husband and wife. In Book One (as in Book Fifteen) Zeus accuses Hera of causing trouble, and Hera stoutly defends herself. Neither is entirely candid, for Zeus has been concealing his plans from Hera and she has been slyly meddling in order to pursue her own agenda. What we have here is a classic marital disagreement, which quickly escalates. Zeus breaks forth in anger, threatening Hera who at first defends herself and then falls silent, sulking. In *Paradise Lost* Eve, like Hera, declares her blamelessness and blithely tries to shift the responsibility to her husband: "who knows / But might as ill have happ'n'd thou being by, / Or to thyself perhaps" (9.1146–48). Moreover, she argues, if he was so certain of her danger, why didn't he forbid her to go? Now in earnest the winds of high passion rise—"Anger, Hate, / Mistrust, Suspicion, Discord" (9.1123–24).

Adam is "incenst" (1162) and accuses Eve of ingratitude: "Is this the Love, is this the recompense / Of mine to thee, ungrateful Eve" (9.1163–64). But he also angrily denounces the female sex: "Thus it shall befall / Him who to worth in Woman overtrusting / Lets her Will rule" (9.1182–84). Milton may well be echoing those Renaissance commentators on *Iliad* Fifteen who commonly added an antifeminist gloss when remarking on Hera's female deviousness.[13] But there is more here than simply the recollection of the warring Zeus and Hera in these quarreling Edenic spouses. It was not Zeus, but Achilles, who was indignant at ingratitude, angry that Agamemnon had not valued his loyal service and had accused him of deviousness. Had he not come to Troy to assist Agamemnon and Menelaus? Was this the reward he received? The onslaught of abuse that follows in Book One of the *Iliad* culminates in the division of general and warrior, who stand apart from each other. So too, in *Paradise Lost*, Adam and Eve, now contentious adversaries and not loving spouses, stand apart from one another. Each accuses the other: "And of thir vain contest appear'd no end" (9.1189).

In the *Iliad* Homer has contrasted divine and human anger. Before the towering rage of the god everything gives way: not so with human anger which festers, causing endless suffering. In Book One of the *Iliad* the quarrel of Hera and Zeus quickly ends with Hephaestos's intervention. But the quarrel of Achilles and Agamemnon escalates, despite Nestor's attempted conciliation, causing suffering for the Achaeans and ultimately redounding on Achilles himself. Similarly, the anger of Adam continues to consume him, even after the Son has descended to pronounce judgment on the human pair.

As Adam resembles Achilles in sacrificing his life for his companion, so he also resembles him in the unrelenting anger that possesses him throughout Book Ten. That Adam's anger is directed not toward an erstwhile commander or an adversary in battle but toward that very same beloved companion is all the more ironic. Milton focuses in Book Ten on the climax of Adam's rage and its final appeasement. Similarly, the denouement of the *Iliad* deals with the end of Achilles' anger. Although Achilles has killed Hector in Book Twenty-two, he continues to rage against Hector's lifeless body, his wrath not appeased until Book Twenty-four, the final book of the epic. In both epics another person central to the plot must intervene in order to turn the hero from his destructive wrath. Priam appeals to Achilles, Eve to Adam, each selflessly abasing himself or herself to make the turnabout possible. By accepting Priam's offer of ransom and releasing the dead body of his son, Achilles purges the anger that has consumed him from the beginning of the epic. Similarly, in accepting Eve's plea for peace and forgiving her, Adam gives up his own heart-rending anger. Between former enemies and estranged spouses comes a healing peace that makes closure possible in both epics.

In the *Iliad* and in *Paradise Lost*, the gods prepare the grounds for reconcilement. Zeus sends Thetis to Achilles, commanding him to surrender Hector's body. God sends the Son to judge Adam and Eve.[14] Yet, despite judgment from above, both Adam and Achilles nurse their anger, refusing to eat or sleep. At the opening of Book Twenty-four Achilles lies outstretched, shedding tears for Patroclus and still committing outrages on Hector's lifeless body. When Achilles' mother, Thetis, comes to him, she urges him not to persevere in his rage and to cease from his weeping:

> τέκνον ἐμόν, τέο μέχρις ὀδυρόμενος καὶ ἀχεύων
> σὴν ἔδεαι κραδίην, μεμνημένος οὔτε τι σίτου
> οὔτ' εὐνῆς; ἀγαθὸν δὲ γυναικί περ ἐν φιλότητι
> μίσγεσθ'. οὐ γάρ μοι δηρὸν βέῃ, ἀλλά τοι ἤδη
> ἄγχι παρέστηκεν θάνατος καὶ μοῖρα κραταιή.

> My child, how long will you eat your heart out
> With weeping and sorrow, thinking neither on
> Food or sleep. It would be good for you

To embrace a woman in love-making.
For you do not have long to live;
Already death stands near and powerful destiny.   (*Il.* 24.128–32)

On other occasions Thetis succeeded in comforting her son; now she is
unable to assuage his sorrow or end his self-destructive anger. She wins his
promise, however, to release the body of Hector as the gods demand. When
Priam comes to Achilles, he is still sitting apart from his companions.

Although the gentle pleas of Thetis failed, those of Priam finally turn
Achilles' heart from anger and bring him peace. Priam has ignored danger
and difficulties and is utterly transcendent in his sole purpose to convince
Achilles to yield. On entering Achilles' hut, he assumes the posture of a
suppliant, grasping Achilles' knees:

ἀλλ᾽ αἰδεῖο θεούς, ᾿Αχιλεῦ, αὐτόν τ᾽ ἐλέησον,
μνησάμενος σοῦ πατρός. ἐγὼ δ᾽ ἐλεεινότερός περ,
ἔτλην δ᾽ οἷ᾽ οὔ πώ τις ἐπιχθόνιος βροτὸς ἄλλος,
ἀνδρὸς παιδοφόνοιο ποτὶ στόμα χεῖρ᾽ ὀρέγεσθαι.

Come, Achilles, revere the gods and have pity on me.
Remember your father, for I am still more pitiable;
I have endured what no other human being has;
I have lifted my hand to the lips of the man who killed my son.
(24.503–506)

In response to Priam's words, Achilles relents. He sees in Priam his own
father; he also sees an extraordinary man who has suffered as he himself has.
Raising Priam to his feet, he comforts him, marveling that Priam had the
courage to come alone to his tents. He feels, as Kevin Crotty has remarked,
pity for another human being:

Achilles' experience of *eleos* [pity] "purifies" his most painful emotions of their bru-
tality, so that they become an occasion, rather, for insight into the quality of his own
and others' grief. To invoke Aristotle, Achilles' experience of pity is a *katharsis*—a
cleansing or purification of his rage and grief.[15]

Yet even as he pities Priam, Achilles tells him that his grieving is futile; he
cannot bring his son back to life. Indeed, as Achilles remarks, "Sooner you
will endure another woe." Neither he nor Priam can alter the decree of the
gods—Achilles must die and Troy must fall. But as human beings they can
bring comfort to one another.

In Book Ten Adam sits apart from Eve, despairing of reconcilement
with God: "hid in gloomiest shade, / To sorrow abandon'd, but worse felt
within / And in a troubl'd Sea of passion tost" (10.716–18). As with Achilles,
he feels no relief from his grief or from the desolation of his situation; Adam

only hopes that death will end him—as swiftly as possible. There is even the sense that he remembers, as Achilles does, the great glory once promised him when, highly favored, he was supreme above all the beings on earth:

> Oh miserable of happy! is this the end
> Of this new glorious World, and mee so late
> The Glory of that Glory?   (*PL* 10.720–22)

Like Achilles, he appreciates his own uniqueness, especially now that he is unique in misery.

Before he repents, however, Adam gives way once more to anger, which, in its relentlessness, rivals the extremes of Achillean rage. He turns on Eve when she approaches him seeking reconcilement, offering "soft words to his fierce passion" (10.866). Critics are quick to remark on the classical parallels in the passage that follows, pointing out that Adam's words echo the cynical pronouncements of Euripides' Jason on the deficiencies of the female sex.

> O why did God,
> Creator wise, that peopl'd highest Heav'n
> With Spirits Masculine, create at last
> This novelty on Earth . . .
> Or find some other way to generate
> Mankind?   (10.888–91, 894–95)

Adam, however, is no Jason, who pleads his case against Medea with sophistic nonchalance and coldly dismisses her. In contrast, Adam passionately hurls epithets at Eve, reviles her, and refuses her mercy: "Out of my sight, thou Serpent, that name best / Befits thee" (10.867–68). Just as Achilles refused Hector's dying request with insults—"Don't beg me, dog, by knees or by parents" (*Il.* 22.345)—Adam returns "fierce passion" to Eve's soft words and repels her with "stern regard" (*PL* 10.865–66). Only when Eve supplicates him anew, falling at his feet and embracing his knees, does he relent.

Of course, neither the persons nor the circumstance in *Paradise Lost* replicate those of Homer's epic. Priam is a reverend old man and Achilles' enemy, not his erstwhile beloved companion. Priam seeks the return of his son's body, not Achilles' forgiveness. Ostensibly, Priam and Eve seek different ends. But both take the same risk, and in action, in gesture, what happens in these two scenes is parallel. With a gesture of supplication and supplicating speech, the action is reversed—suddenly. In the face of anger, Priam and Eve risk rejection but attain instead acceptance and peace.

By clasping the knees of Adam, Eve has taken the posture of a Homeric suppliant. In the very beginning of the *Iliad*, Homer made Thetis assume this posture before Zeus, as she begged a favor for her son. Throughout the epic, moreover, Homeric warriors clasped the knees of their enemy when they asked for mercy. Homer has made the kneeling Priam resemble Thetis and the suppliants who have gone before him. When we turn to *Paradise Lost*, however, this gesture, so appropriate in Homeric epic, seems at first completely out of context in pastoral Eden. But Milton knows what he is doing as he brings the classical precedent visually before our eyes.

> But *Eve*
> Not so repulst, with Tears that ceas'd not flowing,
> And tresses all disorder'd, at his feet,
> Fell humble, and imbracing them, besought
> his peace. (10.909–13)

Eve's words also suggest the Homeric suppliant:

> thy suppliant
> I beg, and clasp thy knees . . .
> . . . On me exercise not
> Thy hatred for this misery befall'n,
> On me already lost, mee than thy self
> More miserable. (10.917–18, 927–30)

Eve's lowly plight, as does her immovable posture kneeling before him, moves her husband: "in *Adam* wrought / Commiseration; soon his heart relented" (10.939–40). Like Achilles he feels pity for another human being.

Aristotle's term for a reversal in fortune in tragedy would be *pertipeteia*. Often accompanied by *anagnorisis*—a recognition that indicates a change from ignorance to knowledge—it produces love or hate, reverses the action, and brings about closure.[16] Milton has incorporated many classical devices into his Christian epic, not the least of them these. Adam experiences something like a tragic *anagnorisis* as he turns from his wrath and re-admits Eve as wife. He accepts the tragedy of their situation, but now he accepts it with understanding and with hope and love—those two indispensable virtues of the Christian triad.

> But rise, let us no more contend, nor blame
> Each other, blam'd enough elsewhere, but strive
> In offices of Love, how may light'n
> Each other's burden in our share of woe. (10.958–61)

Nothing has changed in one way—Adam and Eve still face expulsion from Eden and the burden of the world's woe. But in another way, everything has changed. Just as Achilles and Priam accept the unacceptable in the human condition, so do Adam and Eve. They too choose to go on.[17]

There is a difference, of course, between the man who raises Priam from the ground and commiserates with him and the one who raises Eve. However, reading the scene of Adam's reconcilement with Eve in terms of Achilles' scene with Priam deepens our sense of how Milton has used Homer's epic in his own. Milton follows the ancient poet in bringing his Adam and Eve to a Homeric crisis—in breaking the wrath of Adam with pity, and making possible the closure of the final books.

At two points in the tragic action of his epic, Milton has made Eve play the role that a male character plays in the *Iliad*. Eve takes the place of the beloved companion that Achilles loses; she effects the resolution of the epic by assuming the role that Priam had played in the *Iliad*. Of course, Eve is the only female protagonist in an epic otherwise ruled, as the *Iliad* is, by male protagonists. But she is one who changes the course of the epic in a way that neither Briseis, the effective cause of the quarrel between Agamemnon and Achilles, nor Hector's wife, Andromache, pleading in vain to have a voice in war, nor even Helen does. Yet Milton takes the cue from Homer in turning over the concluding tableau of his epic to the female voice. It is Eve who has the final word in *Paradise Lost*, as she and her husband leave Eden hand in hand. Did Milton remember how Homer at the funeral of Hector brought his epic to a close with a trio of female voices—Andromache, Hecabe, and Helen?

The funeral of Hector closes the *Iliad*, the expulsion from the garden *Paradise Lost*, both fitting conclusions. About the bier of Hector the survivors gather. Though Priam speaks the last words of the *Iliad*, as he orders the wood for the funeral fire, the dirge of the women that precedes his closing injunction puts the female perspective on a battle epic ruled by men's actions. Hector's sister Cassandra sees Priam from afar approaching with Hector's body and calls the people to assemble and do him final homage, for, as she says, he was a great joy to the city and all its people: "ἐπεὶ μέγα χάρμα πόλει τ᾽ ἦν παντί τε δήμῳ" (*Il.* 24.706). Now the three women closest to Hector—his wife, his mother, and his sister-in-law—gather to bewail the fallen hero.

Their dirges are personal, but they also speak of what Hector's loss means to Troy, now bereft of its protector and doomed to fall. Andromache looks forward to a bleak future as a captive woman, either taking her infant son with her into exile or seeing him killed by a Greek taking vengeance on the child for Hector's manslaying ways. She laments that she has even been deprived of attending Hector at his death, when he might have stretched out his arms to her and spoken a condoling word to comfort her in her grief. Hecabe likewise looks back in regret, having lost the dearest of her sons. She can only find comfort now in tending his dead body, lying fresh on his bier after having been terribly abused by Achilles. Helen's lament, the last of the three, is in a way the most poignant. To her Hector was the dearest of her husband's brothers, who never spoke a spiteful word to her but who defended her against the reproaches of others. In weeping for him, she also weeps for herself.

> οὐ γάρ τίς μοι ἔτ᾽ ἄλλος ἐνὶ Τροίῃ εὐρείῃ
> ἤπιος οὐδὲ φίλος, πάντες δέ με πεφρίκασιν.

> Truly there was no one else in wide Troy
> Either gentle or kind; all others shudder at me.　　(24.774–75)

Relentlessly, their dirges look back on a happiness gone and forward to a future that offers no dawning hope or reprieve from misery.

It is true that darkness begins to fall over Eden as the angel catches the lingering Adam and Eve by the hand and hastens their descent from paradise. In some ways the prospect for the human couple, exiled from paradise, is no less gloomy than that which the Trojan women face. When she first hears of the coming exile, Eve exclaims, "O unexpected stroke, worse than of Death!" (*PL* 11.268). Her words could almost be Andromache's, who at the end of the *Iliad* imagines the hollow ships waiting to speed her and the captive women away. But by the end of Book Twelve, though facing a future fraught with woe, Eve can exclaim: "Lead on; / In mee is no delay" (12.614–15). *Paradise Lost* closes looking ahead to the future, with only the slightest glance behind at "Paradise, so late thir happy seat" (12.642).

It is Eve who sets the tone for the final passage of the epic. Like Helen in the *Iliad*, she is the last female speaker, and rightly so, for she knows that she has been the cause of woe, the one for whose "wilful crime" they are banished. But unlike Helen she does not look backward. Helen wishes that she might have died before causing such woe: "ὡς πρὶν ὤφελλον ὀλέσθαι" (*Il.* 24.764). But Eve does not renew her thoughts of suicide. Here Milton, who has found so many fruitful parallels between the ancient epic and his own, insists on the difference between his and Homer's vision. Eve carries with her a Christian consolation that Andromache and Helen are denied, a mark of favor, a promise that "though all by mee is lost, / Such favor I unworthy am voutsaf't, / By mee the Promis'd Seed shall all restore" (*PL* 12.621–23).

Thus Milton closes his dialogue with Homer on a note of difference. Throughout the *Iliad*, but especially in its final scenes, Homer shows us how the human heart is tested in the cauldron of wrath and pity. Milton brings his epic to a close, as Homer had, with a new and more profound understanding of the human condition, insisting on his own sense of the heroic, while never denying the poignant humanity of the Greek epic that has so often lit his way through Eden.

Southern Illinois University, Edwardsville

NOTES

My thanks to Richard DuRocher for his careful and judicious commentary on this article; also to Wendy Furman-Adams and Stephen Buhler for helpful suggestions when I delivered a version of this paper in Florence in 2000. I wish to dedicate this paper to the late David Belmont, Department of Classics, Washington University, my first teacher of Homer.

1. See, for example, Charles Martindale's treatment of the epic encounters of the war in Heaven in *John Milton and the Transformation of Ancient Epic* (London, 1986), 93–102; also Francis C. Blessington, *Paradise Lost and the Classical Epic* (London, 1979), 8–9.

2. See John M. Steadman, *Milton and the Renaissance Hero* (Oxford, 1967), 18; Blessington, 8.

3. *Aristotle's Theory of Poetry and Fine Art, The Poetics*, trans. S. H. Butcher (London, 1895). See especially section 1449b.

4. Aristotle comments how Homer, like the tragic poet, centers his epic on one action, rather than many (*Poetics*, 1451a).

5. See Steadman, *Milton and the Renaissance Hero*, 9–10. Steadman also points out that Renaissance critics sometimes felt that Achilles' valor was tarnished by brutishness and violence. See "Achilles in Renaissance Tradition," *Milton and the Paradoxes of Renaissance Heroism* (Baton Rouge, 1987), 44–45.

6. Blessington comments, "Satan never lands a successful blow." The Son "emerges from the battle in heaven as the archetype of the classical warrior, just as Satan was his distortion. The Son, no longer the humble and self-sacrificing intercessor of the council in heaven, is the true Achilles." "Here," he goes on to say, "real displacement occurs. The wrath of Achilles has become the wrath of God. . . . The vengeance that Achilles arrogated to himself is no longer acceptable in the epic poem" (Blessington, 8, 10, 38–39).

7. Ironically, however, in commenting on the superficial likenesses between Satan and Achilles, Blessington perpetuates the connection between the two: "Just as Achilles withdraws and refuses to show 'αἰδῶς' to Agamemnon, Satan rebels and refuses to yield homage to God. Both refusals begin the action that leads to tragedy in both poems. The wrath of Achilles belongs to Satan, 'But his doom / Reserv'd him to more wrath' (1.53–54), the wrath that he first brings to hell and later to Eden" (10).

8. Martin Mueller, "*Paradise Lost* and the *Iliad*," *Comparative Literature Studies* 6 (1969), 292–316.

9. Homer, *Iliad*, ed. D. B. Monro (Oxford, 1893–94). Translations of the *Iliad*, unless otherwise noted, are mine.

10. John Milton, *Complete Poems and Major Prose*, ed. Merritt Y. Hughes (New York, 1957), 826.

11. See Martindale's discussion of these scenes (88–93); also see Mary Nyquist, "Textual Overlapping and Dalilah's Harlot-Lap," *Literary Theory/Renaissance Texts*, ed. Patricia Parker and David Quint (Baltimore and London: Johns Hopkins Press, 1986), 341–72. Although she mentions the Paris-Helen scene, Nyquist's focus is on the relationship of Milton's Adam to Homer's Zeus and the alleged parallelism of both patriarchs deceived by their wives.

12. Martindale comments that the Zeus-Hera episode had roused criticism both in ancient times and in the Renaissance: "Plato had condemned it for showing Zeus so overcome by passion that he indulged it lying on the ground (*Republic* 3.390 B–C). To Spondanus it was particularly offensive that Zeus should boast about his extra-marital successes" (89). See Joannes Spondanus,"Commentarius," *Homeri Quae Extant Omnia* (Basel, 1583), 268.

13. See Spondanus' comments on Hera's deception of Zeus in *Homeri Quae Extant Omnia*, 275.

14. Later in Book Eleven, God sends down prevenient Grace so that Adam and Eve will be moved to repent.

15. See Kevin Crotty, *The Poetics of Supplication: Homer's Iliad and Odyssey* (Ithaca, 1994), 15. Also see 3–23, 70–88.

16. See *Aristotle's Theory of Poetry and Fine Art, The Poetics*, 36–39 (sections 1452a–1452b). See the discussion of *peripeteia* and *anagnorisis* in John M. Steadman, *Epic and Tragic Structure in Paradise Lost* (Chicago, 1976), 41–59, 67–68, 99–100. Steadman defines *peripeteia* as a change of state in a relatively short space, *anagnorisis* as a recognition of guilt. Mary Nyquist astutely points out that in Book Nine Adam and Eve are represented as undergoing a change in fortune before they have any consciousness of having done so (Nyquist, 344).

17. Aristotle notes that *peripeteia* combines with *anagnorisis* to produce pity and fear in those viewing the drama (1452b). Here the pity is produced in the character involved in the action as well as in the audience.

"IMPREGN'D WITH REASON": EVE'S AURAL CONCEPTION IN *PARADISE LOST*

Kent R. Lehnhof

IN HIS STUDY of sexual attitudes at the time of Milton, James Grantham Turner reviews several interpretations of the Genesis myth in early modern England. He demonstrates that a number of these explications equate Eve's Fall with some sort of sexual transgression. Both Paracelsus and Cornelius Agrippa, for example, interpretively conflate the forbidden fruit with Adam's phallus and identify Eve's sin as an act of copulation. According to this outlook, Satan brings about the Fall of humanity by fostering in Eve a lust that leads to unlawful union with Adam.[1] Although Milton rejects this particular formulation of the Fall, *Paradise Lost* nevertheless participates—at least in part—in this sexualization of humanity's first sin. Milton's erotic interpretation of the Genesis account, however, substitutes sexual companions. Instead of Adam, Satan serves as Eve's first forbidden sexual partner. Rather than simply prompting Eve to carnally enjoy her husband, Satan usurps Adam's role, in a certain sense copulating with Eve and causing her downfall. In this approach, Milton aligns himself with another exegetical tradition also examined by Turner. As Turner notes, rabbinical commentators often instructed that Eve brought sin into the world by having sex with the serpent. Catharist heretics who elaborated on this idea even stipulated the physical particulars of this sex act, teaching that the serpent penetrated Eve with his tail.[2] In his epic eroticization of the Temptation, Milton is not nearly so aggressive. In Milton's account, the physical is displaced onto the verbal. Milton not only substitutes Satan for Adam but also substitutes discourse for intercourse. In *Paradise Lost* Satan inseminates Eve not with his phallus or with his tail but rather with his tongue. Using his mouth as an instrument of generation, Satan impregnates Eve through her ear, causing her to conceive sin and death.

The idea of oral insemination is not original to Milton, nor is it foreign to the exegetical tradition of his Christian subject matter. For centuries certain branches of Christianity have fostered a tradition of aural impregnation in connection with the Incarnation, contending that the Virgin Mary conceives

38

the Son of God through the ear. According to this understanding, the Annunciation does not foretell a conception to befall Mary in the future but actually effects that very event. The Virgin Mother conceives the Christ-child immediately upon hearing the divine declaration/decree, "Thou shalt conceive." As John Wall indicates, the feasting calendar of the medieval and early modern church implicitly institutionalizes this idea, for the Feast of the Annunciation is celebrated on March 25—exactly nine months before the day of Christ's birth.[3] The idea of aural conception is explicitly addressed in the writings of a number of Christian authors, ranging from the imposing to the obscure. For instance, the Breviary of the Maronites proclaims: "The Father's Word entered through the ear of the Blessed One,"[4] and a hymn believed to have been written by either Thomas à Becket or St. Bonaventure intones: "Rejoice, Virgin, mother of Christ, / Who conceived by the ear, / By Gabriel's message."[5] St. Agobard is included in the list of auricular advocates, asserting: "He came down from heaven sent from the Father's citadel, he entered in through the Virgin's ear into our realm."[6] The idea also appears in texts tentatively attributed to St. Ephrem. The "Homily on the Nativity" instructs:

> Just as the bush on Horeb bore
> God in the flame,
> so did Mary bear
> Christ in her virginity.
> Perfectly God,
> He entered the womb through her ear,
> in all purity the God-Man
> came forth from the womb into creation.[7]

Even St. Augustine is supposed to have espoused this interpretation of the Annunciation, straightforwardly stating: "God spoke through the angel and the Virgin was impregnated through the ear."[8]

The idea of aural impregnation that underwrites these exegetical interpretations also informs artistic approaches to the Annunciation. Several visual representations of the scriptural scene re-create the episode in terms of oral insemination and aural penetration. Often, the angel is identified as the inseminating instrument. In Simone Martini's *Annunciation* (Figure 1), the words issuing from Gabriel's mouth proceed directly into Mary's ear. Demurely receiving these words, Mary demonstrates the modest reluctance yet eventual acceptance appropriate to an obedient virgin submitting to the paternal wishes of an authoritative male.[9] In the Annunciation panel of Nicolas of Verdun's *Klosterneuburg Altar* (Figure 2), a ray of light emanating from Gabriel's outstretched index finger enters Mary's ear. The angel leans forward as an astonished Mary raises her hands in surrender. The presentation in this manner associates the Annunciation with the operation of an irresistible impregnating force.[10] In Jacopo Torriti's mosaic (Figure 3), the angel also stretches out his finger towards Mary, but the ray of light comes not from the angel's finger but rather from the Father's mouth. Visible in the heavens above, the Father speaks forth an inseminating stream that carries the dove of the Holy Ghost directly into Mary's ear. With its wings tucked in and its beak foremost, the dove dives directly at the Virgin, emphasizing a penetrative approach to the Annunciation.[11] The *Netze Passion Altar* (Figure 4) also shows a stream of light leaving the Father's mouth and carrying a dove in the direction of the Virgin's ear, but the head of the dove is no longer visible, having already entered Mary's ear. The ray of light emanating from the Father's mouth also carries an embryonic Christ, or homunculus. The idea of aural invasion indicated by the diving, half-visible bird is duplicated in the posture of the homunculus. Like the dove that precedes him, the infant descends headlong in the direction of Mary's ear. Indeed, the divine child shoulders a miniature cross that seems positioned to serve as a battering ram, better enabling the child to penetrate the Virgin's ear and immediately enter her womb.[12]

In Master Bertram's portrayal of the Annunciation (Figure 5) not just one but both of Mary's ears are being invaded. A scroll of words unraveling from Gabriel's finger penetrates the Virgin's left ear, while a dove and a Christ-child issuing from the Father's mouth in heaven enter her right ear.[13] Perhaps the most explicit expression of Mary's auricular conception, however, is found in the Lady Chapel of the Würzburg Cathedral. The stone relief above the north door of the chapel (Figure 6) shows the Father blowing into a phallic-like tube, the other end of which is inserted into Mary's ear. The phallic symbolism of the tube as an instrument of insemination is indicated by the anatomical route it traces, emerging from between the Father's legs. Emphasizing the aural endpoint of this tube, the artist has pulled back the Virgin's long tresses in order to clearly expose her intricately carved ear. A dove is pictured at the precise moment of entering this ear. Having traveled the length of the tube, the dove's beak is just beginning to pierce the Virgin's auditory canal. A little higher up, Christ as a homunculus slides head-first along the tube. With his hands clasped in front of him, the homunculus assumes the position of a diver preparing to break the surface of the water. Following the course of the bird of the Holy Spirit, the Christ-child readies himself to plunge into Mary's womb by means of her ear.[14]

The notion of aural conception in the theology, artwork, and religious practices of the medieval and early modern eras has its counterpart in secular drama; Shakespeare's texts often refer to the ear as an orifice of conception.

Figure 1. Simone Martini. *Annunciation* (detail, center panel).

Figure 2. Nicolas of Verdun. *Klosterneuburg Altar* (detail).

Figure 3. Jacopo Torriti. *Annunciation.*

Figure 4. *Annunciation* (detail of Netze Passion Altar).

Figure 5. Master Bertram of Minden. *Grabow Altar* (detail).

Figure 6. *Annunciation* (from the North portal of Marienkapelle Cathedral). Würzburg, Germany.

Cleopatra, for example, tells Antony's messenger to "Ram thou thy fruitful tidings in mine ears, / That long time have been barren" (*Antony and Cleopatra* 2.5.24–25).[15] Philippa Berry demonstrates that the idea is also present in *Hamlet*. According to Berry, much of the play's imagery evolves out of "an implicit quibble upon 'earing' as copulation."[16]

In the tragedy of *Othello*, however, the idea of aural impregnation is not simply implicit—it informs the plot of the entire play. In his very first soliloquy Iago invokes images of auricular impregnation, claiming that he has "engend'red" a scheme and explaining that by "abus[ing] Othello's ear" he will "bring this monstrous birth to the world's light" (1.3.395–404). Michael Long follows this trail of insemination, incubation, and delivery, emphasizing that the plot of the play imitates a repulsive pregnancy: "a hideous birth, whose conception takes place in Act One and delivery in Act Five." According to Long:

At first it is remote and small in "the womb of time", then "engender'd" in the brain of Iago: "Hell and night / Must bring this monstrous birth to the world's light" (1.3.397–98). Thereafter we hear of its foetal formation—"'tis here, but 'tis confused"—and later Othello senses its quickening and growth in the womb of Iago's brain: "As if there were some monster in his thought / Too hideous to be shown," (3.3.111–12); "As if thou then hadst shut up in thy brain / Some horrible conceit" (3.3.118–19).

Long observes that by Act Three, Iago has successfully transplanted this embryonic evil into Othello: "Emilia and Desdemona now sense its growth as 'some unhatch'd practice', some 'conception' now felt to be in the brain of Othello." Long claims that Othello originally fears Iago's conception:

But then, with the vaginal ragings of "a cistern for foul toads / To knot and gender in" and "the gate of hell," the thing begins to be born in him. Desdemona's "Alas, what does this gentleman conceive?" is her bewildered response to its coming, and then his eyes roll and his frame is shaken and we get "the strong conception / That I do groan withal."[17]

The fact that Othello's "strong conception" has come through the ear does not escape John Wall. He accurately avers that in the course of the play:

Othello's ear and Iago's tongue become displaced organs of generation, and Iago is revealed as the Moor's aural-sexual partner. Iago's words thus become the seed which impregnates Othello's mind through his ear so that it will produce the "monstrous birth" of jealousy, the "green-eyed monster." . . . It is Othello's mind, assaulted through his ear, which gives birth in this play, and not Desdemona's abandoned, and thus barren, womb.[18]

Moreover, Wall not only connects Othello's conception to the ear but also envisions the way in which this aspect of the play intersects with accounts of the

Annunciation that evoke the idea of aural impregnation. Wall claims that Iago is "a demonic Gabriel, creat[ing] through his words a 'monstrous birth,' a 'dangerous conceit' borne to Othello's ear." According to Wall, Shakespeare carefully connects Othello's temptation to Mary's Annunciation, showing through this juxtaposition that language is capable of bringing about both redemption and damnation. Shakespeare employs the idea of aural impregnation, then, in order to "remind us of the doubleness of human words."[19]

Milton utilizes in his own writings this tradition of auricular conception. Throughout *Paradise Lost* Milton patterns Eve's Temptation after Mary's Annunciation, presenting the Temptation in terms of oral insemination and aural impregnation. Milton's account of the Fall in this way indicates that Eve and the Temptation are typological precursors to Mary and the Annunciation.

Milton's desire to link Eve and the Temptation to Mary and the Annunciation surfaces in several places in the poem. For instance, Albert C. Labriola observes that the appellations applied to Eve by both Adam and the epic narrator are customarily associated in early modern literature with the Virgin Mother.[20] When Raphael first meets Eve in Book Five, this implicit typology is asserted openly, for Raphael's salutation to Eve is identical to Gabriel's later greeting to Mary. The narrator takes pains to emphasize the overlap, stressing that the *"Haile"* bestowed by Raphael on Eve is, indeed, "the holy salutation us'd / Long after to blest *Marie, second Eve" (PL* 5.385–87).[21] Milton's typological intent is manifest in the simple fact that Mary is only mentioned by name twice in the entire epic, yet each time she is identified as an antitype of Eve: "blest *Marie, second Eve"* and *"Mary second Eve"* (5.387; 10.183).[22] In his concerted effort to connect Eve and Mary, Milton engages with a number of patristic authors who elaborate at length a typological relationship between the two women.

In his study of Mariology in the patristic tradition, Walter Burghardt claims that the typological vision of Mary as the New Eve constitutes "the primordial patristic insight with respect to the Mother of Christ."[23] Burghardt traces this typology all the way back to the first century, when Bishop Papias appears to have asserted that the Annunciation took place on the same day as the Temptation.[24] In the following centuries, analogies between Eve and Mary were developed and disseminated by authorities in both the East and the West. According to Burghardt, the three most significant literary figures of the second and third centuries all championed the concept that Mary is the Second Eve. In Burghardt's view, Irenaeus occupies a prominent position in this exegetical tradition, for he is the first to integrate the Eve-Mary analogy with a formal theology.[25] In *Adversus haereses* Irenaeus instructs:

Just as Eve, wife of Adam yes, yet still a virgin . . . became by her disobedience the cause of death for herself and the whole human race, so Mary too, espoused yet a virgin, became by her obedience the cause of salvation for herself and the whole human race. . . . The point is, what is tied together cannot possibly be untied save by inversion of the process whereby the bonds of union have arisen, so that the original ties are loosed by the subsequent, and the subsequent set the original free. . . . And so it was that the knot of Eve's disobedience was loosed by Mary's obedience.²⁶

The formulation of the Mary-Eve analogy found in *Adversus haereses* is particularly pertinent insofar as Milton is concerned, for Milton mentions the tract in his own writings. In *Of Prelatical Episcopacy*, Milton points to the very passage cited above, criticizing Irenaeus for claiming that Mary's obedience is "the cause of salvation for . . . the whole human race." Maintaining that this salvific role belongs solely to the Son, Milton accuses Irenaeus of idolatry and refuses to recognize his authority in doctrinal debates (YP 1:642).²⁷

Although Milton rejects the veneration of Mary informing Irenaeus's interpretation of the relationship between Mary and Eve, he does not deny that the two women are typologically tied to one another. Milton in fact avails himself of the idea that Eve's experience in Eden foreshadows the supernatural conception experienced by Mary, adapting the analogy to conform with and express his own theological convictions. He appropriates for his own ends the Marian traditions of patristic authors in the same way that he drafts into service the pagan myths of classical eras. Christianizing the pagan and Protestantizing the Catholic, Milton syncretizes that which advances his epic aims.

In this Protestant appropriation of the typology of the Second Eve, Milton indicates that the Temptation in Eden constitutes a corruption of the kind of conception enacted at the Annunciation. Although Mary's union with God preserves her purity, Eve's relations with Satan in *Paradise Lost* compromise her chastity. Whereas Mary's conception in the New Testament is undeniably literal, Eve's conception in the epic vacillates between the metaphorical, the allegorical, and the real. Thus, the Temptation in Eden constitutes a vitiated and debased version of the Annunciation. Eve's aural conception parodically prefigures the Annunciation, wherein God impregnates Mary through the ear.

Satan's role as an oral author in this typological tale of aural impregnation is evident from the outset—even before he has been expelled from Heaven. Immediately after the Father has announced the begetting of his Son, Satan seeks out his sub-commander and engages him in precisely the type of oral/aural intercourse that we will see in Eden. Whispering into the ear of Beelzebub, Satan metaphorically impregnates his second in command. As Raphael explains, Satan "infus'd" into "th' unwarie brest / Of his Associate" the "deep malice" and "bad influence" that he has only a few lines earlier been "conceiving" within himself (5.666, 694–96). After sowing sinful thoughts in Beelzebub's breast, the Adversary trains his "potent tongue" on the other angels under his command (6.135). "With calumnious Art / Of counterfeted truth," Raphael recounts, Satan "thus held thir ears" (5.770–71). Abusing the ears of his subordinates, Satan implants in his cohorts the envy he feels within himself. He uses insidious speech to refashion heavenly inhabitants after his own likeness, transforming upright angels into duplicates of his own disobedient self.

When Michael rebukes Satan on the battlefields of Heaven, he foregrounds the reproductive significance of Satan's deeds, adopting a terminology of propagation. Vilifying Satan as the "Author of evil" (6.262), Michael exclaims:

> how hast thou disturb'd
> Heav'ns blessed peace, and into Nature brought
> Miserie, uncreated till the crime
> Of thy Rebellion? how hast thou instill'd
> Thy malice into thousands, . . .
>
> . . . .
>
> Hence then, and evil go with thee along
> Thy ofspring, to the place of evil, Hell,
> Thou and thy wicked crew.   (6.266–70, 275–77)

The ideas of insemination and creation that underwrite Michael's accusation are appropriate, for Satan has indeed impregnated his companions with evil. In the same way that Sin is to Satan both a lover and a child, the angels that Satan impregnates are simultaneously his sexual partners and his progeny. In keeping with the epic's confusion of demonic genealogies, the fallen angels assume the role of parent (the agent who conceives) and offspring (the new being that issues from the conception). After conceiving Satan's evil through the ear, the fallen angels become Satan's children. No longer known as the "Sons of Heaven" they are identified instead as the "sons of Darkness" (1.654; 6.715).

Although the Son eventually fulfills Michael's wish to exile Satan and his "ofspring," the Adversary eventually escapes the confines of Hell. Satan's journey from Hell to Eden emphasizes at many points his intention to pervert creation by promoting and perpetrating improper propagation. When he encounters his children, Sin and Death, at the edge of Hell, Satan succeeds in re-seducing his former sexual partner. Persuading Sin to unlock the Gates of Hell, Satan gains entry into the realm of Chaos. Michael Lieb alerts us to the sexual implications of this trespass by reminding us that Chaos is repeatedly referred to as a womb, particularly the womb of God.[28] In this light, Satan's invasion of Chaos "takes on the character of a sexual offense to a realm associated with impregnation and procreation." As Lieb writes: "The privacy of the Abyss as a womb is violated in Satan and Sin's perverted indiscretion."[29] Satan's own description of his journey supports this interpretation; the villain boasts that he "plung'd in the womb / Of unoriginal *Night* and *Chaos* wilde," forcing "uncouth passage" (10.475–77).

Lieb notes that Satan's arrival on earth is similarly associated with a sexual violation, for Milton's description of the new world is anatomically suggestive: "The insulated world . . . that Satan approaches becomes in itself a living organism that takes on characteristics of bodily functions." According to Lieb, Milton deliberately chooses words with corporeal connotations in his description of the landscape leading up to Eden in order to "[place] the whole description within the human context." These bodily images turn Satan's trespass into a type of rape: "Sexually, Satan assumes the posture of an assault: he is about to attempt to penetrate and thereby defile a pure, unfallen, womb-like area that shelters and sustains what exists within."[30]

This demonic mission of sexual penetration eventually targets the matrimonial bower of Adam and Eve. Intending to "violate sleep, and those / Whose dwelling God hath planted here in bliss," Satan sneaks into Adam and Eve's boudoir (4.883–84). Although the bower is so "sacred and sequesterd" that "other Creature here / Beast, Bird, Insect, or Worm durst enter none," Satan nevertheless invades this privatized and enclosed interior of marital intimacy (4.703–6). The fiend then essays another invasive act, one that hearkens back to the aural impregnation associated with the Annunciation. Satan speaks forth a stream of words in an attempt to penetrate Eve's ear and gain access to her inner organs. As the narrator informs us, Satan crouches

> Squat like a Toad, close at the eare of *Eve*;
> Assaying by his Devilish art to reach
> The Organs of her Fancie, and with them forge
> Illusions as he list.   (4.800–803)

Describing the encounter in terms of penetration, the narrator presents Satan and Eve's interaction as a simulacrum of sexual intercourse. Satan's tongue acts as a phallus, and Eve's ear—as the orifice that Satan penetrates and through which he intends to introduce the seeds of sin—functions as a vagina. The anatomical reordering herein effected finds numerous parallels in early modern discourses of the body.

As Carla Mazzio points out, early modern expositions on the tongue often contemplate "the isomorphic relations between the tongue and the penis, that other bodily member with an apparent will of its own." In *Pathomyatomia* (1649), for instance, John Bulwer speculates that there is a connection between "the Egresse of the Tongue out of the mouth and of *Pria-*

pisme."[31] Jacopo Berengario's *Microcosmographia*, appearing in translation in London in 1664, also explores the analogical relationship between the extension of the tongue and the erection of the penis:

> Yet there are many that say, that the Tongue is not moved to the outward parts voluntarily, but meerly naturally from the imagination, as the Yard; and some say that it, and also the Yard are moved of muscles, and of the imagination together, and some of the imagination only, which by means of the spirit causeth a windinesse, dilating, and erecting the Yard, and in like manner the Tongue, with bringing it out of the mouth.[32]

Although comparisons of this kind can be found in medieval texts, Mazzio claims that early modern authors elaborated on the tongue-penis homology with increasing detail and specificity. According to Mazzio, "associations between the tongue and the penis became more explicit in the sixteenth and seventeenth centuries," as did "the imagined relationship between rhetorical and sexual performance."[33] *Paradise Lost* appears to participate in this analogical approach, implying that Satan's tongue is a penetrative instrument of insemination. In the same way that Renaissance texts conflate rhetorical performance with sexual performance, Milton's account of the dream temptation blurs the boundaries between discourse and intercourse.

As Eve engages in verbal/sexual congress with Satan, her ear comes to stand in for her vagina. This kind of anatomical reordering, substituting one female orifice for another, also appears in early modern texts. Karen Newman demonstrates that Renaissance writers continually confuse the vagina with the mouth, identifying immoderate consumption and excessive speech with sexual impropriety. In early modern texts, Newman explains, "women's two mouths are conflated. . . . An open mouth and immodest speech are tantamount to open genitals and immodest acts."[34] Although Newman only addresses the equivalency of mouth and vagina, early modern exhortations to virtue mention other orifices as well. Stephen Gosson, for instance, informs his female audience: "If you doe but listen to the voyce of the fouler, or joyne lookes with an amorous gazer, you have already made your selves assaultable, and yeelded your cities to be sacked."[35] Gosson's lesson on chastity advises women to shut their mouths, but commands them to seal up other openings as well:

> The best councel that I can give you is to keepe at home, and shun all occasion of ill speech. The virgins of Vesta were shut up fast in stone walles to the same end. You must keepe your sweete faces from scorching in the sun, chapping in the winde, and warping in the weather, which is best perfourmed by staying within; and if you perceive your selves in any danger at your owne doors, either allured by curtesie in the day, or assaulted with musike in the night, close uppe your eyes, stoppe your eares, tye up your tongues.[36]

Commending the corporeal impermeability of the walled-in virgins of Vesta, Gosson worries over every female orifice. Requiring women to close their eyes, their ears, and their mouths, Gosson suggests that each bodily opening potentially betokens the vagina. In *Paradise Lost* Milton plays upon this signifying potential, turning Eve's ear into a symbolic vagina.[37] When Satan inserts his phallic tongue into Eve's receptive ear, the Adversary initiates an act of intercourse that oscillates between the sexual and the verbal, the analogical and the actual. As he tries to inseminate Eve through her ear, Satan imitates the method through which the Father impregnates Mary. Indeed, Satan's "Devilish art" of "inspiring venom" is the demonic counterpart to the Father's creative pronouncements at the time of the Annunciation (4.801, 804).

The dream that Satan creates for Eve further reinforces the relationship between the temptation in the bower and the Annunciation. In her dream, Eve is approached not by a toad (Satan's actual form at the moment) but by a beautiful angel. J. M. Evans is on the right track when he tentatively proposes that the gorgeous angel appearing in Eve's dream mirrors the magnificent Gabriel who appears to Mary at the Annunciation. Although Evans ultimately backs away from his speculation, I believe that he is correct in his initial proposition: "It is just conceivable that Milton wished to strengthen the standard typological parallel between Eve and Mary by giving Eve an experience analogous to Mary's vision of Gabriel at the Annunciation."[38]

A. B. Chambers also picks up on the correlation between dream and Annunciation. Linking Eve's dream with the tradition of Mary's conception through the ear, Chambers explains that Eve conceives sin and death through the words of a hellish angel in the same way that Mary conceives life and salvation through the words of a divine angel. As Chambers writes: "By means of his unwitting parody of Gabriel's relationship to Mary, Satan does cause an imaginative version of the conception of sin to occur."[39]

Satan's choice of bestial vehicle in the bower also suggests an aural seduction and impregnation, for medieval and early modern ideas about toads tie them closely to lust, sexuality, and copulation. Francis Klingender claims that during the twelfth century artists in France "degraded the ancient Earth-Goddess nourishing infants or serpents at her breast into the hideous nightmare of Lust devoured by toads and serpents."[40] Roland Frye notes that numerous medieval depictions of Hell identify lustful women by portraying them with toads attached to their breasts or vaginas.[41] Adolf Katzenellenbogen claims that sculptors of the Romanesque period take a similar approach: "the breasts and abdomen of the lustful woman are sucked out by toads and repulsive serpents."[42] Brueghel utilizes this iconography in the *Fall of the Rebel Angels*, and Bosch employs it repeatedly in such works as the

Seven Deadly Sins, the *Hay Wain* triptych, and the *Garden of Earthly Delights* triptych.[43]

This artistic tradition of attaching toads to female genitals speaks to Satan's nocturnal transformation. As a toad in the bower, Satan strives to penetrate Eve's ear with a stream of sinful suggestions. In this interchange, Eve's ear substitutes for her vagina, serving as the orifice through which Satan's seed is intromitted. As Eve's ear becomes a vagina, the gardens of Milton and Bosch converge. Bosch's toads attached to the (genital) vagina in the *Garden of Earthly Delights* correlates to Milton's toad attached to the (aural) vagina in the Garden of Eden. In both works, the presence and precise anatomical position of the toad signal an evil or illicit union. Gesturing toward the iconographic significance of the toad as a marker of sinful concupiscence, *Paradise Lost* transmogrifies Satan into a toad to imply a sexual impurity in his interaction with Eve.

Although Frye claims that the toad symbolizes lechery only when specifically situated on the genitals, Peter McCluskey persuasively argues for a more widespread association between toads and lust, demonstrating that early modern texts often equate toads with loathsome sexuality.[44] Shakespeare's Ajax, for instance, claims "I do hate a proud man, as I do hate the engend'ring of toads" (*Troilus and Cressida* 2.3.158–59). When Othello vilifies Desdemona as "a cestern for foul toads / To knot and gender in," the verbal association of toads and lust coalesces with the visual custom of using toads to label the lascivious (*Othello* 4.2.61–62). Othello's phrase not only accuses Desdemona of possessing the repugnant lust of "foul toads," but also riffs on the iconographic idea that toads attached to a woman's vagina indicate her immorality. Othello revises the iconography, however, by locating the toads on the interior rather than the exterior of Desdemona's vagina: it is Desdemona's womb that serves as the receptacle that Othello calls a "cestern." In what Michael Long accurately terms Othello's "vaginal ravings," Othello contends that his wife not only exhibits but also teems with toadsome lust.[45]

It is no accident that Othello in his jealousy refers to the exact animal that squats at Eve's ear in the bower of Book Four. The toad appears in both *Othello* and *Paradise Lost* because both texts are concerned with aural conception and oral insemination. To explain why both Shakespeare and Milton would associate the image of the toad with the idea of oral/aural reproduction, we turn to Edward Topsell's *History of Serpents*, first published in 1608 and reissued as a slightly revised version in 1658.[46]

In his scientific account of the animals that make up the serpent family, Topsell acknowledges the aforementioned association of toads and lust by devoting a great deal of attention to their reproductive activities. In the course of this discussion, Topsell acknowledges a pervasive opinion that toads inseminate their mates with their mouths rather than with their genitals. Some have thought, Topsell relates, that the male performs the act of copulation "by the mouth." Topsell himself believes that the male services the female with "the instrument of generation," but his discussion in other ways associates the toad with aural sex (719).[47] Explaining that "with their croaking voyces the male provoketh the female to carnal copulation," Topsell turns the voice of the toad into a sexual instrument, diminishing in this manner the distance between oral and genital impregnation (719). Both Milton and Shakespeare gesture toward this understanding of the toad as an oral inseminator (or, at least, as an oral seducer) by invoking the image of the toad in situations suggestive of oral/aural propagation.

Topsell's text is especially illuminating insofar as Milton's toad is concerned, for *The History of Serpents* identifies the toad not only with oral insemination but also with Satanic influence. Once again witnessing the toad's significance as an emblem of lust and debauchery, Topsell talks at length of "the conception of Toads in Women." Topsell reports "it hath also been seen, that women conceiving with childe, have likewise conceived at the same time a Frog, or a Toad, or a Lizard." Topsell piously proclaims: "But what should be the reason of these so strange and unnatural conceptions, I will not take upon me to decide in nature, lest the Omnipotent hand of God should be wronged." Nevertheless, he cannot resist speculating. Pointing to apocalyptic prophecies "that Frogs and Locusts should come out of the Whore of *Babylon*," Topsell triumphantly reports that all of these toad births have taken place in Italy (728). These monstrous deliveries, Topsell avers, testify to Satan's grip on the Roman Catholic Church. Satan's power over papal countries is witnessed by the corruption of human reproductive behavior. Topsell's observations easily align themselves with the implications of what takes place in the bower of *Paradise Lost*. Were Satan to succeed in impregnating Eve through the ear while she sleeps, the issue would perhaps resemble the toad form its father took during the act of impregnation. Eve's delivery of a toad would illustrate her abasement. Her transformation into a Whore of Babylon would be made manifest by her monstrous maternity.

Moreover, Satan's strategy for engaging Eve in aural/sexual reproduction is perfectly harmonious with the reproductive behavior Topsell attributes to toads. As Peter McCluskey points out: "Topsell's moralistic description of the engendering of toads almost reads as a gloss of Satan's first temptation of Eve." As Topsell tells it, when toads emerge from hibernation:

With their croaking voyces the male provoketh the female to carnal copulation, . . . and this they perform in the night season, nature teaching them the modesty or shamefastnesse of this action: And besides in that time they have more security to give themselves to mutual imbraces, because of a general quietnesse, for men and all other their adversaries are then at sleep and rest. (719)

In Milton's account, Satan acts just like one of Topsell's toads. The Adversary uses the cover of night to provoke Eve to a copulation confusingly located somewhere between the carnal and the symbolic. And Eve's physiological response might attest to the success of Satan's croaking. When Eve awakens in Book Five, her face is flushed. Satan's actions seem to have elicited the secondary sexual response of increased blood flow. Eve's "glowing Cheek" perhaps signifies both her sexual arousal and her unconscious participation in Satan's carnal fantasy (5.10). Before Satan succeeds in "ingendring," however, Ithuriel and Zephon stop the scene, prodding the Adversary in such a way as to startle him (4.809). The narrator compares Satan's reaction to a pile of gunpowder touched with a spark:

> up he starts
> Discoverd and surpriz'd. As when a spark
> Lights on a heap of nitrous Powder, laid
> Fit for the Tun som Magazin to store
> Against a rumord Warr, the Smuttie graine
> With sudden blaze diffus'd inflames the Aire.   (4.813–18)

Forced to withdraw from Eve's ear before effecting the kind of conception he intends, Satan's paternally minded pronouncements go up in smoke. The piercing ray of light that appears in portrayals of the Annunciation is dissipated in the account of the dream temptation, turning into a short-lived burst of unfocused and undirected light that quickly fades. In contrast to the Father's words, which directly penetrate the ear of the virgin, Satan's words flare up and fizzle out.

But the gunpowder simile involves heat as well as light, and when we read the passage in terms of Galenic models of reproduction, we uncover another way in which the simile suggests activities associated with impregnation. According to Galenic medical models prevalent during early modern times, sexual reproduction is a function of heat: the chafing of intercourse heats blood in both the male and the female. The blood heated in this fashion becomes the "male seed" and the "female seed" that unite to form a fetus.[48] In this physiological framework, then, semen is closely associated with heat. As a few bold readers have been ready to point out, Milton employs this Galenic equation of heat and semen in A Mask. The throne on which Comus confines the Lady is "smear'd with gumms of glutenous heat" (917), a substance that scholars such as John Shawcross and William Kerrigan have identified as semen.[49] Milton's practice in A Mask of using "heat" to euphemistically denote "semen" illuminates the epic simile of *Paradise Lost*. If heat signifies semen, then the gunpowder simile describing Satan's premature retreat from Eve's ear can be seen to enact a type of *coitus interruptus*. Because Satan is compelled to terminate his intimate interaction with Eve before reaching his desired end, the words that he has attempted to introduce into Eve's ear/vagina are errantly expelled into the open. Satan releases into the air a burst of heat and energy suggestive of the vital heat of semen. In this way, the Galenic elements of Milton's simile reinforce the notion that the bower temptation sketches out a simulacrum of sexual intercourse aiming at aural conception. The inseminating stream of words that Satan directs upon Eve in the second scene of temptation, however, is not misdirected.

As Milton begins the book that will eventually describe the second temptation of Eve, he briefly digresses from his epic plot in order to acknowledge the divine source of his verse. The poet gratefully recognizes the beneficence of his "Celestial Patroness," who grants him "nightly visitation[s] unimplor'd, / And dictates to me slumbring, or inspires / Easie my unpremeditated Verse" (9.21–24). The digression establishes a heavenly origin for Milton's epic but simultaneously revives the model of auricular conception that had been conveyed five books earlier in the account of Eve's bower temptation. The process of poetic composition that Milton claims for himself closely parallels the events of Satan and Eve's initial encounter in Eden, when the uninvited Adversary visits the sleeping Eve and strives to influence the "Organs of her Fancie," by "forg[ing] / Illusions" and "inspiring venom" (4.802–4). Milton's lines on the nightly visitation of his inspiring Muse gently gesture backwards, reminding the reader of Eve's own nocturnal visitor. Declaring that he obtains his poetry from an otherworldly visitor who "brings it nightly to my Ear," Milton resurrects the idea of auricular conception, preparatory to the telling of the second temptation. Foregrounding in the first parts of Book Nine a model of literary creation based upon aural conception, Milton prompts the reader to recognize the aural aspects of the Temptation that will soon take place. Soon after priming the reader to perceive the way in which Eve's temptation becomes an insemination through the ear, Milton launches into an account of Satan and Eve's second encounter.

As was the case in the first meeting, Satan and Eve's second encounter occurs in a highly sexualized setting. The site of the second temptation is likened to mythical gardens of amorous activity. Alluding to "those Gardens feign'd / . . . of reviv'd *Adonis*" the text evokes Ovid's myth of Venus and her boar-slain lover, traditionally read as an allegory of the dangers of lust (9.439–40). As a footnote in the Oxford Authors edition points out, the reference in these lines also resonates with Spenser's version of the tale, identifying Eden with "the secret garden where Adonis and Venus make love."[50] The comparison to the garden "not Mystic, where the Sapient King / Held dalliance with his faire *Egyptian* Spouse" further identifies the setting in Paradise with sexual activity, linking it to the site of Solomon's famous affairs (9.442–43).

These erotic undertones are heightened as Satan advances upon Eve. Albert C. Labriola points out, for instance, that Milton has deliberately insisted throughout the epic that Eve—although naked—is nonetheless "clad" in honor, righteousness, and innocence (4.289). When Satan first sees the solitary woman in Book Nine, this paradoxical state of naked modesty is maintained, for Eve is clothed by a fragrant bank of flowers that render her only half visible. Amidst the roses, Eve is "veild in a Cloud of Fragrance"; she is only "half spi'd, so thick the Roses bushing round / About her glowd" (9.425–27). Labriola notes, however, that Eve is disrobed and exposed as Satan comes closer. Initially, "Eve appears clothed by the roses that surround her," Labriola writes, "but as Satan approaches her, she is figuratively undressed and fully naked to his view":

> What pleasing seemd, for her now pleases more,
> She most, and in her look summs all Delight.
> Such Pleasure took the Serpent to behold
> This Flourie Plat, the sweet recess of *Eve*. (9.453–56)

According to Labriola, the "Flourie Plat" or "sweet recess of *Eve*" that Satan takes such pleasure in contemplating is Eve's pudendum: "the middle of Eve's body." Separated from her husband and protector, Eve's sexualized body is exposed to the Adversary's voyeuristic gaze. As Labriola remarks: "Satan's view of Eve . . . arouses his concupiscence and debases her."[51]

Wolfgang Rudat believes that Satan's lustful concern with Eve's sexual organs manifests itself in his dialogue with her. Rudat stresses the sexual significance of 9.626–29, where the serpent responds to Eve's interrogative about the location of the magical tree:

> Empress, the way is readie, and not long,
> Beyond a row of Myrtles, on a Flat,
> Fast by a Fountain, one small Thicket past
> Of blowing Myrrh and Balme.

According to Rudat:

This is a description of the landscape of a woman's body, similar to a description likewise set in a seduction scene, namely, to the words with which in Shakespeare's *Venus and Adonis* the goddess of love had tried to seduce the young man: "I'll be a park, and thou shalt be my deer: / Feed where thou wilt, on mountain, or in dale; / Graze on my lips, and if those hills be dry, / Stray lower, where the pleasant fountains lie."

Rudat believes that the passage in *Paradise Lost*, like the lines in *Venus and Adonis*, transforms topography into anatomy. In Milton's epic, "the anatomically descending order from the 'row of Myrtles' (breasts) over the 'Flat' (abdomen) and the 'Thicket' (pubic hair) to the 'Fountain'" suggests a caress that concludes at the female genitalia—the fountain just beyond the thicket. By way of this titillating topography, "Milton presents Satan as trying to get to Eve's 'Fountain.'"[52]

When Satan is likened to both Jupiter Ammon and Jupiter Capitolanus in lines 507–10, the sexual expectancy of the scene is enhanced, for the comparison classifies the imbruted Adversary with other legendary lovers who have assumed the serpent's shape in order to have sex with and impregnate the objects of their desire. The phallicization of the Satanic serpent is furthered in other moments as well. Calling to mind the image of an erect penis emerging from curling pubic hair, Satan is said to advance upon Eve, "erect / Amidst his circling Spires" (9.501–02). Writing of the way in which the imbruted Adversary approaches Eve, Wolfgang Rudat emphasizes the sexual echoes of the text. He claims that Milton's description at this point deliberately calls to mind Augustine's contention that prelapsarian man could completely control his sexual member, moving it with the same dexterity that we now move our fingers or our mouths. According to Rudat: "In his description of the controlled movement of the Satanic Serpent . . . Milton appropriates, and transforms into poetry, the prosaically graphic description of a phallic demonstration which he had found in *The City of God*."[53] This pervasive phallicism also informs the idea of tumescence underlying the description of Satan as he begins his assault in earnest: "to highth upgrown / The Tempter all impassiond thus began" (9.677–78).

With the onset of Satan's temptation, the devilish art of aural/vaginal penetration begins anew. Indicating an invasion of Eve's interior spaces, the narrator notes that Satan's words "replete with guile / Into her heart too easie entrance won" (9.733–34). Reproaching Eve for granting Satan "too easie entrance," the narrator calls Eve's chastity into question, accusing her of insufficiently policing her bodily openings. This sexualized account of the Temptation reaches its climax in the succeeding lines, as Eve contemplates the forbidden fruit:

> Fixt on the Fruit she gaz'd, which to behold
> Might tempt alone, and in her ears the sound
> Yet rung of his perswasive words, impregn'd
> With Reason, to her seeming, and with Truth.   (9.735–38)

As she accommodates within herself the "perswasive words" implanted by Satan, Eve performs a symbolic act of conception. The sexual significance of this act is signaled by the idea of impregnation expressed in lines 737–38. Although a strict reading of these lines suggests that the sexually charged participle "impregn'd" modifies the words that Satan speaks, Lara Bovilsky insists that the idea of impregnation is also valid insofar as Eve is concerned:

Though, literally, Satan's argument is the impregnated object in lines 437–38 [sic], its insertion through Eve's ear into her heart suggests that his "truth" germinates within her as well, as another Satanic birth. The "easy entrance" of Satan's speech, its designs to awaken Eve's "eager appetite," and its impregnation in her heart define a trajectory which mimics coitus—and conception.[54]

The conceptual trajectory established in Book Nine progresses rapidly from insemination to gestation. After giving ear to Satan's pregnant and impregnating rhetoric, Eve mulls over the Adversary's invitation: "Pausing a while, thus to her self she mus'd" (9.744). This introspective interval acts as a gestational period, in which Satan's conceit grows within her. Eve's meditative gestation hearkens back to the moment of incubation Sin mentions in her description of the conception and delivery of Death:

> Pensive here I sat
> Alone, but long I sat not, till my womb
> Pregnant by thee, and now excessive grown
> Prodigious motion felt and rueful throes.   (2.777–80)

As was the case with Sin, Eve's gestational period does not last long. Dilating upon Satan's disobedient dialogue, Eve approaches the tree and eats: "Her rash hand in evil hour / Forth reaching to the Fruit, she pluck'd, she eat" (9.780–781).[55]

Eve's disobedience is accompanied by terrestrial tremors, as Nature, "sighing through all her Works gave signs of woe" (9.783). The pangs that Nature feels are not unlike the pains that Sin describes in her own account of labor: the "signs of woe" in Book Nine echo the "rueful throes" of Book Two. The Earth's obstetric earthquake emulates Eve's own conception and delivery. Drawing upon the pathetic fallacy, Milton puts Paradise through parturition at the precise moment of the Fall to reinforce the idea that Eve's intercourse with Satan has caused her to conceive and deliver sin. Satan has succeeded in using seductive words to bring about an aural impregnation like unto that associated with the Annunciation. In the same way that God's words impregnate Mary, Satan's words "impregn" Eve.

In this symbolic conflation of sin and conception, *Paradise Lost* parallels Milton's description of iniquity in the *Christian Doctrine*. In the *Christian Doctrine* Milton also explains the descent into sin in terms of insemination, gestation, and delivery. He writes that the soul is genuinely fallen "when it has conceived sin, when it is heavy with it, and already giving birth to it" (YP

6:332).[56] Milton's equation of sin with sexual reproduction in the *Christian Doctrine* appears to grow out of the writings of St. Paul. Milton's metaphor immediately follows a reference to the first chapter of James, where Paul describes sin and death as the issue of several unseemly conceptions. Apparently providing Milton with a pattern for the sexualizing of sin, Paul declares: "When lust hath conceived, it bringeth forth sin: and sin, when it is finished, bringeth forth death."[57] A. B. Chambers asserts that Milton was not the only early modern exegete attracted to Paul's maternal metaphors. Chambers claims that many of Milton's contemporaries pick up on the propagative nature of Paul's definition and develop in their own writings the connection between sin and sexual reproduction. Robert Jenison's *The Height of Israels Heathenish Idolatrie* (1621) typifies this type of writing. Teasing out Paul's reproductive images, Jenison explains that in the course of sin, the soul first

lyeth open to the Deuils suggestions. *Secondly, wicked thoughts* . . . cast in by Satan, are as the *seed* in the wombe. Then, *sudden delight* is as the *retention* of the seed in the wombe. *Fourthly, Consent* is the *conception* of sinne. *Fifthly*, a more *permanent* and *enduring delight* vpon consent, is as the *fashioning* and *articulation* of it. Then, *Sixtly, purpose* to commit sinne is as the *springing* of the child in the wombe, hastning the birth and egresse. Then *Seuenthly*, follows the *act* it selfe, as the birth of sinne. These are the degrees about the breeding and hatching of sinne.[58]

As Chambers points out, Milton's approach to the Temptation of Eve parallels this model of sin-as-pregnancy: "The process described by Jenison is a reasonably accurate account of what happens to Eve in Book Nine."[59] Jenison's description, however, does not simply delineate the sexualized trajectory of the Fall in *Paradise Lost*. It intervenes importantly in Milton's narrative, for the connection Jenison makes between conception and consent ("*Consent* is the *conception* of sinne") indicates the way in which Eve's agency is asserted in the act of sin, in spite of the numerous suggestions that the Fall is a verbal/sexual ravishment.

Relying upon such classical authorities as Galen and Aristotle, the early moderns asserted the existence of a female seed analogous to the male semen. Although the female seed was believed to be weaker and less pure than the male seed, it was nevertheless considered vital for conception. Conception, it was thought, could only occur if both the male and the female seeds were discharged during the sexual encounter. Because they believed that a female only emits her seed upon attaining orgasm, the early moderns insisted that conception could only come about if a woman enjoyed the sexual act. Thus, conception came to constitute concrete proof that a woman acted as a desiring, consenting participant in any given episode of intercourse. This putative connection is codified in Renaissance rape laws. As Sir Henry Finch professes in the enormously influential *Law, or a discourse thereof* (1627): "Rape is the carnal abusing of a woman against her will. But if she conceives upon any carnal abusing of her, that is no rape, for she cannot conceive unless she consent."[60] Richard Burns reiterates the idea in his guide for English magistrates, citing classical authorities to establish that "a woman can not conceive unless she doth consent."[61] According to Thomas Laqueur, the belief that pregnancy proves complicity was so entrenched in English society that its physiological basis was not even questioned until the second half of the eighteenth or the first half of the nineteenth century.[62] The medico-legal maxim that conception requires consent alleviates concerns about Eve's agency in Eden. When Eve conceives at Satan's suggestion, she conclusively demonstrates to an early modern audience that her will has not been violated, for "a woman can not conceive unless she consent." Suspicions that Satan has overwhelmed or abrogated Eve's agency are undone by the simple fact of her conception. Eve's impregnation establishes that she has not only consented in her relations with Satan but has also derived delight from them.

After the once-erect serpent succeeds in effecting through Eve's ear the conception of sin, it undergoes a post-coital detumescence: "Back to the Thicket slunk / The guiltie Serpent" (9.784–85). Eve's return is even more significant, pointing to a disastrous deflowering. Emphasizing the idea that Eve has in some sense aurally conceived as a result of her discursive intercourse with Satan, the narrator recounts:

> *Adam*, soon as he heard
> The fatal Trespass don by *Eve*, amaz'd,
> Astonied stood and Blank, while horror chill
> Ran through his veins, and all his joynts relax'd;
> From his slack hand the Garland wreath'd for *Eve*
> Down drop'd, and all the faded Roses shed.   (9.888–93)

Playing upon the traditional association of female chastity and maidenhood with flowers, the passage points to Eve's despoiling, for the "faded Roses" of the Garland are irreparably "shed."[63] The encounter with Satan deprives Eve of that which she has possessed only a few hundred lines earlier: "Virgin Majestie" (9.270). As the narrator remarks, Eve has been "Despoild of Innocence" (9.411). Adam, immediately intuiting the sexual pollution of his spouse, bewails Eve's deflowering: "How art thou lost, how on a sudden lost, / Defac't, deflourd, and now to Death devote" (9.900–01).[64]

The union with Satan, however, does more than merely compromise Eve's chastity and transfer her individual allegiance from the Father to the Adversary. Eve's intercourse with Satan also affects the race that is to spring from her womb. Because Satan succeeds in insinuating himself into Eve's creative life, he is able to assume a quasi-paternal relationship in regard to Eve's offspring. Satan's ability to usurp this paternal role unsettles the patterns of obedience that pertain in the prelapsarian Garden, for Edenic obedience is predicated upon subordinating one's self to one's creator(s).

The importance in Eden of submitting to one's creator is illustrated by the fact that Adam's first utterance in the Garden does not proceed for more than a line and a half before referring to "the power / That made us, and for us this ample World" (4.412–13). When he and Eve narrate the stories of their "births," we learn that both sought to learn the source of their existence and the nature of their creator immediately upon gaining self-awareness.[65] Adam's account registers not only his desire to discover the source of his existence but also explains the motive that drives that desire. Imploring the animals to reveal to him the identity of his "Maker," Adam exclaims: "Tell me, how may I know him, how adore, / From whom I have that thus I move and live" (8.280–81). Adam wants to know his creator so that he can adore him. He intuitively recognizes that in Eden, relations of obedience are forged according to creation.

This concept is made even more concrete in Adam and Eve's recorded prayers, the nightly orison of Book Four and the matinal invocation of Book Five. Both prayers follow the same basic form: a lengthy catalog of all that God has created followed by declarations of devotion directed at the "Maker Omnipotent" (4.725). Each prayer suggests that adoration arises from an appreciation of the Father's creativeness. Adam and Eve worship the Father because he has given them (and all other inhabitants of Eden) the gift of life.

Instances of lawgiving in *Paradise Lost* also demonstrate that structures of obedience in Eden are founded upon creation. Just before informing Adam of the terms and conditions of his paradisal state, God proclaims: "Whom thou sought'st I am, / . . . Author of all this thou seest / Above, or round about thee or beneath" (8.316–18). No additional justification for the succeeding prohibitions is offered or asked: God's status as Adam's creator fully legitimizes his authority as lawgiver. Raphael's later visit, designed to reiterate the injunction against eating the forbidden fruit, similarly structures its prohibition around assertions of authorship. The angel begins his admonition by reminding Adam and Eve that they "proceed" from "one Almightie" (5.469–70). Asserting that Adam and Eve have been fashioned from the primary matter by the Father, Raphael simultaneously establishes their obligation to obey the Father. From this point, the angel need do nothing more than explain what the Father requires, for his unfallen audience fully accepts the burden of obedience they owe their creator. As Adam fervently professes: "We never shall forget to love / Our maker, and obey him whose command / Single, is yet so just" (5.550–52). Adam acknowledges the justice of his maker's authority so completely that he cannot even imagine opposing him: "Can we want obedience then / To him, or possibly his love desert / Who formd us from the dust?" (5.514–16).

The obedience that Adam owes to his Maker is fairly straightforward, for God acted alone in forming the first man from the dust of the earth. Since none but the Father and the Son had a hand in his genesis, Adam need recognize no other authority than that of God. Eve's obligations are a little more complex. As Adam is quick to tell his wife, he contributed to her creation: "To give thee being, I lent / Out of my side to thee, neerest my heart / Substantial Life" (4.483–85). Because he donated "his flesh, his bone" to Eve's creation, Adam is in some ways Eve's second father (4.483). As Adam reminds her, Eve is "Daughter of God and Man" (4.660). As a result of Adam's collaboration in her creation, Eve must submit herself not only to God, her primary creator, but also to Adam, her secondary creator. Possessing multiple makers, Eve must acknowledge multiple masters. This state of affairs is outlined in Book Four, when the differences between Adam and Eve's respective "formations" are said to produce differences in their respective responsibilities. Whereas Adam answers to one creator, Eve obeys two: "Hee for God only, shee for God in him" (4.299). On several occasions, Eve acknowledges her numerous obligations and simultaneously recognizes that these obligations arise from the conditions of her creation. In Book Four, for instance, Eve's declaration of submission to Adam accounts for and explains this submission by pointing to the fact that Adam "authored" her: "My Author and Disposer, what thou bidst / Unargu'd I obey; so God ordains" (4.635–36). Adam is one of Eve's masters because he is one of Eve's makers. In Eden, authorship and authority are inextricable.

Had Adam and Eve remained faithful in Eden, their children would have been born into this straightforward system of allegiance. Adam and Eve, made fertile by the Father, would have brought forth a race of humans who would consequently have recognized three authors: God, Adam, and Eve. Owing obedience to these authority figures (and only these), the children of Adam and Eve would have readily perceived their devotional obligations to God the Father. They would have constituted the "Race of Worshippers" that Raphael describes in 7.630. Satan muddies this model of metaphysical obedience, however, when he impregnates Eve with evil. When Eve turns her back on her husband and her God in order to unite with Satan, she affords the Adversary a role in the authorship of the human race. Supplanting the Father as co-creator of the human race, Satan becomes one of humanity's multiple authors. In this position of quasi-paternity, Satan commands from Eve's children an amount of filial obedience. Like Sin, the children of Eve must now acknowledge (albeit to a lesser degree) the presence of Satan in their pedigree. Because Edenic obedience is structured according to authority, Eve's children must in some ways echo Sin's statement to Satan:

> Thou art my Father, thou my Author, thou
> My being gav'st me; whom should I obey
> But thee, whom follow?   (2.864–66)

Eve recognizes this condition when she laments that her children will be compelled by nature of their creation to render obeisance to the Adversary. Eve bewails the fact that her impure loins can bring nothing into the world other than "a woful Race" subject to Sin, Death, and Satan (10.984). As Eve herself realizes, "all by mee is lost" (12.621). The syntax of this assessment neatly conveys the complexity of the situation, encouraging two complementary interpretations. At one level, Eve acknowledges her primary guilt in the fall of humanity: all is lost by (i.e., because of) me. At the same time, she recognizes that sin has perverted her reproductive potential and made it so that her tainted womb can only produce fallen children: all by me (i.e., begotten by me) is lost.

Adam confirms Eve's conclusions when he claims that as a couple they can no longer beget anything other than a "propagated curse" (10.729). Indeed, Adam seems to be fully aware that Eve's sin has brought about a state of reproductive contamination. Reproaching Eve in Book Nine for giving "eare" to their enemy, Adam calls attention to the orifice through which Eve is deflowered but also punningly points to the reproductive repercussions of that deflowering: "O *Eve*, in evil hour thou didst give eare / To that false Worm" (9.1067–68). Remembering that in early modern pronunciation "ear" and "heir" are homonyms, we become aware of a crucial quibble in Adam's statement.[66] Entertaining the serpent's sexualized invitations, Eve allows Satan to impregnate her. By giving "ears" to Satan, Eve gives "heirs" to Satan. Having seduced Eve, Satan can in some sense claim her posterity. Her offspring become his offspring, owing him the kind of obedience due to a creator.

On this point *Paradise Lost* alludes to the theory of the *inquinamentum*, or the physical contamination of Eve. The theory is often expressed in rabbinic biblical commentary and folklore. As Robert Graves and Raphael Patai point out in their investigation of Hebraic myth: "Some [commentators] say that Samael disguised himself as the serpent and, after vengefully persuading man to eat from the Tree of Knowledge, fathered Cain upon Eve; thus defiling all the offspring of her subsequent union with Adam."[67] Within the Christian tradition, Origen is one of the first to elaborate the idea. According to Origen: "The serpent . . . had beguiled Eve and by spreading the poison of sin in her with his inbreathed encouragement had infected the whole of her posterity with the contagion of the Fall."[68] In *Paradise Lost*, Satan's success-ful temptation of Eve pollutes both her person and her progeny. As the Son explains in Book Three, the serpent's intercourse/discourse with Eve con-taminates the human family. The Son foresees that when Satan retreats from Eden, he will do so "with revenge accomplish't and to Hell / Draw after him the whole Race of mankind, / By him corrupted" (3.160–62).[69]

Eve's first-born child testifies to the corruption of the human race. Cain's wickedness clearly establishes that metaphysical allegiances have been al-tered as a result of Satan's ability to insinuate himself into Eve's acts of reproduction. Succumbing to Satan's temptation, Eve fails to "multiply a Race of Worshippers," but rather gives birth to the first murderer (7.630). Killing his own brother, Cain performs the function of Death, further liter-alizing the doubled relationship between Satan's two sexual partners, Sin and Eve. Sin begets an allegorical murderer of humankind; Eve begets an actual murderer of humankind.[70] But Cain's submission to Satan is just the begin-ning. The sequence of visions that Michael shows to and narrates for Adam in Books Eleven and Twelve is little more than a long march of Hell-bound progeny. For several hundred lines, it appears that Satan's aural impregnation of Eve has captured for him all of humankind.

But then comes a vision that arrests the procession. The Father unites with Mary to beget "the true / Anointed King *Messiah*" (12.358–59). The manner in which the Father impregnates Mary provides a perfect counter-point to the Adversary's earlier actions, for the Annunciation of Book Twelve simultaneously re-enacts and outstrips Satan's insemination of Eve. In Book Nine Satan's impregnation of Eve occupies a shadowy area between allegory, metaphor, and reality. God's impregnation of Mary, on the other hand, is irrefutably literal. Whereas Satan's coupling with Eve effects a deflowering, the Father's union with Mary preserves virginity. Most importantly, Mary's virginal conception, in which "God with man unites," overturns Eve's de-spoiling, for it brings about a second creation of humanity (12.382).

This second creation of humankind is outlined in Book Three, when the Father tells the Son that those who follow him, "live in thee transplanted, and from thee / Receive new life" (3.293–94). "Receiv[ing] new life" from the Son, the disciples of God are reborn, or regenerated. The process of rebirth is spelled out in the *Christian Doctrine*, where Milton teaches that the earthly mission of the Son creates afresh the human race, allowing each man and each woman to become a "new creature" (YP 6:461). Those who take advan-tage of the atonement, Milton explains, "are said to be regenerated and born again and created anew" (YP 6:394). "The old man is destroyed," Milton writes, "and . . . the inner man is regenerated by God . . . as if he were a new creature" (YP 6:461).

In many ways, humanity's second creation is identical to its first creation. Soon after forming the Earth, the Father gives life to the human family through the instrumentality of the Son. Acting as the Father's agent, the Son is sent to Earth from Heaven and successfully performs the creative task enjoined upon him by the Father. When the Father undertakes to create the human family a second time, he uses the same method, again sending the Son to Earth with a creative assignment. The Son's second trip to the terrestrial world, like his first trip, centers in the act of creating the human race. When Adam prophetically foresees the life of the Son, it is telling that he immediately understands the Son's salvific mission to be an act of creation. Adam identifies the regeneration of the human race as an act of creation similar—but superior—to the original act of creation that produced the earth:

> O goodness infinite, goodness immense!
> That all this good of evil shall produce,
> And evil turn to good; more wonderful
> Then that which by creation first brought forth
> Light out of darkness!   (12.469–73)

Because structures of obedience and authority in the epic are established according to creation, the Son's ability to recreate or regenerate the human race successfully redraws structures of filial obedience. When Satan inserts himself into Eve's reproductive life, he in part enables himself to command from Eve's children the kind of loyalty that creatures owe to their creators. When the Son recreates humanity, however, he gives the penitent individual the chance to break with the corrupted race over which Satan presides as co-creator and graft him or herself into a new family, of which God alone is head. The Son's atonement establishes an alternate race into which the saved soul can be adopted. This alternate race acknowledges God alone as its creator and, consequently, recognizes no authority other than God. When adopted into this new family springing from the Son's sacrifice, then, each individual returns to his or her elementary condition of straightforward submission to God. The regeneration wrought by the Son restores humanity's original relationship to God: "Regeneration means that the old man is destroyed and that the inner man is regenerated . . . so that his whole mind is restored to the image of God, as if he were a new creature" (YP 6:461). In sum, the Father overturns Satan's paternal usurpation of the human family by begetting a divine child upon a human mother. Responding to the Temptation with the Annunciation, the Father regains his human family by showing himself to be the superior creator.

In order to encourage the reader to recognize the cause-effect, point-counterpoint relationship that links the Temptation and the Annunciation, Milton presents the Temptation as a debased and weakened version of the Annunciation. Incorporating into his account of Eve's sin the idea of an auricular conception, Milton ties the Temptation to traditional accounts of the Annunciation and transforms the Temptation into a parodic version of the Annunciation. This parodic relationship prompts the reader to juxtapose the conception of Eve and the conception of Mary and thereby perceive their interrelatedness. In many ways, the epic constructs its accounts of the Temptation and the Annunciation in a method similar to the country-western contest of dueling banjos (to employ an anachronistic and utterly undivine analogy). Using the female body as a procreative instrument, the Adversary and the Father strive to best one another through increasingly impressive demonstrations of paternal power. In this dueling banjo format, Satan is the first to pick out his part. Using his "potent tongue" Satan impregnates with false reason the mother of all humankind and thereby perverts her progeny (6.135). The Father, however, upstages the Adversary with a virtuoso performance of supreme omnipotence. Surpassing at each point Satan's earlier attempt at sireship, the Father reasserts his paternal power with an unparalleled procreative act. The magnificence of the Annunciation in this way exposes the Temptation to be yet another perverse attempt on the part of Satan to emulate godly power. Imitating the process without possessing the virtue that makes that process efficacious, Satan falls short yet again. Satan attempts to rival the Father by inseminating a virgin through the ear, but his parody of divine paternity is overturned and overshadowed by the Father's omnipotent ability to beget a Messiah upon the Virgin Mary.

The passages in the poem that proclaim the Father's triumph over the Adversary exploit early modern homonyms to subtly emphasize the way in which the auditory canals of Eve and Mary constitute in some sense the cosmic battleground between good and evil. When the Father tells the fallen couple that the seed of the woman shall bruise the head of the serpent, the epic narrator interjects:

> So spake this Oracle, then verifi'd
> When *Jesus* son of *Mary* second *Eve*,
> Saw *Satan* fall like Lightning down from Heav'n,
> Prince of the Aire; then rising from his Grave
> Spoild Principalities and Powers, triumpht
> In open shew, and with ascension bright
> Captivity led captive through the Aire,
> The Realm it self of Satan long usurpt,
> Whom he shall tread at last under our feet.   (10.182–90)

Explicitly identifying Mary as the "second *Eve*," the passage connects Eve's and Mary's respective conceptions. In less explicit fashion, though, the text takes steps to reiterate the importance of the ear in these women's maternal roles. Earlier in the epic, Adam plays upon the homonymic relationship between "ear" and "heir"; at this point in the poem the epic narrator draws upon another set of homonyms—"air" and "ear"—in order to explain the way in which aurality impinges upon the epic's eschatology.[71] In the passage cited above, the epic narrator exploits "air" and "ear" to punningly paraphrase the way in which oral insemination operates in the epic as a means of either usurping or regaining power in the counterposed events of the Annunciation and the Temptation. According to the narrator, Satan commandeers a part of God's kingdom and becomes a temporary ruler ("Prince of the Aire") by commanding Eve's ear ("Prince of the Ear"). His appropriation of Eve's ear marks out both the air and the ear (the air because of the ear) as "the realm . . . of Satan long usurpt." Inseminating Mary through the ear, however, the Father sets in motion the series of events that will end Satan's reign, effectively "spoil[ing] Principalities and Powers." When the aurally begotten Son deposes the Father's enemy, "Captivity [is] led captive through the Aire." "Aire" describes the ethereal medium through which the captive is carried but also homonymically indicates the means whereby he is toppled. Satan is made captive "through the Ear"—through the ear of the Virgin who auricularly conceives Christ.

But the epic narrator is not the only voice in the epic to play on "air" and "ear." Indeed, the pun receives divine sanction in Book Three, when the Son employs this very homonymic pair. After volunteering to mediate for humankind, the Son assures the assembled hosts of angels that he will not fail to subdue with finality Heaven's enemy. Proleptically describing his eventual victory, the Son declares: "I through the ample Air in Triumph high / Shall lead Hell Captive maugre Hell" (3.254–55). As the epic narrator will do after him, the Son quibbles on "air" and "ear" to depict Satan's defeat while simultaneously describing the incarnational moment that begins the Adversary's overthrow. Referring to the "air" that is ample enough to accommodate his flight, the Son punningly points to the "ear" that was ample enough to provide for his entry into Mary's womb. Moreover, the Son utilizes the pun to chart the complete course of his condescension. His return to Heaven takes place only after he has detoured or passed through the "ample Air/Ear" of Mary. Abasing and reducing himself to such an extent as to be able to enter the Virgin through an orifice as small as her ear, the Son eventually resumes his former godlike grandeur. He returns to "Triumph high" after passing "through the ample [ear]." Recapitulating the depths to which he willingly descended, the Son uses the air/ear pun to contrast the indignity of the Incarnation with the divine splendor to which he returns.

The epic narrator is not the only one to notice the Son's deft manipulation of "air" and "ear." Michael (who presumably overheard the Son's punning performance in Book Three) also employs the homonymic pair. After revealing to Adam in Book Twelve a vision of the redemptive life of the Son, Michael shows the first man how the Son "shall surprise / The Serpent, Prince of aire" (12.453–54). Informing Adam that God will defeat once and for all the rebel ruler of the Air/Ear, Michael teaches, "Then to the Heav'n of Heav'ns he shall ascend / With victory, triumphing through the aire / Over his foes and thine" (12.451–53). The Son's triumphant flight through the air is made possible by the Father's paternal intercession through the ear. Through the ear of the Virgin Mary ("through the aire"), God recuperates the human family temporarily lost when Satan aurally invades Eve. Imitating the Son's divine wordplay with the homonyms "air" and "ear," Michael informs Adam that the Father and the Son triumph through the ear/air over their foes and ours.

In short, Milton's epic utilizes the idea of aural conception in order to transform the Temptation into a parodic prefiguration of the Annunciation. The relationship of reverse typology calls attention to the inadequacies of the Adversary while emphasizing the superiority of the Father. Both Satan and God impregnate virgins through the ear. Satan, however, succeeds only in siring temporary death and destruction. The Almighty God, on the other hand, fathers everlasting life and redemption. Through the ears of Eve and Mary, the epic shows how the demonic virility of Satan, the "great Potentate," is met and overmatched by the divine fecundity of the Father, the "Maker Omnipotent" (5.706; 4.725). In the end, God does indeed triumph "through the aire/ear."

Duke University

NOTES

I wish to thank Lara Bovilsky for initiating the thought processes that produced portions of this essay. My understanding of Eve's temptation has been greatly influenced by her work. See " 'Female for Race': Pregnancy in *Paradise Lost*," in *Inroads: Proceedings of the Seventh Annual Duke University Women's Studies Graduate Research Conference*, ed. Kate Manuel (Durham, 1997): 128–33. I would also like to acknowledge the tireless assistance of Albert C. Labriola, who patiently critiqued numerous drafts of this essay.

Simone Martini's *Annunciation* and Jacopo Torriti's *Annunciation* are used by permission of Alinari/Art Resource, New York. The images from the Klosterneuberg Altar by Nicolas de

Verdun, from the Netze Passion Altar, and from the North portal of the Marienkapelle, Würz-burg Cathedral are used by permission of Foto Marburg/Art Resource, New York. The detail of the Grabow Altar, photographed by Elke Walford, is used by permission of Hamburger Kunsthalle, Hamburg, Germany.

1. James Grantham Turner, *One Flesh: Paradisal Marriage and Sexual Relations in the Age of Milton* (Oxford, 1987), 157–61.

2. Turner, *One Flesh*, 156.

3. John N. Wall, "Shakespeare's Aural Art: The Metaphor of the Ear in *Othello*," *Shakespeare Quarterly* 30.3 (Summer 1979): 366.

4. "Verbum patris per aurem benedictæ intravit." The Latin translations in this essay were generously performed by Andrew S. Jacobs, Duke University Department of Religion.

5. "Gaude, Virgo, mater Christi, / Quae per aurem concepisti, / Gabriele nuntio." Quoted from Ernest Jones, "The Madonna's Conception Through the Ear," in *Essays in Applied Psycho-Analysis* (New York, 1964), vol. 2, 269.

6. "Descendit de caelis missus ab arce Patris, introiuit per aurem Virginis in regionem nostram." St. Agobard, *Opera Omnia, Corpus Christianorum*, ed. L. Van Acker, *Continuatio Medieaeualis* series, vol. 5 (Turnholti, 1981), 341.

7. St. Ephrem, "Homily on the Nativity," in *The Harp of the Spirit*, trans. Sebastian Brock, Studies Supplementary to Sobornost series, vol. 4 (London, 1975), lines 13–20.

8. "Deus per angelum loquebatur, et virgo auribus impraegnabatur." St. Augustine, "In Natali Domini, V," in *Patrologiae Cursus Completus*, ed. Jacques-Paul Migne, Latin series, vol. 39 (Paris, 1844–65), 1988. The attribution of this text to Augustine is also somewhat uncertain.

9. Simone Martini, *Annunciation* (Florence, Musée des Offices).

10. Nicolas of Verdun, *Klosterneuburg Altar* (Vienna, Monastery of Klosterneuburg).

11. Jacopo Torriti, *Annunciation* mosaic (Rome, Santa Maria Maggiore).

12. *Netze Passion Altar* (Westphalia, district of Waldeck Evangelical Parish Church). In passages describing angelic locomotion, Milton gestures toward this image of the Christ-child carried on a beam of light. In Book Four the narrator recounts Uriel's arrival in this manner: "Thither came *Uriel*, gliding through the Eeven / On a Sun beam, swift as a shooting Starr" (4.555–56). The angel departs on the same ray of light on which he arrived: "*Uriel* to his charge / Returnd on that bright beam, whose point now raisd / Bore him slope downward to the Sun now fall'n / Beneath th' *Azores*" (4.589–92).

13. Master Bertram of Minden, *Grabow Altar* (Hamburg, Hamburger Kunsthalle).

14. Tympanum of the North Portal of the Marienkapelle (Würzburg, Würzburg Cathedral). For additional discussion of the appearance in art of the Virgin's auricular conception see Ernest Jones, "The Madonna's Conception Through the Ear," in *Essays in Applied Psycho-Analysis* (1951) (New York, 1964), vol. 2, 268–72; and Gertrud Schiller, *Iconography of Christian Art*, trans. Janet Seligman (Greenwich, Conn., 1971), vol. 1, 43–46.

15. All references to Shakespeare's texts come from *The Riverside Shakespeare*, ed. G. Blakemore Evans, second edition (Boston, 1997) and are cited parenthetically by act, scene, and line number.

16. Philippa Berry, "Hamlet's Ear," in *Shakespeare Survey* 50, ed. Stanley Wells (Cambridge, 1997), 59.

17. Michael Long, *The Unnatural Scene: A Study in Shakespearean Tragedy* (London, 1976), 47–48.

18. Wall, "Shakespeare's Aural Art," 361–62.

19. Wall, "Shakespeare's Aural Art," 366. Peggy Muñoz Simonds claims that Wall's work on the image of auricular insemination in *Othello* "can be applied equally well to *Cymbeline*, a later work in which a noble husband's ear is also poisoned against his innocent wife by deliberate

calumny." In *Cymbeline*, however, the aurally conceived evil is ultimately aborted by the descent of Jupiter, whose first words frustrate the villainous project of abusing unguarded ears: "No more, you petty spirits of region low, / Offend our hearing; hush!" (5.4.93–94). According to Simonds, *Cymbeline* "goes beyond dramatizing the tragic fall of a good man seduced into irrational violence by a vice figure adept at verbal persuasion," for the play "also demonstrates that verbal and musical sound can elevate, even save, the human soul, when it is sufficiently harmonious and properly directed toward moral ends." Peggy Muñoz Simonds, "'No More . . . Offend Our Hearing': Aural Imagery in *Cymbeline*," *Texas Studies in Literature and Language* 24.2 (Summer 1982), 137.

20. Albert C. Labriola, "The Aesthetics of Self-Diminution: Christian Iconography and *Paradise Lost*," in *Milton Studies* 7, ed. Albert C. Labriola and Michael Lieb (Pittsburgh, 1975), 298.

21. All references to Milton's poetry come from *The Riverside Milton*, ed. Roy Flannagan (Boston, 1998) and are cited parenthetically by book and/or line number.

22. For additional evidence of a Mary-Eve typology in *Paradise Lost*, see Mother Mary Christopher Pecheux, "The Concept of the Second Eve in *Paradise Lost*," *PMLA* 75.4 (September 1960): 359–66.

23. Walter J. Burghardt, "Mary in Western Patristic Thought," in *Mariology*, 3 vols., ed. Juniper B. Carol (Milwaukee, 1955), vol. 1, 110.

24. Walter J. Burghardt, "Mary in Eastern Patristic Thought," in *Mariology*, ed. Juniper B. Carol (Milwaukee, 1957), vol. 2, 88–89.

25. Burghardt, "Mary in Western Patristic Thought," 110–13.

26. Quoted from Burghardt, "Mary in Western Patristic Thought," 112.

27. All references to Milton's prose come from *The Complete Prose Works of John Milton*, 8 vols., ed. Don M. Wolfe et al. (New Haven, 1953–82) and are cited parenthetically as YP, followed by volume and page number.

28. See 2.150, 2.911; 5.181, and 10.476.

29. Michael Lieb, *The Dialectics of Creation* (Amherst, 1970), 26.

30. Lieb, *The Dialectics of Creation*, 69.

31. John Bulwer, *Pathomyatomia, or a dissection* (London, 1649), 231.

32. Jacopo Berengario, *Microcosmographia or, a description of the body of man*, trans. Henry Jackson (London, 1664), 235–36.

33. Carla Mazzio, "Sins of the Tongue," in *The Body in Parts*, ed. David Hillman and Carla Mazzio (New York, 1997), 59.

34. Karen Newman, *Fashioning Femininity and English Renaissance Drama* (Chicago, 1991), 11.

35. Stephen Gosson, *The Schoole of Abuse* (1579), Shakespeare Society of London Publications, vol. 15, no. 2 (Nendeln, 1966), 49.

36. Gosson, *The Schoole of Abuse*, 51.

37. *Paradise Lost* is not the only place where Milton participates in the early modern substitution of female orifices. As Jean Graham demonstrates, Milton's masque is also involved in this approach. She observes that when Comus captures the Lady and threatens her with sexual violation, his libidinal aggression targets the Lady's mouth and ears. Urging the Lady to open her mouth to his charmed drink and her ears to his lascivious invitations, Comus conflates the oral and the aural with the sexual. Accordingly, the Lady signals her chastity by closing both her mouth and her ears. As Jean Graham writes: "Through the Lady's assertions of silence and deafness, she proclaims her purity." Jean E. Graham, "Virgin Ears: Silence, Deafness, and Chastity in Milton's *Maske*," in *Milton Studies* 36, ed. Albert C. Labriola (Pittsburgh, 1998), 1.

38. J. M. Evans, Paradise Lost *and the Genesis Tradition* (Oxford, 1968), 255.

39. A. B. Chambers, "Three Notes on Eve's Dream in *Paradise Lost*," *Philological Quarterly* 46.2 (April 1967), 192.

40. Francis Donald Klingender, *Animals in Art and Thought to the End of the Middle Ages*, ed. Evelyn Antal and John Harthan (Cambridge, Mass., 1971), 302.

41. Roland Mushat Frye, *Milton's Imagery and the Visual Arts* (Princeton, 1978), 99.

42. Adolf Katzenellenbogen, *Allegories of the Virtues and Vices in Mediaeval Art* (1939), trans. Alan J. P. Crick (New York, 1964), 58.

43. Pieter Brueghel, *Fall of the Rebel Angels* (Brussels, Musées Royaux des Beaux-Arts); Hieronymous Bosch, *Seven Deadly Sins* (Madrid, Museo Nacional del Prado), *Hay Wain Triptych* (Madrid, El Escorial), and *Triptych of the Garden of Earthly Delights* (Madrid, Museo Nacional del Prado).

44. Peter M. McCluskey, "The Toad at Eve's Ear," paper presented at the 1999 Conference on John Milton at Middle Tennessee State University, Murfreesboro, Tennessee. My reading of Satan's shape in the bower scene owes much to Professor McCluskey's work, and I gratefully recognize his influence.

45. Long, *The Unnatural Scene*, 48.

46. All references to Topsell, indicated parenthetically, come from a facsimile version of the 1658 edition. Edward Topsell, *The History of Four-Footed Beasts and Serpents and Insects* (1658), 3 vols. (New York, 1967), vol. 2.

47. My discussion of Topsell does not differentiate between frogs and toads because Topsell himself does not recognize any distinction, identifying the toad as simply "the most noble kinde of Frog" (726).

48. For a discussion of Galen's influence in early modern ideas about reproduction, see Stephen Greenblatt, "Fiction and Friction," in *Reconstructing Individualism*, ed. Thomas C. Heller et al. (Stanford, 1986), 30–52; and Thomas Laqueur, *Making Sex* (Cambridge, Mass., 1990), 25–62.

49. John Shawcross, "Two Comments," *Milton Quarterly* 7.4 (December 1973), 98; William Kerrigan, *The Sacred Complex: On the Psychogenesis of* Paradise Lost (Cambridge, Mass., 1983), 47.

50. *John Milton*, ed. Stephen Orgel and Jonathan Goldberg, Oxford Authors series (Oxford, 1991).

51. Labriola, "The Aesthetics of Self-Diminution," 292–97.

52. Wolfgang E. H. Rudat, "Ovid's *Art of Love* and Augustinian Theology in *Paradise Lost*," *Milton Quarterly* 21.2 (May 1987), 63.

53. Wolfgang E. H. Rudat, "Milton, Freud, St. Augustine: *Paradise Lost* and the History of Human Sexuality," *Mosaic* 15.2 (1982), 111.

54. Lara Bovilsky, " 'Female for Race': Pregnancy in *Paradise Lost*," in *Inroads: Proceedings of the Seventh Annual Duke University Women's Studies Graduate Research Conference*, ed. Kate Manuel (Durham, 1997), 131.

55. In the same way that Milton draws upon iconographic traditions to juxtapose the Temptation and the Annunciation, he subtly manipulates the iconography to signal dissimilarities between the two events. Albert Labriola asserts (and his assertion is borne out by the artistic examples included earlier in this study) that portrayals of the Annunciation typically display a Virgin whose posture suggests modesty and demure reluctance: "The Virgin is often glancing downward or away from Gabriel. . . . Her arms are sometimes crossed with the palms of her hands against her breast, or her arms are clasped in prayer, or an arm is extended outward in a gesture of modesty and humility." Milton, however, places Eve in the opposite position. In order to pluck the fruit, Eve must elevate herself to her fullest extent and lunge forward, for the

forbidden fruit is found on branches so "high from ground" that they "require / [Her] utmost reach" (9.590–91). Labriola, "The Aesthetics of Self-Diminution," 300.

56. The *Christian Doctrine* is not the only prose text in which Milton metaphorically connects sin to sexual reproduction. In *The History of Britain*, for instance, Milton relates that when "evil was embrac'd for good" the English people became "in falshood and wicked deeds pregnant and industrious" (YP 5:139–40). In the *Reason of Church Government*, Milton identifies the Roman Catholic Church as the maternal source of sinful offspring: "the very wombe for a new subantichrist to breed in" (YP 1:783). The biological model behind Milton's anti-Catholic accusation is spelled out a little earlier in the tract. Presenting papal apostasy as a series of grotesque generations, Milton explains: "Heresie begat heresie with a certain monstrous haste of pregnancy in her birth, at once borne and bringing forth" (YP 1:781).

57. James 1:15.

58. Quoted from Chambers, "Three Notes on Eve's Dream in *Paradise Lost*," 191.

59. Chambers, "Three Notes on Eve's Dream in *Paradise Lost*," 191.

60. Sir Henry Finch, *Law, or a discourse thereof*, 1678 edition (Buffalo, N.Y., 1992), 204.

61. Quoted from Thomas Laqueur, *Making Sex* (Cambridge, 1990), 161–62.

62. Laqueur, *Making Sex*, 161.

63. The roses of Adam's garland contrast starkly with the roses showered upon the couple in their matrimonial embrace. When prelapsarian Adam and Eve retire to their bower in Book Four, the narrator tells us: "On thir naked limbs the flourie roof / Showrd Roses, which the Morn repair'd" (4.772–73). Unlike the instantly "repair'd" roses of the bower, the blooms in Adam's garland are forever faded.

64. Wolfgang Rudat also emphasizes the sexual significance of the word "deflourd" but explains that Adam's use of the word anticipates an eventual deflowering that will occur only after Adam has eaten and he and Eve have engaged in lustful, postlapsarian sex. As Rudat writes: "We can read the *deflow'r'd* proleptically: in the lapsarian sex act, Eve will lose the sexual token of her innocence." I suggest that Adam's pronouncement is not simply a prophecy of Eve's impending deflowering—it is an assessment of her current condition, arising from her interaction with the Satanic serpent. Rudat, "Milton, Freud, St. Augustine," 110–11.

65. See 4.449–52 and 8.270–81.

66. For evidence of the homonymic relationship in early modern English between "air" and "heir," see Helgë Kökeritz, *Shakespeare's Pronunciation* (New Haven, 1953), 64–65.

67. Robert Graves and Raphael Patai, *Hebrew Myths: The Book of Genesis* (Garden City, 1964), 85. In the Hebraic tradition, "Samael" is another name for Satan. See, for instance, *The Oxford Dictionary of the Jewish Religion* where the entry for "Samael" reads: "the prince of demons in Jewish folklore; identical with Satan." *The Oxford Dictionary of the Jewish Religion*, ed. R. J. Zwi Werblowsky and Geoffrey Wigoder (New York and Oxford, 1997).

68. Origen, *The Song of Songs: Commentaries and Homilies*, trans. R. P. Lawson, Ancient Christian Writers 26 (Westminster, Md., 1957), 225.

69. The plight of the rebel angels parallels not only Eve's auricular conception but also her resultant contamination. Like Eve, the rebel angels unwisely offer their ears to Satan, who uses devilish rhetoric to impregnate them with sin. Conceiving evil through their ears, the rebel angels are polluted in the same way that Eve is. Abdiel perceives this pollution, observing that among his followers Satan has the "contagion spred / Both of [his] crime and [his] punishment" (5.880–81).

70. Eve's connection to Sin is suggested by the fact that after her fall Eve is accused of possessing the snake-like shape that characterizes Sin. As Albert Labriola reminds us: "At the birth of Death, her offspring by Satan, Sin became serpentine from the waist downward (2.650–

53, 782–85). After Eve has fallen to Satan, Adam describes her as if she had been transmogrified: 'thou Serpent, that name best / Befits thee with him leagu'd' (10.867–68)." Labriola, "The Aesthetics of Self-Diminution," 299.

71. For evidence of the homonymic relationship between "air" and "ear," see Berry, "Hamlet's Ear," 58.

MURDER ONE: THE DEATH OF ABEL. BLOOD, SOUL, AND MORTALISM IN *PARADISE LOST*

Raymond B. Waddington

> Whereat hee inly rag'd, and as they talk'd,
> Smote him into the Midriff with a stone
> That beat out life; he fell, and deadly pale
> Groan'd out his Soul with gushing blood effus'd.[1]   (*PL* 11.444–47)

OVER TWO DECADES AGO, Roland M. Frye identified a crux in the first vision of the future that the angel Michael presents to Adam: "I cannot explain why Milton chose to describe the murder in terms that are at once so bizarre and so inherently improbable, but he did not haphazardly introduce such details and there must be a richness of meaning here which I have been unable to discover."[2] Genesis 4:8, "Cain rose up against Abel his brother, and slew him," specifies neither the murder weapon nor the fatal wound, but a well-defined iconographic tradition had supplied the deficiencies. Cain strikes Abel's head with a wooden club, an animal bone (most frequently the jawbone of an ass), or, more rarely, a farm implement.[3] Alternatively, the weapon of choice is sometimes a stone.

Golda Werman asserts that "Cain's use of a stone as a murder weapon is peculiar to Jewish sources," pointing particularly to the Midrash *Pirkei de-Rabbi Eliezer*, which "notes that Abel is hit in the forehead with a stone."[4] She perhaps exaggerates somewhat in narrowing this invention to Jewish sources. Frye has adduced a stoning similar to Milton's on Byzantine ivory carvings, trade goods exported to Western Europe, but concludes that this iconographic tradition seems "so narrow and so restricted" as to have dubious relevance.[5] Much more immediately pertinent would be the example of Cowley's *Davideis:* "I saw him fling the *stone,* as if he meant, / At once his *Murder,* and his *Monument*" (1.16.3–4). What the couplet occludes, Cowley's textual note makes clear; on commonsense grounds, he has selected the same target as that favored by the Midrashim. In the absence of scriptural directive, "I had the Liberty to choose that which I thought most probable; which is, that he knockt him on the head with some great stone, which was one of the first ordinary and most natural weapons of *Anger.*"[6] The con-

fluence of minority traditions in commentaries, art, and poetry argues that
Milton surely was aware that Abel might have died by stoning, but his particular conception—a traumatic blow to the diaphragm with a stone, causing
massive hemorrhage—is virtually unprecedented. Frye finds it puzzling on
two counts—first, the impracticality (p. 302: "It would be hard to find a less
efficient method for killing a man."), and, second, the significance of the
deviation from tradition.

The first point is the more easily disposed of. Renaissance physicians
and anatomists still viewed the body as a hierarchy, and the diaphragm or
"midriff" performed a crucial division or linkage between lower and higher.
In a 1616 lecture William Harvey asserted, "In so far as it is the partition
between the bellies its use is to divide the noble from the ignoble, the vital
from the natural and the inferior from the superior parts of the body."[7] In this
Harvey is at one with such contemporaries as Helkiah Crooke, who attributes
the value distinctions to Plato and Aristotle.[8] Like Harvey, who noted the
"very great sensitivity" of the diaphragm, most medical practitioners were
conscious of its vulnerability. The *Treasury of Health* (1550?) advises that "A
wounde in the braynes, hert, midrife, . . . or lyuer is deadly" (Aiii). John
Woodall, Harvey's colleague at St. Bartholomew's and master of the Barber-
Surgeons Company, defined a wound broadly as "a recent solution of continuitie," then distinguished puncture wounds from contusions, "when a
weighty thing offending (as timber) falling downe or violently cast downe (as
a stone), the flesh being bruised and broken." In his experience,

If the great Veynes and Arteries in the Breast be offended, an immoderate flux of
blood, defection of virtue in all the faculties, a cold and an vnsaourie sweat doth ensue,
and death within a few houres.

The solution of continuitie in the sinowie parts of the *Diaphragma* causeth
convulsion, difficile respiration, an acute feuor, rauing, and death.[9]

It appears unlikely, then, that Milton's contemporaries would have found an
inherent improbability in the fatal wound that he describes. Indeed, in the
first printed commentary on this episode, Patrick Hume observed, "Our
Author has followed the most probable Opinion, that Cain killed his Brother
with a blow on the Breast with a great Stone . . . that beat the Breath out of his
Body."[10]

Allowing that a ruptured diaphragm and a cracked skull could render
Abel equally dead, however, does not explain why Milton might have wanted
to choose the former. Milton's retelling of sacred history is deeply informed
by Augustine's vision of the temporal order and by a Protestant conception of
typology, emphasizing Old Testament prefigurations of Jesus Christ; together
these give shape and meaning to Books Eleven and Twelve.[11] It seems rea-

sonable, therefore, to consider Milton's handling of the Cain and Abel episode as the first movement in this scheme. Gilbert Cope has remarked that
"Abel, the good shepherd who makes an acceptable sacrifice, and who is then
put to death, clearly can be thought of as a type of the Shepherd-Priest who is
also the Lamb of God: in the same way Cain can be thought of as pre-figuring
Judas Iscariot."[12] Sir Thomas Browne, contemplating "the holy line" culmi-
nating in Jesus Christ, alludes to the Savior "that was mystically slain in
Abel."[13]

Such a direct typology of figures particularly was strong in traditions of
popular iconography—through the woodblock prints of the *biblia pauperum*,
the *bibles moralisée*, and in manuscript illuminations of virtues and vices.[14]
An illustration of temperance and wrath, for example, pairs Jesus, the Lamb
of God, with Abel, struck dead by Cain.[15] One remarkably illuminated, moralized bible, *Codex Vindobonensis 2554*, although double-columned, follows
the typical format of biblical text and image above and the commentary text
and image immediately below. For Genesis 4:8, the biblical text states, "Here
Cain kisses his brother in betrayal and says to him: Come play with me in the
fields, and he does so, and kills him in betrayal." The image, in simultaneous
narrative, represents in the left background of the roundel the fraternal kiss
as the two emerge from a portal; in the right foreground, Cain strikes down
Abel with a grub hoe. Below, the commentary text explains, "That Cain kissed
his brother in betrayal signifies Judas who kissed Jesus Christ in betrayal and
had Him delivered over to death on the Cross."[16] The parallel commentary
roundel illustrates the Judas kiss, left, and, right, two executioners on ladders,
fastening Jesus to the cross.

In writing an episode that is framed as a vision, not surprisingly, Milton
seems deliberately conscious of the visual tradition. Genesis 4:4 does not say
how the Lord indicated approval of Abel's sacrifice. "His Offr'ing soon propi-
tious Fire from Heav'n / Consum'd with nimble glance, and grateful stream"
(*PL* 11.441–42), however, follows the pictorial convention of the descending
fiery column.[17] Milton's Abel is a "Shepherd . . . / More meek" (436–37), an
obviously typological description; he sacrifices "On the cleft Wood" (440), an
altar evocative of the cross on which Jesus would die. Contrastingly, Cain's
presentation as "A sweaty Reaper" (434) both highlights his fallen condition
(cf. Gen. 3:19) and foreshadows, in Marvellian fashion, his role of death-
bringer.[18] To account for the failure of Cain's sacrifice, Milton draws upon
two lines of commentary.[19] Not only is the offering itself scant (435–36); in
common with Protestant authorities, Milton finds Cain's motive suspect, "for
his was not sincere" (443). In consequence, Cain "inly rag'd" (444) at the
favor accorded to his brother's sacrifice. The conceptions of both characters

are entirely consistent with those in the tradition of the moralized and typological illustrations.

Interpreting Abel as a type, of course, is authorized by Jesus himself who cites Abel as the first prophet whose righteous blood has been shed upon the earth (Matt. 23:34–35; Luke 11:50–51). The Lord's rebuke to Cain, "the voice of thy brother's blood crieth unto me from the ground" (Gen. 4:10), thus becomes a prophecy of the Eucharist.[20] The New Testament offers two versions of the death of Judas. In Matthew 27:5, he hangs himself, providing the exemplar for suicides who have despaired at their alienation from God;[21] but in Acts 1:18, Judas "purchased a field with the reward of iniquity; and falling headlong, he burst asunder in the midst, and all his bowels gushed out."[22] Reading backward, from truth to shadowy type, suggests that Milton has devised a parallel between the deaths to reinforce the typological relation. The manner of Judas's death, "burst asunder in the midst," becomes retribution for the fatal blow that Cain, the first Judas, inflicted on his brother, "Sm[iting] him into the Midriff with a stone" (*PL* 11.445). The parallelism extends to the field, described by the commentators as barren,[23] into which Cain led Abel and from which God hears Abel's blood crying out, and the godforsaken "field of blood" (Acts 1:19) where Judas died. Hyam Meccaby observes, "The graphic picture of Judas's blood and entrails spilling on to the raw earth of an open field evokes the story of Cain and Abel."[24]

The linkage of Genesis and Acts by blood throws into relief another unconventional aspect of Milton's narrative: "he fell, and deadly pale / Groan'd out his Soul with gushing blood effus'd" (11.446–47).[25] As Abel groans, his soul departs in the effusion of blood; in other words, his soul is in the blood. Mosaic law forbade the eating of blood, "For the life of the flesh *is* in the blood" (Lev. 17:11), which in the Vulgate reads "quia anima carnis in sanguine est." *Anima* in this sense probably means no more than "vital principle," justifying the Geneva and King James translations as "life"; but it was difficult for Latinate Englishmen not to see *anima* as "soul," as it had been in the Wycliffe and Coverdale translations. Expounding Colossians 1:14, "In whom we have redemption through his blood," John Donne poses the question, "Is effusion of bloud the way of peace?" He notes that "bloud being ordinarily received to be *sedes animae*, the seat and residence of the soule; The soule, for which, that expiation was to be, could not be better represented, nor purified, then in the state, and seat of the soule, in bloud." Donne reflects on the progression from Law, with the blood sacrifice of animals, to Grace, with the sacrifice of Christ's blood, concluding "so all bloud is his; no nor his, as the bloud of all the Martyrs was his bloud, (which is a neare relation and consanguinity) but his so, as it was the precious bloud of his body, the seat of his soule, the matter of his spirits, the knot of his life."[26] For Donne, plainly *anima* means more than life force; blood is the location of the soul itself.

In Renaissance philosophy and physiology, to say the soul is in the blood meant something precise, stemming from the traditional faculty psychology of three souls—vegetative, sensitive (or organic), and intellective. The last, consisting of intellect, will, and conceptual memory, constituted the rational powers, whereas the sensitive soul encompassed the perceptual and motive faculties.[27] The entire body is animated by *spiritus,* a subtle vapor or exhalation generated from blood and distributed through the body by it. Marsilio Ficino, both physician and philosopher, described the indeterminacy of this "first instrument" of the soul: "Spirit is a very tenuous body, as if now it were soul and not body, and now body and not soul."[28] Donne concisely summarized this doctrine of an infinitely refined intermediary between body and soul in a famous stanza of "The Extasie": "As our blood labours to beget / Spirits, as like soules as it can, / Because such fingers need to knit / That subtile knot, which makes us man" (61–64).[29] In philosophical and theological discourse, the argument that the sensitive soul existed throughout the human body, in each and every part thereof, was expressed in a venerable Latin tag—*tota in toto et tota in qualibet parte corporis.*[30] By the 1640s Richard Overton only could express his impatience with the ubiquitous topos, grumbling that, if we ask where the soul is, "They *flap* us i'th mouth with a Ridle, *tota in toto, & tota in qualibet parte,* the whole in the whole, and the whole in every part."[31]

During the sixteenth and seventeenth centuries both theology and natural philosophy tended to simplify explanations and to make them increasingly materialistic. Amidst the general collapsing of distinctions, "a small but growing number of philosophers . . . described the organic soul as material . . . and identified it with *spiritus.*"[32] Even more radically, one could simplify and materialize by eliminating the sensitive soul and identifying the intellective soul with *spiritus. Paradise Lost* goes far in this direction with Raphael's tutorial speeches,[33] explaining to Adam and Eve that "Your bodies may at last turn all to spirit" (5.497) and describing the sexual embrace of angels in language that plays allusively on the Latin formula: "Total they mix" (8.627), *tota in toto;* "and obstacle find none / Of membrane, joint, or limb" (8.624–25), *tota in qualibet parte corporis.*[34] But if Milton could imagine bodies of spirit, Thomas Hobbes went in the opposite direction. In *Leviathan* (1651), he restored the suspect translation of *anima,* "*Eate not the Bloud, for the Bloud is the Soule,* that is, *the Life*" (Deut. 12:23), using it to maintain that the soul cannot be a "*Substance Incorporeall.*"[35]

As John Henry has commented, "By the seventeenth century, there was a tradition, well established in spite of its potentially heretical nature, which tended to identify souls with medical concepts of 'spirit.'"[36] The confused assessments of *spiritus* or "soul" in the blood provide the background to contemporary controversies over Harvey's discovery of the circulation of the blood. In the mid-1960s, Christopher Hill argued that this event generated a number of radical political and religious consequences, for Harvey and others, aligning circulation of the blood with both mortalism and republicanism. His essay provoked a furious rebuttal from Gweneth Whitteridge, defending Harvey's consistent royalism, itself leading to a more measured, but unabashed, response from Hill.[37] One historian of science, in conversation, characterized the debate as "proving that Hill knows nothing about Harvey, and that Whitteridge has no imagination." Initially, Hill had argued that the *De motu cordis* (1628) celebrates the heart in expressly monarchical terms, but *De circulatione sanguinis* (1649) and *De generatione animalium* (1651) "dethrone the heart," instead bearing an implication that "can only be described as republican."[38] In the face of Whitteridge's strictures, Hill gives some ground, and specifies that the central issue is less what Harvey thought than the reception of his discovery by contemporaries.

The drive to simplify concepts of the soul was not restricted to theology and philosophy but affected medical theory, as well:

The rejection by many Protestants of the learned tradition, now seen as Catholic, the emphasis on personal reading of the scriptures, which so often led to personal interpretation, the preference for the Old Testament in place of the *ethnicae* authorities, led [Robert] Fludd, as it seems to have led his Protestant contemporary Daniel Sennert (at Wittenberg), to abandon the complex of Greek philosophical ideas about soul, *anima*, or *psyche*. . . . In place of the Platonic or Aristotelian *psyche*, Fludd and Sennert saw the soul in Old Testament terms as the blood.[39]

Accordingly, Fludd, in the heat of the weapon-salve controversy, reviewed all the biblical texts pertaining to blood, concluding in an echo of Donne's sermon a decade before, "the Blood is the seate of the Soule or vitall Spirit."[40] So also Jean Baptiste van Helmont, who asserts that "We therefore who have the like humanity, its no wonder if we contain Blood and a Spirit of a co-like Unity; and that the action of the Blood is merely spiritual: Yea therefore in *Genesis*, it is not called by the Etymology of *Blood* but is made remarkable by the name of a *Red Spirit*."[41] Fludd, a member of the College of Physicians who heard Harvey's lectures and witnessed his demonstrations, was the first person to approve in print Harvey's theory of circulation with his *Medicina catholica* (Frankfurt, 1629). He was predisposed to do so because, five years before Harvey, he had arrived at a concept of the general circulation of the spirit in the blood. He was led to this from his reading of Psalm 19:4–6, "he set a tabernacle for the sun, / which *is* as a bridegroom coming out of his chamber, *and* rejoiceth as a strong man to run a race. / His going forth *is* from the end of the heaven, and his circuit unto the ends of it." In the microcosm of man, the sun is the heart; but, as Allen G. Debus has explained, "Yet, as early as 1617, we find that Fludd's primary concern is not with an anatomical study of the heart, but rather with the blood which has the all-important function of carrying the spirit of the Lord to all parts of the body."[42] Van Helmont's similar understanding of biblical texts as stating that the soul is in the blood caused him to oppose Harvey on the issue of blood-letting.[43]

Roger French has insisted that people in the mid-seventeenth-century tended to accept or reject Harvey's doctrines, not on some objective standard of verification, but by whether they could be used to confirm their own visions of reality.[44] This is demonstrated strikingly by two poems, both of which celebrate the circulation of the blood. Henry More, the Cambridge Platonist, was a determined opponent of mortalism, having written *Antipsychopannychia, or . . . a Confutation of the Sleep of the Soul after Death*, as the third book of his Spenserian *Psychozoia, or the Life of the Soul* (1642). More, in principle an avowed dualist, expressed his own pneumatology in both poems and philosophical treatises, including *The Immortality of the Soul* (1659). These writings contain inconsistencies and confusions resulting from his positions in controversies with Descartes on the one hand and Hobbes on the other.[45] On mortalism, however, he does not waver. A necessary correlative of his opposition to mortalism can be seen in his contemptuous dismissal of the belief that he calls "Holenmerian":

The other Mound of Darkness laid upon the nature of a *Spirit*, is by those who willingly indeed acknowledge that *Spirits* are *somewhere;* but add further, that they are not only entirely or totally in their whole *ubi* or place, (in the most general sense of the word) but are totally in every part or point thereof, and describe the peculiar nature of a *Spirit* to be such, that it must be *Totus in toto & totus in qualibet sui parte.*[46]

More's Latin poem, *Circulatio Sanguinis, Ad celeberrimum Medicum G. Harvaeum Inventorem,* although not published until 1679, may have been written as early as 1651.[47] So closely does the poem follow a sequence of proofs from *De motu cordis,* that More must have had it before him as he wrote. He describes the effect of bloodletting (*De motu cordis,* chap. 11), significantly with no adverse comment on the procedure (ll. 59–62). In the most telling omission, the poem is completely devoid of biblical allusion. More celebrates Harvey's achievement, first through the time-honored analogy of microcosm to macrocosm: as our ancestors have charted the orbits of the heavens, so Harvey teaches us the circuits of blood in silent dance throughout the body (ll. 1–15). The second verse paragraph shifts from macrocosm to geocosm: the course of blood through the body to the heart is like the subterranean rivers of the world leading to the ocean (ll. 16–32).[48] More carefully has avoided any possible association of blood with the soul, thereby purifying Harvey's work from the taint of mortalism.

John Collop, the quirky and highly independent physician, published his *Poesis Rediviva* in 1655, revealing a lively interest in his colleagues and in the state of his profession. There are two dozen poems praising or blaming individual doctors, on aspects of physiology, and disapproving various practices. Poems salute, in addition to Harvey himself, George Ent, "Great *Harvy's* second"; Francis Glisson's contributions to circulation theory; and *Religio Medici*, in which Thomas Browne confessed his youthful flirtation with mortalism ("More zeal and charity *Brown* in twelve sheets shows, / Then twelve past ages writ, or th' present knows").[49] Collop's admiration for Harvey is unstinting: "Thou set'st up sail, swim'st through the purple flood, / Which blush'd before, 'cause never understood. / Thou circlest through our *Microcosm*, and we / Learn more then th' world, our selvs, new worlds by thee" ("*On Doctor* Harvey," 14–16); and he responds immediately to the publication of *De generatione animalium* (1651), but through his own vision. Although he satirizes J. B. van Helmont and his disciple Noah Biggs, Collop shares their biblical belief that the soul is in the blood; and he "borrows phrases" from Biggs' *The Vanity of the Craft of Physick* (1651) "in almost every one of the medical poems."[50] Thus, Collop's "Of the Blood," standing in sharp contrast to More's poem, presents a curious amalgam of Harvey and Biggs:

> Sure in these purple streams the Sun doth glide,
> And in his Crimson Chariot blushing ride,
> While he doth circle through the lesser world,
> Through veins of earth in strange *Meanders* curl'd.
> Now in a full tide channels doth disdain,
> Flows into flesh, and then ebbs back again.
> Thus blood, Sun-like, gives motion, life and sense,
> Spirit, and innate heat are nought from hence.
> Distinct from Blood, who can the Soul ought call;
> 'Tis all in every part, and all in all. (3–12)

The soul-in-body topos, which Collop also quotes in "On the Soul" (l. 29: "Th' soul's all in all, and all in every part."), probably comes directly from Harvey's *De generatione animalium:*

And lastly, the *blood* doth so surround, and pierce into the whole body, and impart *heat* and *life* to all its *parts*, that the *soul* may justly be counted resident in it, and for his sake, *Tota in toto & tota in qualibet parte*, to be all in *all*, and all in every *part* (as the old saying is).[51]

The beginning of Collop's poem echoes Biggs, "According to Scripture, the *soul* or *vital* strength, rides in the Chariot of the bloud" (*Vanity,* 139–40), whereas the ending, "Gods Tabernacle thus plac'd in the Sun, / That Giant races must with th' whole world run" (ll. 39–40), envelops Harvey in the mystically medical reading of Psalm 19, with the "tabernacle for the sun" and the "strong man to run a race." Consistent with this, in two poems against phlebotomy, he sides with Biggs, who follows van Helmont in denouncing bloodletting on the biblical authority that blood is "the seat . . . chamber and magazine of life" and, consequently, phlebotomy will result in "the fall or losse to the whole ocean of strength" (*Vanity,* 162).

Given the importance that Francis Glisson assigned to spirits,[52] Collop's assertion that Harvey and Glisson together caused "Knowledge by circling" to progress may imply a similar emphasis in their concepts of the circulatory system. However selective his understanding, Collop could well have taken the value assigned to blood directly from Harvey, who wrote that blood "like a Tutelar Deity, is the very soul in the body."[53] D. P. Walker once observed that "by the time we have finished reading the *De Generatione Animalium,* we realize that something very odd has happened. The spirits are indeed gone; but blood has not only taken their place, it has also taken over all their functions, including sensation, and has acquired their divine and celestial nature."[54] Christopher Hill may have been right in maintaining that, even with Harvey, the distinction between "the soul is in the blood" and "the soul is the blood" is not always as clear as it might be.

In light of the extended, vocal, and extensively published medical-theological controversy on the soul in the blood, I find it difficult not to accept that Milton consciously evoked the belief when he described Abel "Groan[ing] out his Soul with gushing blood effused." Thomas Corns has remarked that "Groan'd out his Soul" is "a curious phrase for a mortalist,"[55] but the converse is true. An awareness of seventeenth-century discourse on blood and soul serves to confirm its mortalism. The mortalist stamp of the passage further is emphasized by Milton's elision of Genesis 4:10, "the voice of thy brother's blood crieth out unto me from the ground." Here, avoiding the possible implication that the spirit in the blood does not die with the body, only the voice of Adam, reacting to the vision, cries out in protest.

Milton's mortalism is a subject that has fallen into abeyance in recent years. Norman T. Burns importantly traced to Milton a tradition of mortalism in native English theology.[56] Hill's 1964 article on Harvey mentioned in passing Milton's mortalism, returning to the subject more seriously in a subsequent book in which the circulation of the blood and Milton are cited as parallel, not connected, expressions of mortalism.[57] Hill presents a Milton in constant dialogue with Interregnum radicals, "both emotionally and intellectually very close to the enthusiastic activists of the Revolution,"[58] from whom he ingested mortalist ideas. Burns emphasizes more Milton's indebtedness to the longer tradition, but allows the possibility that he had read Richard Overton on *Man's Mortalitie* (1643). Like Hill, Burns remarks the contemporary circulation of mortalist thought: "The more one knows of the currency of mortalist ideas in Interregnum England, the more hesitant one becomes to suggest that Milton was stimulated by any particular person or book to examine the Scriptures for proof of soul sleeping."[59] Whether Milton's interest in mortalism first was sparked by Overton or, as seems more likely, by his own study of Lucretius,[60] is, one might say, immaterial. By the time that he wrote *Paradise Lost*, mortalism indisputably had engaged his mind.

The decline of interest in the topic of mortalism may have commenced with the resurgence in the 1980s of conservative British historiography, spearheaded by Conrad Russell and Kevin Sharpe, which has reduced Hill's social revolution to a civil war, largely caused by the incompetence of the ruling class. In the nineties the controversy over the authorship of *De Doctrina Christiana* may have put the mortalism issue on hold,[61] since discussion of Milton's mortalism customarily begins with *De Doctrina* and works back to *Paradise Lost*. In view of the provisional finding from stylometric analysis that "[t]he relationship of *De Doctrina Christiana* to the Milton oeuvre must remain uncertain,"[62] we cannot at present say whether the mortalist chapters of the treatise represent Milton's own thoughts or simply ideas in which he was interested. Consequently, his beliefs must be represented from the poetry itself.

No one yet has discerned mortalist beliefs in Milton's poetry earlier than *Paradise Lost*. William Kerrigan examined Milton's early attraction to assumption—i.e., immediate translation of both soul and body as Enoch and Elijah experienced—shrewdly noting the point of connection with mortalism: "neither . . . permits the body to be severed from the soul in time or in eternity."[63] Hill cites four mortalist loci in *Paradise Lost*: first, the Son of God predicting that "Though now to Death I yield," the Father "wilt not leave me in the loathsome grave / His prey, nor suffer my unspotted Soul / For ever with corruption there to dwell" (3.245, 247–49). Second, Adam, struggling to understand the penalty of death, considers the dreadful possibility that "the Spirit of Man / Which God inspir'd, cannot together perish / With this corporeal Clod," and concludes that "All of me then shall die" (10.784–86, 792). Third, the Father's own explanation that immortality is forfeit: "Death becomes / His final remedy" until man is "to second Life, / Wak't in the renovation of the just" (11.61–62, 64–65). Fourth, Michael's description of Christ's victory over Sin and Death, redeeming humans from temporal death, "a death like sleep, / A gentle wafting to immortal Life" (12.434–35).[64] To these now must be added the death of Abel.

Hill further associated mortalism and the circulation of the blood with radical political theory.[65] The mortalist Hobbes describes the circulation of money as the life-blood or soul of the commonwealth:

> . . . the same passeth from Man to Man, within the Common-wealth; and goes round about, Nourishing (as it passeth) every part thereof, In so much as this Concoction, is as it were the Sanguification of the Common-wealth: For naturall Bloud is in like manner made of the fruits of the Earth; and circulating, nourisheth by the way, every Member of the Body of Man.[66]

In direct debate with Hobbes, James Harrington's *Oceana,* similarly but more idealistically, adapts Harvey's medical theory to the body politic of the commonwealth, "for in motion consisteth life, and the motion of a commonwealth will never be current, unless it be circular." That being the case, "So the parliament is the heart which, consisting of two ventricles, the one greater and replenished with a grosser store, the other less and full of a purer, sucketh in and gusheth forth the life blood of Oceana by a perpetual circulation."[67] Here the lifeblood is the political system, not commerce. In the belief that the health of the body politic could be maintained by the principle of "rotation" or what we would now call "term limits," Harrington himself was anticipated by the radical republican John Streater, former officer in the New Model Army, pamphleteer and printer, in which capacity he printed *The Commonwealth of Oceana.*[68] Two years earlier, in eleven weekly parts from 4 April to 4 July 1654, Streater's *Observations Historical, Political, and Philosophical upon Aristotles first Book of Political Government* were published. In the body politic, Streater argues that "the ministers of State and the Magistrates may be likened to the veins and Sinews in the body of a man." Their function is "to convey justice and vertue to every part of the body, and be as staies and helps to the motion of the Commonwealth." The health of the body should be maintained, however, "by renewing of blood" through annual elections.[69]

A decade before this, in the most idealistic phase of his republicanism, Milton had registered his own sense of what circulation through the body politic means. The *narratio* of *Areopagitica* initiates the famous extended metaphor: "For Books are not absolutely dead things, but doe contain a potencie of life in them to be as active as that soule was whose progeny they are . . . a good Booke is the pretious life-blood of a master spirit, imbalm'd and treasur'd up on purpose to a life beyond life." The homicide or massacre of books "ends not in the slaying of an elementall life, but strikes at that ethereall and fift essence, the breath of reason it selfe, slaies an immortality rather than a life." Toward the end of the treatise, Milton describes the English people as a nation of writers, "musing, searching, revolving new notions and idea's wherewith to present," and readers, "trying all things, assenting to the force of reason and convincement," before he returns once more to the blood metaphor:

For as in a body, when the blood is fresh, the spirits pure and vigorous, not only to vital, but to rationall faculties, and those in the acutest, and the pertest operations of wit and suttlety, it argues in what good plight and constitution the body is, so when the cherfulnesse of the people is so sprightly up, as that it has, not only wherewith to guard well its own freedom and safety, but to spare, and to bestow upon the solidest and sublimest points of controversie, and new invention, it betok'ns us not degenerated, nor drooping to a fatall decay. . . .[70]

Here the spirit in the blood comprises not just the sensitive soul but the rational or immortal soul itself. The lifeblood of the commonwealth is the free interchange of ideas; the veiled warning to parliament implies that the tyranny of censorship kills not simply individual books, but, like repeated courses of bloodletting, endangers the very soul of the state itself. For Milton in the emergent print culture of the Interregnum,[71] the circulation of ideas through books and pamphlets is the lifeblood of the body politic. In the Bible and in *Paradise Lost*, the death of Abel also is the death of a possibility, that of an innocent commonwealth. Cain, first builder of cities (Gen. 4:17), becomes the type of state planners and tyrants, who cannot escape his mark.[72]

University of California, Davis

NOTES

1. Quoted from *John Milton: Complete Poems and Major Prose*, ed. Merritt Y. Hughes (New York, 1957).

2. Roland M. Frye, *Milton's Imagery and the Visual Arts: Iconographic Tradition in the Epic Poems* (Princeton, 1978), 304.

3. Most helpful on the tradition are George Henderson, "Cain's Jaw-Bone," *Journal of the Warburg and Courtauld Institutes* 24 (1961): 108–14; and A. A. Barb, "Cain's Murder-Weapon and Samson's Jawbone of an Ass," *JWCI* 35 (1972): 386–89. Two later studies focus on Cain's punishment. See Ruth Mellinkoff, *The Mark of Cain* (Berkeley and Los Angeles, 1981) and Ricardo J. Quinones, *The Changes of Cain* (Princeton, 1991).

The possibility seems remote, but Milton could have known the *Genesis B* attributed to Caedmon, since he was acquainted with Franciscus Junius, who first published the poem (*Caedmonis monachi paraphrasis poetica Genesios*, Amsterdam, 1655). On this, see David Masson, *The Life of John Milton: Narrated in Connection with the . . . History of His Time*, 6 vols. (1880. Gloucester, Mass., 1965), vol. 6, 557 n.; and two articles in *A Milton Encyclopedia*, gen. ed. William B. Hunter, Jr., 9 vols. (Lewisburg, Pa., 1978–83): Thomas A. Carnicelli, "Anglo-Saxon Period, Milton's Knowledge of," vol. 4, 174–75 and John J. Roberts, "Junius, Franciscus," vol. 6, 51–53. The *Genesis B* text does not specify a weapon; however, the manuscript (Bodleian Junius 11) has an illustration depicting Cain with a club.

4. Golda Werman, *Milton and Midrash* (Washington, D.C., 1995), 227. This Midrash was translated into Latin by Willem Vorstius as *Capitula R. Elieser* (Leiden, 1644). See Werman, 44–45. The similarity was noticed first by Don Cameron Allen, "Milton and Rabbi Eliezer," *MLN* 63 (1948), 262–63. Louis Ginzberg paraphrases another Midrash: "Not knowing what injury was fatal, Cain pelted all parts of his body with stones, until one struck him on the neck and inflicted death." *The Legends of the Jews*, trans. Henrietta Szold, 7 vols. (Philadelphia, 1909–38), vol. 1, 109.

5. Frye, *Milton's Imagery and the Visual Arts*, 303, and see fig. 220.

6. Abraham Cowley, *Poems (1656)*, Scolar Press Facsimile (Menston, 1971), 8 and 29, n. to stanza 16. The *Davideis* analogue is mentioned by Wayne Shumaker, *Unpremeditated Verse: Feeling and Perception in "Paradise Lost"* (Princeton, 1967), 204–5; and by Frye, 302. Cowley's note is quoted by Don Cameron Allen, *The Legend of Noah: Renaissance Rationalism in Art, Science and Letters*, University of Illinois Studies in Language and Literature 33, nos. 3–4 (Urbana, 1949), 178; and by Alastair Fowler, ed., *Paradise Lost*, 2d ed. (London, 1998), 623 n. According to Elizabeth Minshull, Milton's third wife, he regarded Cowley as the greatest poet among his contemporaries. See J. M. French, ed., *The Life Records of John Milton*, 5 vols. (New Brunswick, N. J., 1949–58), vol. 5, 322–23.

7. Quoted from Gweneth Whitteridge, ed. and trans., *The Anatomical Lectures of William Harvey* (Edinburgh, 1964), 243.

8. See Helkiah Crooke's *[Microcosmographia]: A Description of the Body of Man* (1615), bk. 2, v, "Of the midriffe called Diaphragma," 354; also, Pierre de la Primaudaye, *The French Academie*, trans. T. B. (1618), bk. 2, xxxvii, 449; and Thomas Vicary, *The English-Mans Treasure: With the true Anatomie of Mans Body*, 8th ed. (1633), 40.

9. John Woodall, *The Surgions Mate* (1617), facsimile ed., intro. John Kirkup (Bath, 1978), 125, 126.

10. See Patrick Hume, *Annotations on Milton's Paradise Lost*, in *The Poetical Works of Mr. John Milton* (London: Jacob Tonson, 1695), 300–301. Hume's phrasing ("great Stone") may echo Cowley's note to *Davideis*. I am indebted to an anonymous reader for this citation.

11. See Hugh R. MacCallum, "Milton and Figurative Interpretation of the Bible," *University of Toronto Quarterly* 31 (1962), 397–415; and John R. Mulder, "Typology," in *A Milton Encyclopedia*. For typological readings of the final books, see, e. g., Barbara K. Lewalski, "Structure and the Symbolism of Vision in Michael's Prophecy, *Paradise Lost*, Books 11–12," *PQ* 42 (1963), 25–35; MacCallum, "Milton and Sacred History: Books 11 and 12 of *Paradise Lost*," in *Essays in English Literature . . . Presented to A. S. P. Woodhouse*, ed. Millar MacLure and F. W. Watt (Toronto, 1964), 149–68; and R. B. Waddington, "The Death of Adam: Vision and Voice in Books 11 and 12 of *Paradise Lost*," *MP* 70 (1972), 9–21.

12. Gilbert Cope, *Symbolism in the Bible and the Church* (London, 1959), 199; see also Frye, 300.

13. Thomas Browne, *Pseudodoxia Epidemica: or, Enquiries Into very many Received Tenents And commonly presumed Truths* (1646. 6th ed. London, 1672), bk. 6, vi, p. 345.

14. See, for example, Louis Réau, *Iconographie de l'art chrétien*, 3 vols. (Paris, 1955–59), vol. 2, pt. 1: "Dans les Bibles moralisées, Cain est assimilé à Judas qui 'bailla' son maitre Jesus aux Juifs pour le Crucifier" (961).

15. See Rosemond Tuve, *Allegorical Imagery: Some Medieval Books and their Posterity* (Princeton, 1966), 95, fig. 18; and Pearl F. Braude, " 'Cokkel in oure Clene Corn': Some Implications of Cain's Sacrifice," *Gesta* 7 (1968), 581 and fig. 11.

16. Trans. Gerald B. Guest, *Bible Moralisée: Codex Vindobonensis 2554, Vienna, Österreichische Nationalbibliothek* (London, 1995), 56. See the facsimile, p. 2vC, and Guest's comment on the typology, p. 31. The imputation of the Judas kiss to the Genesis narrative occurs

more than once. The most notable precursor to the typological schemes of the *biblia pauperum* occurs with the altarpiece, attributed to Nicolas of Verdun, for the monastery of Klosterneuburg. One group in blue enamel and black niello against gold, dating from 1330, presents two types: above (*ante legem*), Cain strikes Abel with a hoe; below (*sub lege*), Joab slays Abner. Between them, the antitype shows Judas betraying Christ with a kiss. See Avril Henry, *Biblia Pauperum: A Facsimile and Edition* (Aldershot, 1987), 10–12, and fig. 7b. For a fuller account, see Floridus Röhrig, *Der Verduner Altar* (Vienna, 1955).

17. See Frye, 301–302.

18. For biblical and classical antecedents to the reaper or mower metaphor, see Don Cameron Allen, *Image and Meaning: Metaphoric Traditions in Renaissance Poetry* (Baltimore, 1960), 130–31. As Erwin Panofsky noted, Death "was represented with a scythe or sickle from very early times." See Panofsky, *Studies in Iconology: Humanistic Themes in the Art of the Renaissance* (1939. New York, 1962), 77. The *Codex 2554* illuminator figures Cain as Death by changing the color of his costume from ochre (when he kisses Abel) to blue-black (as he strikes him with the hoe). Although the *Oxford English Dictionary* does not record the epithet "Grim Reaper" before the nineteenth century, the premodern sense of *grim* as "Fiercely angry" (*OED*, s. v. A.1.b) is suggestively like Milton's "inly rag[ing]" reaper.

19. For these, see Arnold Williams, *The Common Expositor: An Account of the Commentaries on Genesis, 1527–1633* (Chapel Hill, 1948), 142.

20. Crucial here is Hebrews 12:24, "and to Jesus the mediator of the new covenant, and to the blood of sprinkling, that speaketh better things that *that* of Abel." For a summary of commentators on this comparison, see Cornelius à Lapide (Cornelissen van den Steen), *Commentarii in Scripturam Sacram*, 10 vols. (Paris, 1858–60), vol. 9, 1007; and, for Abel and Cain as types, see vol. 1, 97, 100. Among Milton's contemporaries, John Bunyan uses Heb. 12:24 to explain, "as by the rule of contraries," the progression from Law to Grace, the blood of Abel to the blood of Christ. See *An Exposition of the First Ten Chapters of Genesis*, in *The Complete Works,* ed. Henry Stebbing, 4 vols. (1859. Marshallton, Del., 1968), vol. 3, 399. Henry Hammond, unusually, argues that Hebrews alludes to Gen. 4:4, Abel sacrificing "the firstlings of his flock": "the first great type of that shedding the blood of *Christ*, this *lamb of God*." See *A Paraphrase and Annotations Upon all the Books of the New Testament* (1653. 4th ed. London, 1675), 765.

21. See Susan Snyder, "The Left Hand of God: Despair in Medieval and Renaissance Tradition," *Studies in the Renaissance* 12 (1965), 53, 55–56.

22. I am grateful to Michael T. Walton for pointing out the relevance of this text. On the different versions, see Kirsopp Lake, "The Death of Judas," in F. J. Foakes Jackson and K. Lake, eds., *The Beginnings of Christianity. Part I: The Acts of the Apostles* (London, 1933), vol. 5, 22–30.

23. See, e.g., Ambrose, *De Cain et Abel*, II, 8, in *Sancti Ambresii Opera*, pt. 1, ed. Charles Schenkl, Corpus Scriptorum Ecclesiaticorum Latinorum, 32 (1897. New York, 1962).

24. Hyam Meccaby, *Judas Iscariot and the Myth of Jewish Evil* (London, 1992), 59.

25. Newton's note on the vision pauses over the conjunction of the blow to the diaphragm and the massive hemorrhage, citing Cowley for the one and Virgil for the other: "Undantique animam diffundit in arma cruore" (*Aeneid* 10.908). See *Paradise Lost*, ed. Thomas Newton, 4th ed. (1749. London, 1757), vol. 2, 352–53. The circumstances in both of Newton's suggestions differ from Milton: Cowley's Cain hurls the stone at Abel's head and Aeneas slashes Mezentius' throat with a sword. Nonetheless, Newton's bracketing may have established the correct range. Virgil's phrase *animam diffundit* echoes Lucretius (3.437), on which see *Aeneid 10*, trans. and commentary by S. J. Harrison (Oxford, 1991), 285, n. to l. 908. It is difficult to imagine that Milton would not have recognized the echo. Book Three of *De rerum natura* expounds on the

mortality of the soul, the relevance of which will become apparent later in this essay. I am grateful to Joe Wittreich for the gift of the Newton edition.

26. Sermon No. 11, "Preached at St. Pauls, upon Christmas day. 1622." *The Sermons of John Donne*, ed. George R. Potter and Evelyn M. Simpson, 10 vols. (Berkeley and Los Angeles, 1953–62), vol. 4, 293, 294.

27. See Katharine Park, "The Organic Soul," in *The Cambridge History of Renaissance Philosophy*, ed. Charles Schmitt and Quentin Skinner (Cambridge, 1988), 464–68. See also Eckhard Kessler, "The Intellective Soul," 485–534, for debate on the question of its immortality.

28. "Ipse vero est corpus tenuissimum, quasi non corpus et quasi iam anima, item quasi non anima et quasi iam corpus." Quoted from Ficino, *Three Books on Life*, ed. and trans. Carol V. Kaske and John R. Clark (Binghamton, N.Y., 1989), bk. III, iii, 256–57. See also bk. I, ii, 111. On *spiritus*, see pp. 42–44; Park, *Cambridge History*, 469; D. P. Walker, *Spiritual and Demonic Magic from Ficino to Campanella* (London, 1958); Robert Klein, "Spirito Peregrino," in his *Form and Meaning: Writings on the Renaissance and Modern Art*, trans. Madeline Jay and Leon Wieseltier (Princeton, 1981), 62–85.

29. Quoted from *The Complete English Poems of John Donne*, ed. C. A. Patrides, Every-man's Library (London, 1985).

30. For this philosophic commonplace, see R. B. Waddington, " 'All in All': Shakespeare, Milton, Donne and the Soul-in-Body Topos," *ELR* 20 (1990), 40–68.

31. Richard Overton, *Man's Mortalitie*, ed. Harold Fisch (Liverpool, 1968), 72. Overton provides the marginal note, "Absurd."

32. See Park, *Cambridge History*, 476–84; quotation, 483. See also Owsei Temkin, *Galen-ism: Rise and Decline of a Medical Philosophy* (Ithaca, N.Y., 1973), 143–49, on Telesius and Campanella.

33. Stephen M. Fallon, *Milton Among the Philosophers: Poetry and Materialism in Seventeenth-Century England* (Ithaca, N.Y., 1991), 98–107, discusses the corporeality of the soul in Raphael's Book Five speeches, arguing that, in effect, for Milton the rational displaces the immortal soul.

34. See Waddington, " 'All in All,' " 56–57.

35. See Hobbes, *Leviathan*, ed. Richard Tuck (Cambridge, 1996), 425. For the contempo-rary reception of the work, see Samuel I. Mintz, *The Hunting of Leviathan: Seventeenth-Century Reactions to the Materialism and Moral Philosophy of Thomas Hobbes* (Cambridge, 1962).

36. John Henry, "Medicine and Pneumatology: Henry More, Richard Baxter, and Francis Glisson's *Treatise on the Energetic Nature of Substance*," *Medical History* 31 (1987), 15–40; quotation, 23. See further D. P. Walker, "Medical Spirits in Philosophy and Theology from Ficino to Newton," in *Arts du spectacle et histoire des idées: Recueil offert en hommage à Jean Jacquot* (Tours, 1984), 287–300.

37. The three essays from *Past and Present*—Hill, "William Harvey and the Idea of Mon-archy," no. 27 (April 1964); Whitteridge, "William Harvey: A Royalist and No Parliamentarian," no. 30 (April 1965); and Hill, "William Harvey (No Parliamentarian, No Heretic) and the Idea of Monarchy," no. 31 (July 1965)—have been reprinted in Charles Webster, ed., *The Intellectual Revolution of the Seventeenth Century* (London, 1974), 182–96. Webster mediates the dispute in judging that, while Harvey's ideas did not change over time, "critics are obliged to accept Hill's basic point that there are distinct differences of emphasis between *De motu cordis* and *De generatione*" (p. 14). Hill's attention to the political uses of the circulation metaphor has been extended by John Rogers, *The Matter of Revolution: Science, Poetry, and Politics in the Age of Milton* (Ithaca, N. Y., 1996), pp. 16–38. Harvey's innovative use of the body politic metaphor is placed in a broad context by I. Bernard Cohen, "The Body Politic: before and after the Scientific

Revolution," in *Experiencing Nature: Proceedings of a Conference in Honor of Allen G. Debus,* ed. Paul H. Theerman and Karen Hunger Parshall (Dordrecht, 1997), pp. 1–7.

38. Christopher Hill, in Webster, *The Intellectual Revolution,* 161, 162. But see Whitteridge, *William Harvey and the Circulation of the Blood* (London, 1971), 215–21, in which she traces Harvey's thought on the primacy of heart or blood; and 191–92 and 223–27 in which she revisits the spirit-in-blood issue.

39. Roger French, *William Harvey's Natural Philosophy* (Cambridge, 1994), 130. For the reception of Harvey's ideas in England, see chap. 6; and on the Continent, chap. 9.

40. *Doctor Fludds Answer unto M. Foster or the Squeesing of Parson Fosters Sponge, ordained by him for the wiping away of the Weapon-Salve* (1631), 68–70; quotation, 70.

41. Jean Baptiste van Helmont, *Oriatrike or, Physick Refined,* trans. J. C. (1662), 793. See also p. 954 on the soul in the blood. Michael T. Walton discusses both Fludd and van Helmont as chemists who read Genesis through the perspective of the Cabala. See "Genesis and Chemistry in the Sixteenth Century," in *Reading the Book of Nature: The Other Side of the Scientific Revolution,* ed. Allen G. Debus and M. T. Walton, Sixteenth Century Essays and Studies, vol. 41 (Kirksville, Mo., 1998), 8–12.

42. Debus, "Harvey and Fludd: The Irrational Factor in the Rational Science of the Seventeenth Century," *Journal of the History of Biology* 3 (1970), 81–105; quotation, 90. See also Debus, *The English Paracelsians* (New York, 1966), 111–14; and French, 123–32.

43. See Peter H. Niebyl, "Galen, Van Helmont, and Blood Letting," in Allen G. Debus, ed., *Science, Medicine and Society in the Renaissance: Essays to Honor Walter Pagel,* 2 vols. (New York, 1972), vol. 2, 13–23.

44. See French, 2.

45. See John Henry, "A Cambridge Platonist's Materialism: Henry More and the Concept of Soul," *JWCI* 49 (1986), 172–95; and Henry, "The Matter of Souls: Medical Theory and Theology in Seventeenth-Century England," in Roger French and Andrew Wear, eds., *Medicine, Religion and Natural Philosophy in the Seventeenth Century* (Cambridge, 1989), 87–113.

46. More, *The Easie, True, and Genuine Notion and Consistent Explication of the Nature of a Spirit,* in Joseph Glanvill, *Saducismus Triumphatus* (2nd ed., 1682), 89–162, quotation, 90; see 112–22, 144, 152–62 for More's extended exposition and confutation of Holenmerianism. *The . . . Notion* translates chapters 27–28 from More's *Enchiridion metaphysicum* (1671). See Henry, "A Cambridge Platonist's Materialism," 192 n. Presumably, the increased association with mortalism caused More to recant his earlier acceptance of the *tota in toto* concept in *Psychathanasia,* 2, canto 2, stanzas 32 and 37.

47. See Geoffrey Bullough, *The Philosophical Poems of Henry More* (Manchester, 1931), 169–72, for the Latin text. In "Henry More's 'Circulatio Sanguinis': An Unexamined Poem in Praise of Harvey," commentary by Wallace Shugg and trans. by Walter Sherwin and Jay Freyman, *Bulletin of the History of Medicine* 46 (1972), 180–89, Shugg concludes that it was written between 1651 and 1653.

48. See Shugg, 186–87, on these analogies.

49. See French, 168–78, on Ent; and, 286–309 on Glisson; also see Henry, "Medicine and Pneumatology." For Browne, see *Religio Medici,* pt. 1, sects. 7–8. Collop is quoted from *The Poems,* ed. Conrad Hilberry (Madison, Wis., 1962).

50. Hilberry, 6.

51. Harvey, *Anatomical Exercitations, Concerning the Generation of Living Creatures* (1653), chap. 51, 280; also cited by Hilberry, 203, n. to l. 12. The modern translation by Whitteridge, *Disputations Touching the Generation of Animals* (Oxford, 1981), 245, eliminates the Latin tag, thereby obscuring the reference. Earlier in chap. 51 Harvey cites the Bible for the assertion that life and soul exist in the blood (Whitteridge trans., 243).

52. "For Glisson the spirits in the body were the instrument of the soul and were informed by it; they were also the chief element of the blood" (French, 304). See further Henry, "Medicine and Pneumatology." Rogers, 104–8, links Glisson and Milton as "like-minded participants in the Vitalist Movement" (108).

53. *Anatomical Exercitations*, chap. 52, 283 (Hilberry's gloss on "Of the Blood," l. 34, "Placing in him this tutelar Deity"). Whitteridge's translation again blunts the point: "and that there the tutelary deities and the soul itself have set up their abode, no man can doubt" (243).

54. D. P. Walker, "The Astral Body in Renaissance Medicine," *JWCI* 21 (1958), 131.

55. Thomas Corns, *Regaining* Paradise Lost (London, 1994), 88.

56. Norman T. Burns, *Christian Mortalism from Tyndale to Milton* (Cambridge, Mass., 1972). See also William B. Hunter, Jr., "Mortalism" in *A Milton Encyclopaedia*.

57. See Hill, *Milton and the English Revolution* (New York, 1977), 317–23.

58. Hill, *Milton*, 333. For an assessment of the thesis, see R. B. Waddington, "Milton Turned Upside Down," *Journal of Modern History* 51 (1979), 108–12.

59. Burns, 168.

60. For the most recent influence study, see Philip Hardie, "The Presence of Lucretius in *Paradise Lost*," *MQ* 29 (1995), 13–24. Hardie's concern, however, is with poetic strategies rather than ideas.

61. But this does not account for all the neglect. A recent volume, *Milton and Heresy*, ed. Stephen B. Dobranski and John P. Rumrich (Cambridge, 1998), proclaims itself committed to the proposition that "Milton's authorship of the treatise is practically indisputable" (7), yet does not mention the word *mortalism*. Both Rogers and Fallon comment on mortalism only in passing, although it is a logical consequence of Fallon's thesis.

62. Gordon Campbell, Thomas Corns, John K. Hale, David I. Holmes, and Fiona J. Tweedie, "The Provenance of *De Doctrina Christiana*," *MQ* 31 (1997), 67–121; quotation, 110. In 1991 William B. Hunter first questioned the attribution to Milton; see now his *Visitation Unimplor'd: Milton and the Authorship of* De Doctrina Christiana (Pittsburgh, 1998). The most vigorous proponent of the attribution has been Barbara K. Lewalski, "Milton and *De Doctrina Christiana*: Evidences of Authorship," *Milton Studies* 36, ed. Albert C. Labriola (Pittsburgh, 1998), 203–28. For the relevant sections of *De Doctrina*, see bk. 1, chaps. 7 and 13.

63. See William Kerrigan, "The Heretical Milton: From Assumption to Mortalism," *ELR* 5 (1975), 125–66; quotation, 145. He notes that both Overton and Hobbes use Enoch and Elijah as proofs of mortalism (145–46).

64. Hill, *Milton,* 317

65. Rogers, 21–24, dismisses Hill's suggestion that Harvey consciously trimmed his political loyalties for patronage, arguing instead that a kind of linguistic feedback occurs: by 1649 the political discourse becomes "a culturally inescapable homology" (24).

66. *Leviathan,* 174. For Hobbes's mortalism, see, e.g., Burns, 183–87. For earlier instances of the metaphor in economic discourse, see Blair Hoxby, "The Trade of Truth Advanced: *Areopagitica*, Economic Discourse, and Libertarian Reform," *Milton Studies* 36, ed. Albert C. Labriola (Pittsburgh, 1998), 179, 185.

67. *The Political Works of James Harrington*, ed. J. G. A. Pocock (Cambridge, 1977), 248, 287. See Pocock's commentary, p. 69. For the most thorough influence study, see I. Bernard Cohen, "Harrington and Harvey: A Theory of the State based on the New Physiology," *Journal of the History of Ideas* 55 (1994): 187–210. William Craig Diamond, "Natural Philosophy in Harrington's Political Thought," *Journal of the History of Philosophy* 16 (1978): 390–97, finds Harrington indebted to Paracelsian and Helmontian concepts of *spiritus*.

68. On Streater, see Pocock, *Political Works,* 9–12; Nigel Smith, "Popular Republicanism in the 1650s: John Streater's 'heroick mechanicks,' " in *Milton and Republicanism*, ed. David Armi-

tage, Armand Himy, and Quentin Skinner (Cambridge, 1995), 137–55; and Adrian Johns, *The Nature of the Book: Print and Knowledge in the Making* (Chicago, 1998), 266–323.

69. Quoted from Johns, 281. For the relation to Harrington's thought, see 289–91.

70. Quoted from *Complete Prose Works,* vol. 2, ed. Ernest Sirluck (New Haven, 1959), 492–93, 554, 557. Smith, 148–50, notes continuities of thought among Milton, Streater, and Lilburne.

71. Sharon Achinstein, *Milton and the Revolutionary Reader* (Princeton, 1994), 58–70, suggestively comments on Milton's construction of a reasoning and judging readership.

72. See Hill, *The World Turned Upside Down: Radical Ideas during the English Revolution* (New York, 1972) 117, and *The English Bible and the Seventeenth-Century Revolution* (London, 1993), 205–15, 239–43, 245–50, 387–89 for the use of the Cain and Abel story to figure governmental oppression and social inequity. Among others, he cites Winstanley, Bunyan, Abiezer Coppe, George Fox, and Sir Henry Vane. Williams, *The Common Expositor,* 220–28, reviews the political lessons drawn from Genesis by the commentators.

READING HISTORY WITH
SAMSON AGONISTES

Lauren Shohet

> How could the God who willed 1649 also will 1660?
> Christopher Hill

WITH THE RESTORATION, erstwhile Reformist Parliamentarians had to relearn how to read. The readerly elect was forced to reinvestigate models of signification and figuration, required by circumstance to reconsider the signs of God's will in Scripture and in history. (Or might God's will not be inscribed in history at all?) Widely varying contemporary theories of historical change and agency testify to the range of available models for a hermeneutics of history, from strictly providentialist to proleptically anthropocentric.[1] They carry with them multiple ways to interpret history, from Matthew Mead's understanding of plague as "the sore Judgment . . . which *so evidentlie declares* Wrath to be gone forth from the Lord against us" (1665) to James Harrington's historiographical method of assuming "sufficient *warrant*, even from God himself . . . to make further use of *humane prudence* wherever I find it *bearing a testimony* unto itself" (1656).[2] Whatever else it may have done, the Restoration forced republicans to adjust their interpretive horizons. Accounting for political defeat could require dissenters to change their self-understanding as the elect, or to revise their more-or-less-millenarian notions of apocalyptic history, or to alter their paradigms of how history signifies. For those—like John Milton—holding both a Christian-apocalyptic view of history and an understanding of the Republican cause as divinely sanctioned, millenarian hermeneutics needed to yield to a different view: to a hermeneutics that could give Scripture its due, could maintain faith in the cause, and yet could accommodate what looked very much like a failed revolution.[3]

Stanley Fish's 1969 "Question and Answer" serves as a foundational modern reading of Milton's *Samson Agonistes* (published eleven years after the Restoration) as a drama of hermeneutics, proposing that *Samson* raises questions (about human motivations, about the relationship between God's will and worldly events) in ways that make them structurally unanswerable.[4]

Joseph Wittreich makes these questions historically specific when he contextualizes *Samson* within early modern interpretive traditions, most centrally typology. Wittreich emphasizes the heterogeneity and self-consciousness of seventeenth-century typology. For him, Milton's drama seeks to make poetry adequate to the problems of addressing history by enfolding and critiquing the oversimplifications of earlier Reformation typology. Wittreich writes that "typology had become the chief culprit in disfiguring and eclipsing the Judges narrative": *Samson* "subject[s] Renaissance generalizations about this story to a relentless testing."[5] Whereas Wittreich augments and qualifies Fish by admitting history into the purview of hermeneutics, Lana Cable extends Fish's analysis in a different direction by focusing on the rhetorical structure of truth.[6] Cable agrees with Fish that worldly inscriptions of divine will are uninterpretable in *Samson*. For Cable, however, the interplay of the desire for knowledge and the frustration of this desire eventually lead to a recognition that "true witness" *is* possible. Although "truth" remains ungraspable, Cable's *Samson* offers the possibility of defining a process of truth seeking. According to Cable, this interplay is paradigmatically metaphoric, insofar as metaphor iconoclastically destabilizes meaning, then invites a resuturing of signifier and sign in a way that is inherently provisional and dynamic.[7]

I argue that *Samson* takes up not only the general problem of epistemology Cable elucidates in her abstract dialectic of desire and frustration, but also the particular problem of interpreting historical identity. Given the upheavals of the mid-seventeenth century, *Samson* seeks to negotiate pressing issues of the relationship between faith and history, trying to discern what interpretive tools can be of use to the faithful as they attempt to evaluate the meaning of historical experience.[8] *Samson* maps the intersection of the three categories that this problematic spans: knowledge, identity, and history. I want to consider the epistemological and rhetorical questions raised by Cable within the context offered by Wittreich. Thomas Gorman rightly remarks that most of *Samson*'s characters "behave as though our postlapsarian conceptual and representational economy were a closed and self-supporting totality," acting "as though truth were a property of the social, political, and cultural field when in fact . . . truth lies wholly beyond its scope and thus remains inaccessible to postlapsarian knowledge and expression in any positive sense."[9] I differ from Gorman in two regards: first, I focus on particularly historical "truth," or truth as it makes itself known and unknown through historical process; and second, I argue that *Samson* constructs the rhetorical strategy of metonymy in particular ways—defining it in contrast to synecdoche—that transform metonymy from what Gorman sees as an inescapably flawed model to a valuable way of representing viable epistemological processes.

I propose that we consider *Samson* as historiography, as a theory of what it means to read or write history.[10] Within this problematic, I focus on both rhetorical and corporeal strategies the drama brings to bear on the question of how history is *inscribed* in the world and in texts. *Samson's* emphasis on corporeality and its focus on how bodies register hermeneutic questions point to the body as the node where history and meaning intersect: the place each of us can know history, the way that history signifies in us. Although Wittreich discusses at length *Samson's* distinctions between acting publicly and as a "private person," he does not fully elucidate what being a private person entails. I examine the ways that *Samson* meditates on being a *self in history*. *Samson* uses circumcision as a figure for the way history is written on the body—the way the self is marked by history. Circumcision constitutes a particular corporeal figure that participates in a larger exploration of how rhetorical "figures" (specifically, synecdoche and metonymy) work as interventions in a debate about interpretive practice.

The primary way that early modern readers theorized these relationships of time, text, and self was, of course, typology: reading Old Testament "types" to prefigure New Testament "anti-types" and also apocalyptic antitypes (in the historical experience of the elect as well as in the book of Revelation).[11] But precisely how seventeenth-century readers approached Scripture is the subject of some controversy, as typology becomes increasingly polyvalent. Wittreich shows that orders of worship readjust dominant readings of the Samson story (among other narratives) by re-pairing Old- and New-Testament passages.[12] More broadly, Wittreich details the fraying of typology proper into an attenuated, looser, more complex, more self-aware mode that he characterizes as "typological symbolism."[13]

However, recent investigations into material practices of reading suggest that various kinds of typological practices historically overlap in the later seventeenth century to a greater extent than Wittreich indicates. On the one hand, Patrick Collinson argues that continuous reading replaces typological cut-and-flip typological indexing.[14] On the other hand, Peter Stallybrass has found evidence to the contrary in portraits, bible marginalia, and letters on scriptural reading practices.[15] Furthermore, Raymond Anselment shows that typological interpretive manuals become increasingly popular beginning in the 1630s (and extending through the end of the century, as demonstrated by the Mather text I quote below).[16] This suggests that residual typology, emergent continuous reading, the often uncogent diversity of practice that attends upon popular proliferation, and the narratological sophistication Wittreich discusses probably coexist as interpretive modes available to *Samson's* primary audience. Indeed, Nathanael Mather's 1683 preface to a posthumously published typological treatise composed by Samuel Mather in the 1660's demonstrates this kind of overlay. Writing some twenty years after the treatise's composition, Nathanael Mather avers:

> It is not expected that every one, much less critical and captious Heads, will subscribe to every thing which they may here meet with . . . [Samuel Mather's] making some of the old legal Ordinances Types of the instituted Church, and Ordinances under the New Testament and our Ordinances the Antitypes of theirs, it may be Some may not assent unto.[17]

But Mather also asserts that "Others there are who go with this our Author."[18] Moreover, he writes, "Nor can it be denied that there is a common Nature wherein *their* Institutions and *ours* agree, the one being a Shadow or darker Adumbration; the other a more lightsome and lively Image of the same Things . . . there is a strict and proper Acceptation of the Word, wherein it may be said, that our Institutions are the Antitypes of theirs."[19] Such debate, then, indicates a multiplicity of practice, demonstrating that *Samson*'s interest in what constitutes proper reading extends beyond the drama's boundaries.

This evidence offers some sense of the difficulty seventeenth-century readers face in evaluating how to read scripture.[20] Engaging this difficulty, *Samson Agonistes*'s complexity derives, I would argue, from the text's placing the character of Samson in three conflicting relationships to the elect reader.[21] First, Samson figures the reader (the Godly hero beset by both Philistines and slothful coreligionists). Second, Samson serves as the limited Hebrew foil to a post-incarnation (elect) version of heroism. Third, Samson figures the perpetual displacement of the second model by the first, as the reader (and Samson) are pressed to understand that no one achieves perfect comprehension or full significance while still living in history.[22] Thus *Samson*'s careful Christian reader first recognizes Samson as himself, then misrecognizes himself as a "perfected" version of Samson, then (ideally) recognizes the misrecognition.[23]

The text expresses these interpretive problems through the rhetorical figure of synecdoche. Using the part to figure the whole, synecdoche emerges as a central strategy for *Samson*'s representation of how (for better and for worse) people make meaning out of fragments, how they relate personal experience to larger narratives, how they understand human history in a divine cosmos. Whereas Cable focuses on metaphor as a sign inscribing meaning, I focus on synecdoche as a sign inscribing history; the epistemological frustration Cable analyzes becomes for my argument the frustration of the desire to understand historical identity. And, as Cable finds to be true of metaphor, the meaning of the self in history (and history for the self) makes the synecdochic problems the text elaborates impossible to resolve. Metonymy eventually emerges as *Samson*'s way to imagine kinds of knowledge and selfhood that can accommodate historical discontinuity. Metonymy connects elements to *something*, making them meaningful, without presuming to identify the "whole." Whereas the text provisionally allows Reformed readers to understand Christian hermeneutics as the "whole" that perfects the Hebrew characters' synecdochic forms of understanding, *Samson*'s ultimately metonymic model of history requires Reformed readers to acknowledge their own place in history as equally incomplete, and hence, as for the Hebrews, only partially comprehensible.[24]

By focusing on these more limited rhetorical strategies in place of a grand unified theory of typology, the drama breaks down elements of a typology that popular practice seems to have muddied. Properly speaking, typology should not take *any* phenomena within history to achieve *forma perfectior*.[25] But early modern practice does not always seem fully cognizant of this theoretical limitation. In an interesting example from the 1630s, the publisher of Thomas Taylor's *Christ Revealed* seems more confident about earthly Christian clarity than the text he brings out. In 1632, Taylor cautions, "Even now, in this marvellous light of the Gospell, we . . . see him afarre off, know but in part, darkly as in a glasse . . . time shall bee, when . . . we shall in heaven see him . . . face to face, clearly, perfectly, immediately, without Sacraments or Types."[26] The "Epistle Dedicatorie" by the text's 1635 publisher, William Jemmat, proclaims perhaps more confidently, "These glorious times of the Gospel shew evidently, how much the truth excelleth the shadow . . . as the manifestation is more cleare, so the grace is more plentifull and comfortable."[27] And Mather's 1683 *Figures or Types of the Old Testament* sounds more certain yet of Christian clarity: "Our [sacraments] are not Typical, are not Shadows of good Things to come, and of the Gospel and *Messias* yet to be exhibited; for they are past and done in our Times."[28] Against the backdrop of such hermeneutic confidence, *Samson*'s working by means of rhetorical strategies (synecdoche and metonymy) does not challenge the actual orthodox framework of typology, but instead offers terms perhaps less vulnerable to misuse, to historiographical overconfidence, than typological ones.

Samson operates as a drama of synecdoche, animated by the effort to recognize isolated incidents, artifacts, and actions as signifying fragments of the "whole" of God's plan. Rhetorically, *Samson* is notably rife with synecdoches—among them, for persons, "feet" (336, 931), "hands" (259, 438, 507, 1260, 1299), "mouths" (452), "hearts" (455), "heads" (677), and "ear" (921); for the Ammonites, "the Ammonite" (285); for Philistia, "Gath" (266); for the Philistines, "fore-skins" (144)—that adumbrate the importance of fragmentation and wholeness in the drama.[29] The text's diction of "parts" points to synecdochic structures as well as actual tropes: Samson "was to do my *part* from Heav'n assign'd" (1217); his "high gift of strength" was "lodg'd" in a "part" (47–8); the Philistines' consequent revenge takes advantage of vision's not being "through all parts diffus'd" (96) (and, to press the point, characters wonder whether God is "parted from [Samson]" [1719]). Indeed, the Samson story inherently emphasizes partiality, sketching out the powers and dangers of parts when it localizes Samson's strength in his hair.[30]

"A person *separate* to God" (32), Samson seems synecdoche personified. He is the "part" of his nation separated out to epitomize the whole; as a Nazarite, his separation to God privileges him, but also divides him from others; his separateness acquires meaning and value only in relation to the appropriate whole (in line 32, "to God"), but the fragmentary nature of partiality endangers the visibility of the meaning-endowing horizon.[31] Or, to put this last point more precisely, Samson's "separateness" privileges him when it really is understood synecdochically as the most pertinent part of his existence which thereby appropriately figures his whole, as the sign of God's partiality to him. But it leaves him isolated from his nation, in alien captivity, when his separateness is taken indexically rather than synecdochically. "Index," that is, "points to" something in direct reference, whereas synecdoche constitutes a figurative use that interpretively selects out the most salient aspect of the whole. When the Israelite governors "yield" Samson "to the uncircumcis'd a welcome prey" (259–60), or indeed when Samson understands himself to be abandoned by God, both treat Samson more as an index (a part—not necessarily the most significant possible part—that points to the collectivity of Israelites) than a synecdoche (the epitome of the Israelite chosen, endowed with particular significance by the synecdoche's crafter). Since, in this case, it is God who crafts the synecdoche of Samson's strength, misrecognizing synecdoche as index ignores God. Since the figurative synecdoche encodes authorial agency, characters who misread it as the more mechanical relationship of index turn a blind eye to the figure's author—God.

Samson presents his initial misery and confusion as temporal fragments, introducing the drama's central concern with continuity and interpretation in ways that underscore his need for a theory like typology—which is, of course, unavailable to him because of his historical location before the New Testament comes to be written. Declaring that his "restless thoughts" "present / Times past, what once I was, and what am now" (19–22), Samson depicts past and present as a collage that confronts him as he attempts to narrate a continuous experience of selfhood across time.[32] These lines likewise foreground the ambiguous relationship between "*times* past" (history) and "what once *I* was" (the historical subject). Proceeding to the problem of prophecy, this speech expands these questions into futurity when Samson asks, "O wherefore was my birth from Heav'n foretold / Twice by an Angel[?]" (23–4). The prophecy's apparent unfulfillment ("wherefore?") reminds us of the drama's double frame of time as it appears to the characters and to the reader. Samson's despair suggests that the time for fulfilling the prophecy is past. The reader knows that, for Samson, it is yet to come (hence might it also be yet to come for the Reformist cause?).

Typology offers a model for reading historical experience by relating past and present, text and event, presence and representation. Critical discussions of typology and *Samson Agonistes* have focused, with varying emphases and degrees of specificity, on how early modern readers would have typologically analyzed the Samson story.[33] But the drama demands that we keep in mind a double perspective. We should keep the view accessible to characters in the drama distinct from the view accessible to the Restoration reader.[34] Indeed, the parallels between Samson's questions that open *Samson Agonistes* and Jesus' more resolved meditations on similar hermeneutic puzzles in *Paradise Regain'd*—the first drama of the two-text volume in which *Samson* was printed—highlight the way that historical location determines interpretive horizons.[35] It is not only differences in ontology (divine versus human), but also differences in historical location that distinguish these figures: living before the incarnation, Samson cannot think about hermeneutics the same way Jesus can. In dramatizing an Old Testament figure (as, in part, a strategy for figuring out English history), *Samson* invites us to attend to the interpretive horizons visible *in medias res* at the same time that we consider more distant readerly perspectives. This is not to say that the Restoration reader's perspective is complete or solid. Indeed, the instability of the reader's hermeneutic experience is created by *Samson's* revealing that successive horizons are only provisional.[36] But acknowledging the diversity of hermeneutic horizons available to different participants in the drama's *agon*—both within the text and outside it—is necessary for understanding the drama's eventual proposals for identifying and organizing parts and wholes, fragments and narratives.[37]

Samson's *hamartia* is hermeneutic, and part of his flaw lies in his inability to recognize Scriptural (hence, for early modern readers, also historical) wholes. When Samson laments, "I was to do my part from Heav'n assign'd, / And had perform'd it if my known offence / Had not disabl'd me" (1217–19), his regret is premature, as the reader recognizes from broader knowledge of the story. Focused on the theatrical sense of his "part"—his role assigned by God—Samson does not recognize that his is only *one* "part" of the divine plan, still unfolding after Samson believes it definitively has failed.

Samson's blindness and captivity figure, among other things, the misguided certainty of a judge who has not finished reading Judges. Hence Samson asks, *"wherefore* was my birth from Heav'n foretold?" (23); *"Why* was my breeding order'd and prescribe'd?" (30); *"what if* all foretold / Had been fulfill'd but through mine own default?" (44–45, all emphasis added).

The signs of God's will are ambiguous to Samson because he does not recognize his embroilment in the dynamics of history. Samson prematurely mourns, *"Promise was* that I / Should *Israel* from *Philistian* yoke deliver" (38–39, first emphasis added), and even when he abandons his interrogatives together with the quietist despair of the *prologos*, he explains the rectitude of his two marriages to Gentiles overconfidently:

> The first [wife] I saw at *Timna*, and she pleas'd
> Mee, not my Parents, that I sought to wed,
> The daughter of an Infidel; they knew not
> That what I motion'd was of God; *I knew*
> *From intimate impulse*, and therefor urg'd
> The Marriage on . . .
> She proving false, the next I took to Wife
> (O that I never had! fond wish too late)
> Was in the Vale of *Sorec, Dalila* . . .
> I *thought it lawful* from my former act,
> And the same end . . . .   (219–32, emphasis added)

Samson here sounds certain about his initial "intimate impulse" (to marry his first Gentile wife), but his declaration that his second impulse was mistaken may cast doubt on the objective validity of his first judgment (in Judges, this comes in more authoritative third-person narrative that serves as an implied backdrop for Samson's self-examination here, and Manoa, for his part, certainly thinks Samson was mistaken).[38] Admitting that he only inferred (mistakenly, he believes) the lawfulness of his second marriage, Samson delineates his interpretive difficulties; moreover, the passage suggests that he is no more than retrospectively inferring that he must have been wrong. The reader knows that what was wrong was not necessarily Samson's marriage, but rather his premature interpretation of God's will through the events of his own life before that life has fully developed in time. Hence Samson's self-correction is itself misguided—when he determines that the Dalila marriage, which proves instrumental to his eventual defeat of the Philistines, was contrary to God's will—once again because his understanding of historical process is inadequate.

Samson's misunderstandings could be corrected by his simply finishing Judges. But the difference between classical dramatic irony and Samson's particular hermeneutic *hamartia* lies in the redoubled ignorance of being in the middle of a book *of* the Old Testament. Could Samson finish Judges, he would know *what* happens to him, but not, entirely, *why*: fuller meaning and interpretability must attend history's completion. Samson's complaint to God emphasizes the distance between Hebrew and post-incarnation horizons. When Samson exclaims, "God of our Fathers, what is man!" (667), he asks precisely the question that, for Reformers, cannot yet be answered. The conventional appellation "God *of our Fathers*" underscores the temporality that leads as far as the knowledge of God's plan available to humans before Christ, but not beyond it; "what is man" cannot yet be answered. This interpretive opacity of the drama's events is not merely Samson's problem, but rather common to all Old Testament characters. For example, Manoa's final benediction after the massacre reads:

> Come, come, no time for lamentation now,
> Nor much more cause, *Samson* hath quit himself
> Like *Samson*, and heroicly hath finish'd
> A life Heroic.   (1708–11)

While this might be a perfectly good testimonial to a classical tragic hero, the tautology "Samson hath quit himself / Like Samson" here suggests the limitations of the interpretation available within the Old Testament horizon. Manoa can say only that Samson has performed in a way sufficient to his identity (and note that the ambiguity of "quit" as "acquitted" and as "departed" makes these lines indicate either "eventual fulfillment" or "typical abandonment" of selfhood). He "heroicly hath finish'd / A life Heroic," but this recursive definition points to the fact that even fully adequate Old Testament action remains bounded by its interpretive horizon. It cannot reach outside itself for the interpretive repertoire to make things definable in ways more meaningful than tautology and recursion.

In addition to misrecognizing historical process, the characters in *Samson* misrecognize their ontological status. Typologically, both types and antitypes function simultaneously as historical agents and as textual or quasi-textual signifiers; *Samson* delineates the ambiguous textual status of a character who does not recognize that he inhabits a story. In the opening speech quoted above, when Samson's thoughts "present / Times past" (21–22), the pun on "present" as verb and as noun points to the way that representing the past makes the past present. Similarly, when Samson asks "O wherefore was my birth from Heav'n foretold / Twice by an Angel[?]" (23–24), the doubling of the annunciation ("twice foretold") can gesture either toward certainty or toward tenuousness. Why does angelic communication of God's will require supplementation? Or, to read the same moment somewhat differently, even angelic repetition fails to illuminate meaning ("wherefore?") when it is confined to the framework of the Old Testament. The diction of "pre-scription" in Samson's query "Why was my breeding order'd and prescribe'd?" (30), like Samson's status as "fore*told* / To *Israel*" (1662–63, emphasis added), offers a further example of the ways that *Samson* thematizes the circumscription of textual as well as historical horizons for its characters, detailing the contrast between perceptions available to characters and to readers.

In the context of questions of historically bounded interpretation, *Samson*'s emphasis on corporeality reminds us that the signifying status of the body-in-history is central for a hermeneutics that, like Christianity, includes both historical and extrahistorical dimensions. Embodied experience defines historical experience; divine incarnation alone enables (elect) humans to have extrahistorical significance. More specifically, the Samson story focuses on corporeality by encoding God's favor as bodily strength, Samson's straying as sexual vulnerability, weakness as blindness. Even more specifically, Milton's *Samson Agonistes* emphasizes corporeality in its concretizing of abstract signifying and interpretive issues into figures of bodily experience, like the simile expressing Samson's experience of doubt as a "deadly swarm / Of Hornets arm'd . . . / [That] rush upon me thronging" (19–21), the pun on the divine tonsorial "dispensation" of God's gift (61), or Samson's despair as "tumors of a troubled mind" (185). Indeed, throughout, *Samson*'s lexicon brims with eyes, hands, muscles, hair, foreskins.[39] With this last element, the foreskin, the corporeal figure of circumcision writes the rhetorical figure of synecdoche onto the body in *Samson*, and the different articulations of circumcision across time (corporeal circumcision for the Hebrew characters, "circumcision in the heart" for the Reformed reader) illuminate what synecdoche can and cannot accomplish as a hermeneutic structure in the drama.[40] "The foreskins" (for "the Philistines") is thus a particularly significant synecdoche. In its initial speech, recounting the pinnacle of the exploits of the "Heroic, . . . Renown'd, / Irresistible *Samson*" (125–26), the Chorus momentously declaims, "A thousand fore-skins fell" (144). In addition to its dramatic position in this passage's chronicle of Samson's past, the contrast between the size of the horde and the diminutiveness of the synecdoche that expresses it draws further attention to the figure. Indeed, the place-name the poem cites, "*Ramath-lechi* famous to this day" (145), commemorates the figure: "Ramath-lechi" means "hill of the foreskins."[41]

Samson's fatal military "circumcision" of the Philistines indicates the intersection of corporeal, rhetorical, and textual elements of historical identity in the drama. If circumcision marks chosenness for the Hebrews, here Samson's weapon writes his own chosenness onto the Philistine bodies, "circumcising" them by inscribing them into the narrative of the triumph of

God's Elect. To pause for a moment over the obvious, there are two differences between this figurative circumcision and an actual *bris*. First, the
bearers of these foreskins die (rather than live on in a privileged covenant
with God); second, "foreskin" here is figurative (standing in for the whole
body) rather than concrete (the foreskin alone). Or, to be more precise, due
to the distinctive character of synecdoche as a rhetorical strategy, it is figurative *as well as* concrete. Unlike either metaphor or metonymy, synecdoche
uses what really is there (in part) to figure what else really is there (*in toto*).
Here, what is important about the Philistines is the foreskin: its presence
marks the absence of divine covenant with their people.

    Samson represents this circumscription of Philistine experience—this
non-covenant—in both textual and rhetorical registers. Textually, this emerges
in Dalila's contention that, on her own terms, her actions are heroic:

> My name perhaps among the *Circumcis'd*
> In *Dan*, in *Judah*, and the bordering Tribes,
> To all posterity may stand defam'd,
> With malediction mention'd, and the blot
> Of falshood most unconjugal traduc't.
> But in my countrey where I most desire,
> In *Ecron*, *Gaza*, *Asdod*, and in *Gath*
> I shall be nam'd among the famousest
> Of Women, sung at solemn festivals,
> Living and dead recorded.   (975–84)

When Dalila predicts fame in the history and memory of her own people, she
proposes a congruity between her nation's texts and traditions and those of
"the *Circumcis'd*." But, over time, Philistine oral culture ("sung at solemn
festivals") does not prove equivalent to Hebrew writing. Like the bodies of
the "*Circumcis'd* / In *Dan*, in *Judah*, and the bordering Tribes," the Samson-
friendly version of this argument will bear the traces of divine inscription.
Being part of the right text because one has been inscribed upon by the true
God puts experience into a different realm of significance, extending beyond
temporal boundaries insofar as the Hebrew characters enjoy the potential to
become signifiers in future texts (the Old Testament, the New Testament, the
history of the Elect), even when this larger framework is not visible to them.
In both its origins and the sequence of transfers it encodes, Samson's circumcising weapon—the jawbone of an ass—indicates this privileged but limited
semiotic status. Jaws produce language—but this jaw comes from an inarticulate species and is, moreover, dead. Reanimated as a tool seized by God's
Nazarite hero, the jawbone serves as an instrument for writing God's will

onto history, but only as the bluntest instrument in a series that extends to the Hebrew *mohel*'s knife and eventually to the Reformed spirit that circumcises the heart.[42]

When Dalila's *apologia* refers to the Hebrews as "the *Circumcis'd*," she shows that "the fore-skins" and "the circumcis'd" are not merely opposites, but rather incommensurable, in terms analogous to the incomparability of Philistine song and Hebrew scripture. This incommensurability involves two steps. First, for the Israelites, circumcision works semiotically precisely as a sign (a signifier plus a referent). It inscribes a differentiating mark (the signifier), which, by convention rather than inherent association, signifies a covenant (the referent). As God instructs Abraham in Genesis 17:11, "And ye shall circumcise the flesh of your foreskin; and it shall be a *token of* the covenant betwixt me and you."[43] Philistine foreskins, by contrast, are not signs. Naturally present, unmarked by cultural signifying systems, they do not mean anything within their own cultural framework (just as elbows do not "mean" anything). Second, the *absence* that circumcision produces introduces another level of semiotic complexity. Again serving as an intriguingly paradigmatic case of signification, in ritual circumcision the act of marking gets rid of what was there before: the foreskin needs to disappear to become a signifier.[44] The text emphasizes this when Harapha, discussing the same conquest that the Chorus recounted with the synecdoche "fore-skins" (144), calls the Israelites "the unforeskinn'd race" (1100). There is no parallel term for "fore-skins" because the foreskin is gone (he can't call them "the unforeskins"); what is left available to Harapha is a participle, with its attendant temporal traces ("unforeskinn'd), a participle moreover modifying "race": the group, the family, the chosen people who share the ritual of foregoing the foreskin (thereby producing cultural and religious affinity—that is, meaning—from it).

Thus, whereas Samson's massacring "circumcision" uses the Philistine foreskin as a synecdoche, in a ritual Jewish *bris*, circumcision works more as signifying metonymy. As a corporeal inscription figuring a covenant, the signifier here points beyond bodily boundaries, enacting the shift of register (from mortal body to God and God's promises) that metonymy (like metaphor) accommodates but synecdoche does not.[45] Although *Samson* privileges synecdoche over index, it elevates metonymy further. The very firmness of synecdoche's ground—the fact that its figurative element operates literally as well, the way it maintains its tenor instead of abandoning it the way metaphor or metonymy does—constructs a semantic stability that this text suggests to be limiting and indeed arrogant. While metonymy is more flexible than synecdoche, it is less ontologically dynamic than metaphor. Metonymy moves to an ontologically related term rather than completely switching registers.[46] This suggests metonymy's usefulness to a text trying to account for history. In its contiguous displacement of tenor by vehicle, metonymy encodes something of a semantic history. We can tell where metonymy comes from— even if the possibilities for metonymy are multiple, indeed infinite, they develop from a predictable set of relations—whereas metaphor is completely unpredictable.[47]

Like the Old Testament, which records the cut-around experience of the Chosen who are separated from other ancient peoples by God's favor, but which is cut off from full interpretability by its historical incompleteness, Hebrew circumcision marks both covenant and incompleteness. Samson certainly understands the absent foreskin as a corporeal sign of chosenness, but the various corporeal signs signaling his incompleteness remain opaque to him. In the same speech that hubristically posits him as "Sole Author" and "sole cause" of his fate (376), Samson represents his situation indexically instead of synecdochically, his overliteralness demonstrating his misunderstanding of the relationship between his body and God's story when he recounts his resistance to telling Dalila "in what part my strength / Lay stor'd, in what part summ'd" (394–95). Samson's first locating gesture here is appropriately synecdochic (his strength is "stored" in a "part"), but figurative synecdoche falters in the second gesture: "in what part summ'd." His strength is saliently not "summed" within his body at all, but rather originates in God. Next, Samson's blindness should act as a message from God, more insistently pointing to Samson's incompleteness. But when Samson questions "why was the sight / To such a tender ball as th'eye confin'd?" (93–94), he offers a complaint about bodily human vulnerability that suggests he still resists understanding how dependent humans are upon God, how human heroes are only a "part" as tender and as fragmented as the eyeball.[48] The corporeal figure in *Samson Agonistes* that finally acknowledges incompleteness is Samson's hair. Unlike the foreskin excised to mark God's favor, or the eyeball destroyed to mark Samson's vulnerability, hair grows back, inflected by time.[49] Early in the drama, Samson fails to understand this, offering a limited analysis of his divinely fortified hair when he suggests that "God, when he gave me strength, to shew withal / How slight the gift was, hung it in my Hair" (58–59). As Samson's hair grows back, eventually allowing him to pull down the temple, God's use of Samson's hair seems less to demonstrate "slightness" than to register the necessity for time to unfold in order for Samson's strength to be fully manifest.

Hair, then, figures Samson's opening to history and hence to a metonymic understanding of his situation. For Samson, comprehension of his own incompleteness is not entirely possible for generic reasons. As an Old-Testament character, he lives in and as a synecdoche, limiting the perceptual horizon. Toward the end of the drama, Samson's evolving relationship to God emerges as dynamic metonymy, the paradigm for perceiving synecdoche *in medias res*. Typology is a synecdochic theory of history (a given moment figures the larger historical context), but typological synecdoche works only from the confident perspective of the discernable end of time. Synecdoche can admit history, but only by reading historical moments in relationship to one another, a hermeneutic practice available only *post facto*.

Since the apocalyptic horizon is not so clear to Samson—or to newly chastened elect historians—metonymy substitutes for synecdoche as the appropriate hermeneutics for pious history. Glimpsing that he does indeed inhabit history, Samson turns to metonymy as the figurative relationship that allows one thing to point to another diachronically, offering a hermeneutic practice that can understand that events relate meaningfully to one another without being able to describe the "wholeness" that awaits completion of the historical horizon.[50] In *Samson*, metonymy articulates a view of history that is, properly, *both* synchronic and diachronic. Divinely directed, parts of history do figure other parts (mandating synchronic interpretation), but history as humans live it is not perceivable as a whole (mandating diachronic interpretation as well).

Samson's turn away from synecdoche as the trope expressing chosenness toward a metonymy that cannot definitely locate its referent constitutes rhetorical *humilitas*; metonymy corrects Samson's propensity to interpretive hubris.[51] Interestingly, *Samson* is not idiosyncratic in associating synecdoche with interpretive competence. Henry Peacham's *Garden of Eloquence* (1593), for instance, takes the relationship between metonymic terms to be given ("by nature"), whereas *"intellectio"* (the Latin term for "synecdoche") constitutes "an understanding"—the latter requiring more of the receiver. Thus Peacham cautions that "the Orator useth this figure [synecdoche] chiefly when he is well perswaded concerning the wisedome of his hearers"; hence "when a part is put for the whole, there [must] be a discreete choise of that part."[52] Similarly, Thomas Wilson's *Arte of Rhetorique* (1553) delineates synecdoche's demand that receivers actively evaluate the figure when he writes that "Intellection called of the Gretians, *Synecdoche*, is a Trope, when wee gather or *Judge* the whole by the parte, or part, by the whole."[53] The move away from synecdoche to metonymy, then, suggests that Samson, *Samson Agonistes*, and perhaps *Samson*'s readers must acknowledge their own limitations. If sloppy typology might take the Old Testament's historical and hermeneutic circumscription as a foil to perfected Christian understanding, *Samson Agonistes* suggests that incomplete comprehension imbricated in historical dynamics describes the situation of the Reformed reader as well.

The prevalent deconcretizing of typological practice Wittreich discusses parallels the New Testament metaphorizing of circumcision. Jeremiah 9:26, for instance, substitutes "circumcision in the heart" for genital surgery; Galatians 5:5 dismisses "circumcision of the flesh," since (in Martin Luther's gloss), "we go far beyond all this to live in the Spirit."[54] In ways analogous to seventeenth-century reevaluations of scriptural and historical interpretation, Reformist "circumcision" remains imperative, but becomes semiotically complex in its inwardness and its potential for ambiguity. This transformation from literal to spiritual understanding is crucial, but it is equally striking that Reformers insist on retaining the diction of "circumcision" even when they abandon the actual practice, indicating the importance of its historical grounding.[55]

Reformist emphasis on "circumcision in the heart" makes cardiac circumcision the marked absence of an absence: a noncircumcision of the penis that, in its nonoccurrence, serves as the crucial metaphoric ground for defining Christian identity. Pious Christians *must* be "circumcised in the heart," but *not* in the "flesh of the foreskin." The uncircumcised foreskin marks their difference from Jews; the circumcised heart marks their difference from the impious. The weight *Samson* gives to the foreskin as the marker of unelection for the Philistines makes the Elect Reformist foreskin all the more remarkable. The identical signifier—the foreskin, shared by the Philistine and the Reformer—signifies entirely differently.[56] It is unsurprising, then, to find that Reformist articulations of circumcision shift the synecdochic term from the foreskin to circumcision itself. Whereas the Old Testament takes the foreskin as a figure for the covenant, Reformist writers like Thomas Taylor take the process of circumcision as a synecdoche for the crucifixion: "in [Jewish] shedding of blood by Circumcision, was represented to their eyes the shedding of Christs blood; not only in the first fruits of his bloodshed in his Circumcision . . . but also the full powring out of all his blood in sacrifice upon the Crosse, wherein the Circumcision of Christ was fully accomplished."[57] Taylor's remark that preincarnation circumcision "represented" the Messiah "to their eyes" offers a gloss on Samson's blindness: the historical circumstances of Hebrew experience limit interpretability, in this figure, to the visual.

Against this visuality, with typical Reformist logic, the difference between circumcised and uncircumcised hearts is both utterly crucial and completely inward, undetectable visually or by any "outside" means. Corporeal similarity (the common foreskin) serves as the sign of spiritual difference. Indeed, in Luther's terms, the New Law does not forbid literal circumcision so much as insist on a semiotic shift. Luther writes,

It is amazing that Paul should say that in Christ Jesus neither circumcision nor uncircumcision counts for anything. He should rather have said, "Either circumcision or uncircumcision counts for something, since these two are contrary to each other." But now he denies that either one counts, as though he were saying, "We must go higher, for circumcision and uncircumcision are far too low to count for righteousness in the sight of God."[58]

Thus whereas Daniel Boyarin writes that "the crucial issue dividing Judaism from Christianity is . . . the relation to the body as a signifier of corporeal existence," we might emphasize instead differences in *reading* corporeal existence as *Samson's* primary concern.[59]

If Samson understands that he is chosen, but not that he is incomplete, Reformist circumcision in the heart is meant to comprehend both chosenness and incompleteness. Taylor insists that circumcision signals us to "take notice of our owne estate to humble us."[60] Moreover, Taylor interprets the ordained timing of circumcision—one day longer than a week—as "leading beyond the weeke of this present life (in which we cannot be perfectly circumcised) unto that eight day in the life to come."[61] Structuring circumcision metonymically, Taylor suggests further ways that understanding circumcision metonymically also entails understanding it temporally. He emphasizes the repeatability of "circumcision in the heart": Christ heals "by his Spirit *daily* sanctifying and circumcising our hearts."[62] Since believers' experience unfolds in historical time, circumcision likewise must extend through time, not as it looks from the endpoint, but rather as it is lived.

Placing our own canon into history reminds us that the material *Samson* made its print appearance in 1671 as "*Paradise Regain'd. A Poem In IV Books. To which is added Samson Agonistes.*"[63] *Samson Agonistes*, which disallows Christians to distinguish definitively between their own hermeneutic acumen and the "incomplete" knowledge of the Jews, comes *after*—completes, has the last word on—the story of the only exemplar of perfect earthly knowledge: the unrepeatable experience of the incarnate Christ. Whereas modern editorial, critical, and pedagogical practice sometimes cuts *Samson Agonistes* apart from *Paradise Regain'd*, the binding together of these two poems with *Samson* last is crucial to its theory of history. Samson's hermeneutic crisis has the last word, because we all live—and read—in history. This is why we must marry Wittreich's interest in historical interpretive practice with Cable's analysis of rhetoric. Reading history turns out to depend upon a rhetorical reading of truth, moving through synecdochic to meto-nymic interpretation. *Samson* provides an occasion for such reading, even as it represents the problem. This suggests Milton's answer to Christopher Hill's question in my epigraph: "How could the same God who willed 1649 will 1660?" The year 1660 is no more an answer to the problem of history than any other date could be. Typological reading—synecdochic reading—reads out-ward from text to history: text is the part, apocalyptic history the whole. The non-apocalypses of 1648, 1649, 1654, 1660 (and Y2K) reveal history to in-stead *be* the part. History and text will merge only at the true end of time; until then, pious historians must read metonymically, humbly allowing his-tory as well as text to confound them. The year 1660 showed English Re-formers that they had been bad readers of history. But 1660 may make them better readers of Scripture—and *hence* of a differently legible history yet to come.

Villanova University

NOTES

For help with researching this essay, I thank the Folger Library reading room staff; for assistance with many questions about Hebrew, I thank Jeffrey Shoulson; for helpful comments on various versions of this essay, I thank my works-in-progress group, as well as Jane Hedley, Nora Johnson, Katherine Rowe, David Glimp, Emmet McLaughlin, Julian Yates, Joan Bennett, Donald Friedman, Lori Ann Ferrell, Joseph Wittreich, Albert C. Labriola, and especially Scott Black.

The opening quotation is from Christopher Hill, *The Experience of Defeat: Milton and Some Contemporaries* (New York, 1984), 307.

1. For analyses of seventeenth-century Protestant historiography, see especially G. W. Trompf, *The Idea of Historical Recurrence in Western Thought: From Antiquity to the Reforma-tion* (Berkeley, 1979), and Achsah Guibbory, *The Map of Time: Seventeenth-Century English Literature and Ideas of Pattern in History* (Urbana, 1986).

2. Matthew Mead, *Solomon's Prescription for the Removal of the Pestilence* (London, 1665), A3, in Laura Lunger Knoppers, *Historicizing Milton: Spectacle, Power, and Poetry in Restora-tion England* (Athens, Ga., 1994), 145, emphasis added; James Harrington, *The Commonwealth of Oceana and A System of Politics*, ed. J. G. A. Pocock (Cambridge, 1992), 28, emphasis added.

3. As Robert Wilcher remarks in *"Samson Agonistes* and the Problem of History," *Renais-sance and Modern Studies* 26 (1982): 108–33, "When men involved in a political and military conflict begin with the premise that their cause is justified by God . . . when their conception of the nature of human history, and of their place in it, rests on deeply held beliefs in the prophetic truth of the Scriptures, the controlling hand of providence, and personal inspiration, then defeat carries with it more than merely political consequences" (123). Barbara Lewalski's "Milton's *Samson* and the 'New Acquist of True [Political] Experience,' " in *Milton Studies* 24, ed. James D. Simmonds (Pittsburgh, 1988), 233–51, poses questions about reading God's will that also are taken up in the present essay.

For arguments on *Samson's* engaging its Restoration context, see also Knoppers, *Historicizing Milton: Spectacle, Power, and Poetry in Restoration England*; Blair Worden, "Milton, *Samson Agonistes*, and the Restoration," in *Culture and Society in the Stuart Restoration: Literature, Drama, History*, ed. Gerald MacLean (Cambridge, 1995), 111–36; Nicholas Jose, *Ideas of the Restoration in English Literature, 1660–71* (Cambridge, Mass., 1984); David Loewenstein, *Representing Revolution in Milton and his Contemporaries: Religion, Politics, and Polemics in Radical Puritanism* (Cambridge, 2001); and Sharon Achinstein, "*Samson Agonistes* and the Drama of Dissent," in *Milton Studies* 33, ed. Albert C. Labriola and Michael Lieb (Pittsburgh, 1996), 133–58. For a contrary view, of *Samson* turning away from contemporary politics, see especially Mary Ann Radzinowicz, *Toward "Samson Agonistes": The Growth of Milton's Mind* (Princeton, 1978); and Joan Bennett, *Reviving Liberty: Radical Christian Humanism in Milton's Great Poems* (Cambridge, Mass., 1989), ch. 5.

4. Stanley Fish, "Question and Answer in 'Samson Agonistes,'" *Critical Quarterly* 11:3 (Autumn 1969): 237–65. Fish's subsequent "Spectacle and Evidence in *Samson Agonistes*," *Critical Inquiry* 15:3 (Spring 1989): 556–86, further develops this hermeneutic analysis.

5. Joseph Wittreich, *Interpreting* Samson Agonistes (Princeton, 1986), 177, 181.

6. Lana Cable, *Carnal Rhetoric: Milton's Iconoclasm and the Poetics of Desire* (Durham, 1995).

7. On *Samson's* hermeneutics, see also Knoppers, *Historicizing Milton: Spectacle, Power, and Poetry in Restoration England*; Anthony Low, *The Blaze of Noon: A Reading of* Samson Agonistes (New York, 1974); William Kerrigan, "The Irrational Coherence of *Samson Agonistes*," *Milton Studies* 22, ed. James D. Simmonds (Pittsburgh, 1986), 217–31; Daniel Lochman, "'If There Be Aught of Presage': Milton's Samson as Riddler and Prophet," in *Milton Studies* 22, ed. James D. Simmonds (Pittsburgh, 1986), 281–318; and Jane Collins, "Authorial Providence and the Dramatic Form of *Samson Agonistes*," in *Spokesperson Milton: Voices in Contemporary Criticism*, ed. Charles Durham and Kristin McColgan (Selinsgrove, Pa., 1994), 179–89.

8. David Loewenstein, *Milton and the Drama of History: Historical Vision, Iconoclasm, and the Literary Imagination* (Cambridge, 1990), argues that *Samson* dramatizes the unreadability of history: history is "ruptured and discontinuous, and God's purposes inscrutable" (130). I agree that history is fundamentally "discontinuous" in *Samson*, but will argue that the drama offers rhetorical strategies that allow its readers some hermeneutic access—albeit incomplete—to "ruptured" history.

9. Thomas M. Gorman, "The Reach of Human Sense: Surplus and Absence in *Samson Agonistes*," in *Milton Studies* 39, ed. Albert C. Labriola (Pittsburgh, 2000), 184–215.

10. We might recall that Milton prepared his *History of Britain* and *Brief History of Moscovia* for publication during the same years that saw the publication of *Samson*. Exploring the ways that *Samson* and these histories mutually illuminate one another lies beyond the scope of the present essay, but these works' shared self-consciousness about historiography and hermeneutics suggests their mutual relevance. On the *History of Britain* as a response to Milton's "disillusionment with the pattern of history by which he had *thought* he discerned the meaning of the past," see French Fogle, "Milton as Historian," in *Milton and Clarendon*, ed. Fogle and H. R. Trevor-Roper (Los Angeles, 1965), 10. On the hermeneutic demands that reading the *History* places upon its reader—comparable in some ways to my discussion of *Samson* below—as well as for other points of contact between *Samson* and the *History*, see Gary D. Hamilton, "*The History of Britain* and its Restoration audience," in *Politics, Poetics, and Hermeneutics in Milton's Prose*, ed. David Loewenstein and James Grantham Turner (Cambridge, 1990), 241–56.

11. See especially Barbara Lewalski, *Protestant Poetics and the Seventeenth-Century Re-*

ligious Lyric (Princeton, 1979), and C.A. Patrides, *The Grand Design of God: The Literary Form of the Christian View of History* (London, 1972).

12. Hence Samson also undergoes a change in political valence. Wittreich shows that the Samson story offers opposing factions "a window during the 1640s, with one side looking through it at its adversary"; in the 1660's, the story becomes "a mirror, with each side now glimpsing itself in the reflection" (*Interpreting* Samson Agonistes, 207). For a contrary argument that "the militant and faithful Samson who represents the godly saint actively at war with the world could have great potency for radical religious culture and writing[,] even after the Restoration," see Loewenstein, *Representing Revolution in Milton and his Contemporaries*, 269.

13. Wittreich, *Interpreting* Samson Agonistes, 184.

14. Patrick Collinson, "The Coherence of the Text: How it Hangeth Together: The Bible in Reformation England," in *The Bible, the Reformation and the Church*, ed. W. P. Stephens (Sheffield, 1995), 84–108.

15. See Peter Stallybrass, "Books and Scrolls: Navigating the Bible," in *Books and Readers in Early Modern England: Material Studies*, ed. Jenny Andersen and Elizabeth Sauer (Philadelphia, 2001), 42–79.

16. Raymond Anselment, in his introduction to Thomas Taylor, *Christ Revealed*, ed. Raymond A. Anselment (1632; Delmar, N.Y., 1979).

17. Samuel Mather, *The Figures or Types of the Old Testament, by which Christ and the Heavenly Things of the Gospel were Preached and Shadowed to the People of God of Old* (1683; London, 1705), iv.

18. Mather, iv.

19. Ibid., iv.

20. As Derek N. C. Wood recently has suggested, *Samson's* Biblical allusions "mime the Christian's difficulty in reading the significance of its great pre-text, the Bible. Milton's tragedy actually enacts the problem of reading the Word of God, itself enmeshed in a formidable network of echoes, glosses, cruxes, and obfuscations." Wood, *Exiled from Light: Divine Law, Morality, and Violence in Milton's* Samson Agonistes (Toronto, 2001), 38.

21. Compare Achsah Guibbory's two categories for Samson's figurative functions: Samson "holds much of the same relationship to Israel as Israel (the chosen people) does to the Gentiles," while "in another way . . . Samson represents Israel" (*The Map of Time: Seventeenth-Century English Literature and Ideas of Pattern in History*, 199).

22. *Samson's* use of typology resonates with Thomas Luxon's discussion of Protestant "history" in *Literal Figures: Puritan Allegory and the Reformation Crisis in Representation* (Chicago, 1995). Luxon writes that "one effect of what the Reformers call typology is not simply a re-historicizing of the ancient Hebrews . . . but also a re-fictionalizing of history more generally . . . neither Jesus, nor the church, nor Christians are final fulfillments any longer. Reality has been pushed beyond a new telic horizon" (43).

23. Thus I disagree with Wittreich's claim that "the narrative embedments in *Samson* indicate that Milton's story aspires to completeness" (*Interpreting* Samson Agonistes, 106); I would argue rather that *Samson* rules out the possibility of completeness.

24. Similarly, my understanding of *Samson's* interest in demonstrating that Christians themselves still live in unperfected history—with its attendant hermeneutic imperfection—emphasizes continuities between Israelite and Christian experience, whereas Wood focuses on contrasts between Christian and "un-Christian" experience (*Exiled from Light: Divine Law, Morality, and Violence in Milton's* Samson Agonistes, 61); see also Wood's discussion of Milton's "vision of Old Testament consciousness" as "rigorous, incomplete, enslaved, literalistic, and uncomprehending" (xx).

25. On the Old and New Testaments offering "correlative types" more than type and

antitype, see Lewalski, *"Samson Agonistes* and the 'Tragedy' of the Apocalypse," *PMLA* 85:5 (Oct. 1970): 1050–1062.

26. Taylor, *Christ Revealed*, A2ᵛ

27. Ibid.

28. Mather, *The Figures or Types of the Old Testament*, 181.

29. All citations of *Samson Agonistes* and *Paradise Regain'd* are from *The Complete Poetry of John Milton*, ed. John T. Shawcross (New York, 1963).

30. John Rogers takes Samson's hair as a central problematic of the poem; for Rogers, the "capital secret" of Samson's hair brings together questions about how directly or mediatedly Samson's strength derives from God with questions about the readability or "secrecy" of God's interventions. See Rogers, "The Secret of *Samson Agonistes*," in *Milton Studies* 33, ed. Albert C. Labriola and Michael Lieb (Pittsburgh, 1996), 111–32. For ways *Samson* "meditates upon the difficulty and tensions inherent in the process of constructing identity through hair," see Will Fisher, "Prosthetic Gods: Subject/Object in Early Modern England" (Ph.D. diss., University of Pennsylvania, 1998), 84.

31. Taylor emphasizes the "separateness" of the Nazarite: "a Nazarite signified one that was seperated and severed from the common course of men to a more holy profession of sanctity, and to a stricter care to avoid all manner of impurity . . . holy and seperate from sinners" (*Christ Revealed*, 55); Rogers reminds us that "Nazarite" derives from the Hebrew *"nazir,"* "separate" ("The Secret of *Samson Agonistes*," 114).

32. Ashraf Rushdy takes Samson's focus on the past in this opening soliloquy to demonstrate Samson's limitations, and the discontinuity in Samson's experiences as the sign of his "disintegration." See Rushdy, *The Empty Garden: The Subject of Late Milton* (Pittsburgh, 1992), especially 284–87. On early modern meditations on "narrating selfhood across time," see also Marshall Grossman, *The Story of All Things: Writing the Self in English Renaissance Narrative Poetry* (Durham, 1998).

33. For interpretations of Samson as a type of Christ, see F. Michael Krouse, *Milton's Samson and the Christian Tradition* (Princeton, 1949), and Christopher Kendrick, "Typology and the Ethics of Tragedy in *Samson Agonistes*," *Criticism* 33:1 (Winter 1991): 115–52. For *Samson* prefiguring the Elect as tragic protagonists of the apocalypse, see Lewalski, *"Samson Agonistes* and the 'Tragedy' of the Apocalypse." On Samson's typological relationship to both Reformers and to Christ, see Radzinowicz, *Toward "Samson Agonistes": The Growth of Milton's Mind*. For a typological reading that emphasizes the limitations of the Hebrew view, see William Madsen, *From Shadowy Types to Truth: Studies in Milton's Symbolism* (New Haven, 1968). On traditions of reading Samson as a type of Milton, see Knoppers, *Historicizing Milton: Spectacle, Power, and Poetry in Restoration England*. Wittreich, *Interpreting* Samson Agonistes, qualifies all of the above.

34. Madsen remarks this in analyzing Milton's interest in "the distance between the various levels of awareness . . . possible to those living under the old dispensation and the level of awareness revealed by Christ" (*From Shadowy Types to Truth: Studies in Milton's Symbolism*, 198).

35. The status of this opening moment as repetition-with-a-difference of Jesus' meditation on interpreting oracles in *Paradise Regain'd*—particularly in light of readerly experiences of moving directly from *Paradise Regain'd* to *Samson* in the 1671 edition—would emphasize the resonance of these issues. Jesus' first words in *Paradise Regain'd* are "O what a multitude of thoughts at once / Awak'n'd in me swarm" (196–97); Jesus proceeds to describe experiences of reading "the Law of God" (207), "hear[ing] / The Teachers of our Law" (211–12), and "revolv[ing] / The Law and Prophets, searching what was writ" (259–60).

36. This is the instability remarked by Fish, "Question and Answer in 'Samson Agonistes'"

and "Spectacle and Evidence in *Samson Agonistes*"; by Cable, *Carnal Rhetoric*; and by Harold Skulsky, *Justice in the Dock: Milton's Experimental Tragedy* (Newark, 1995).

37. Thus I disagree with Kendrick's notion that Samson ultimately "grasps the Gospel semiotic governing his actions" ("Typology and the Ethics of Tragedy in *Samson Agonistes*," 131).

38. Similar arguments about this passage are made in Wittreich, *Interpreting* Samson Agonistes, and Irene Samuel, "*Samson Agonistes* as Tragedy," in *Calm of Mind: Tercentenary Essays on 'Paradise Regained' and 'Samson Agonistes' in Honor of John S. Diekhoff*, ed. Joseph Wittreich (Cleveland, 1971), 235–57.

39. The Protestant ambivalence about the ontological status of the body that Luxon details (*Literal Figures: Puritan Allegory and the Reformation Crisis in Representation*) finds its generic counterpart here in closet drama. If scripted theatrical characters inhabit a liminal kind of text/body, the characters in closet drama push this ambiguity even further, asking readers to animate an embodied spectacle whose embodiment will remain imaginative.

40. On circumcision in *Samson*, see also Michael Lieb, " 'A Thousand Fore-Skins': Circumcision, Violence, and Selfhood in Milton," in *Milton Studies* 38, ed. Albert C. Labriola and Michael Lieb (Pittsburgh, 2000), 198–219.

41. Lieb wittily remarks that in this episode, "Milton's Samson no doubt proved himself the greatest *mohel* of all time" (198). For reasons developed below, Lieb's wording here—"of all time"—registers the difference between his reading and mine; I am particularly interested in the ways that circumcision becomes, "*over time*," a mode of Reformed reading and figuration, producing what Reformers take to be far greater *mohelim* than Samson.

42. Note the resonance between Samson's use of the ass's jawbone and his "blabbing." On the one hand, these are opposites—using the ass's jaw to execute God's will, using his own jaw to derail God's plan. On the other, Samson's eventual effectiveness against the Philistines suggests parallels in their blunt and indirect executions which nonetheless inscribe the divine plan onto history.

43. Emphasis added. The Hebrew term is "*oth*," a word translated in some King James Version verses—including this one—as "token," in others as "sign." Compare Taylor's emphasis that circumcision is not an index, but rather a sign: "neither *Abraham* nor any of his were chosen into the Covenant, because they were cleaner or holier then other; but that they might be holier. Gods election is free, who makes choyce of them that need Circumcision as well as any other" (*Christ Revealed*, 206).

44. On the dialectical ontology of signifier and signified, see Jacques Derrida, "Différance," in *Margins of Philosophy*, trans. Alan Bass (Chicago, 1982), 1–28.

45. Kenneth Burke, *A Grammar of Motives*, 2d ed. (Berkeley, 1969), describes this difference in terms of synecdoche "stress[ing] a *relationship* or *connectedness* between two sides of an equation . . . that . . . extends in either direction," whereas "[metonymy] follows along this road in only *one* direction" (509). My understanding of metonymy as a strategy that encompasses incompleteness, deferral, and irreducible multivalence is similar to Lochman's understanding of riddling as a linguistic strategy adequate to "existence as mixed and ambiguous, irreducible to simple, absolute alternatives" (" 'If There Be Aught of Presage': Milton's Samson as Riddler and Prophet," 195–96). On riddling as linguistic accommodation of radical multivalance, see also John C. Ulreich, " 'Beyond the Fifth Act': *Samson Agonistes* as Prophecy," in *Milton Studies* 17, ed. Richard S. Ide and Joseph Wittreich (Pittsburgh, 1983), 281–318.

46. Noting that "metonymy presupposes a contiguous, extrinsic field of reference that is in some sense already given," Jane Hedley, in *Power in Verse: Metaphor and Metonymy in the Renaissance Lyric* (State College, Pa., 1988), remarks that "metaphor pulls its terms out of context . . . creat[ing] . . . forms that call attention to their status as mental constructs" (113).

47. Delineating the set of predictable relations, Henry Peacham's *The Garden of Eloquence*, ed. William Crane (1593; Gainesville, 1954) includes under metonymic relations "the efficient for the cause," the commander or governor "for those which are under his gouernement," instruments for effects, possessor for thing possessed, "time put for the things done in time," "place put for the things it containeth," and place for "the actions in place" (20–21). Thomas Wilson, *Arte of Rhetorique* (London, 1553), also includes "the author of a thyng, for the thyng selfe," and "that whiche doeth conteyne . . . used for that whiche is conteined" (Fol. 93).

48. Rogers takes Samson's complaint about eyeballs to "question the reason behind the awkward division of labor among the body's parts, [which] is to pursue a dangerous critique of God's secrets" ("The Secret of *Samson Agonistes*," 118). Relatedly, Rogers takes the question of whether Samson's strength is actually stored or more mediatedly figured in his hair as a central crux of the poem.

49. Early modern scientific discussions of hair reveal an ambiguous status that parallels these questions about where Samson's strength actually lies (whether the strength is Samson's or God's: whether hair is repository or signifier). Helkiah Crooke, in *Microcosmographia: A Description of the Body of Man* (London, 1615), reports, "it appeareth, that they [hairs] are onely excrements, and their action is but an improper accretion, utterly deuoide of life, and therefore they are not to be reckoned among the parts of the body; or if they be, it is not because they do participate of life . . . But there are some of *Aristotles* followers, who contend that they have a life, but that of nourishment onely, not of offense" (82). Fisher discusses such ambiguity as signaling ways that hair is not "unambiguously corporeal" (*Prosthetic Gods: Subject/Object in Early Modern England*, 87).

50. Indeed, Burke describes metonymy as an historical process: according to Burke, metonymy paradigmatically "convey[s] some incorporeal or intangible state in terms of the corporeal or tangible . . . If you trail language back far enough . . . you will find that all our terms for 'spiritual' states were metonymic in origin" (*Grammar of Motives*, 506). *Samson* demonstrates the dehistoricizing tendency of synecdoche, by contrast, in the way the text's single metonymic use of "Israel" illuminates the usual use of "Israel" as a dead synecdoche. The drama contains many examples of "Israel" to designate nation (39, 179, 233, 242, 285, 342, 454, 1150, 1663, 1714); the single metonymic line, "*Israel* still serves with all his sons" (240) (metonymic because it doesn't refer to Jacob himself) reminds us both of the history encoded in naming the nation "Israel" and of the erasure of history as the synecdoche becomes lexicalized.

51. Hedley writes, "with metonymy, we need not suppose the higher-level gestalt to be capable of totalization . . . synecdoche presupposes a distinct entity, usually an organism or a system to which organic unity is attributed" (*Power in Verse: Metaphor and Metonymy in the Renaissance Lyric*, 137).

52. Peacham, *Garden of Eloquence*, 18.

53. Wilson, *Arte of Rhetorique*, Fol. 93, second emphasis added.

54. Martin Luther, *Luther's Works*, 55 vols., ed. Jaroslav Pelikan (St. Louis, 1958–86), 27:25. All citations from *Lectures on Galatians* are from 1535 edition. Milton's own articulation of this view comes in the *Doctrine and Discipline of Divorce*: "How vain then and how preposterous must it needs be to exact a circumcision of the Flesh . . . unto an outward signe of purity, and to dispence an uncircumcision in the soul . . . to an inward and reall impurity?" *Complete Prose Works of John Milton*, 8 vols., ed. Don M. Wolfe et al. (New Haven, 1953–82), vol. 2, 302.

55. In Burke's terms, this illuminates how spiritual circumcision is paradigmatically metonymic: "Language develops by metaphorical extension, in borrowing words from the realm of the corporeal, visible, tangible and applying them by analogy to the realm of the incorporeal, invisible, intangible; then in the course of time, the original corporeal reference is forgotten . . .

finally, poets regain the original relation, in reverse . . . back from the intangible into a tangible equivalent . . . and this 'archaicizing' device we call 'metonymy' " (*Grammar of Motives*, 506).

56. This reinterpretation of a signifier retained from an earlier tradition is central to much Reformist practice (reinterpretations of the Real Presence in the Host, for example: the Host still is raised, but it means something different). Most interestingly in the present context, it also suggestively parallels early Christianity's use of codex technology to differentiate Christian from Jewish practice. Stallybrass writes: "Prior to the tenth or eleventh centuries, Christians and Jews actively differentiated themselves from each other through the adoption of the book or the scroll. . . . Christians and Jews read the *same* Jewish scriptures. But whereas Jews read the scrolls of the Torah and of the prophets, Christians read the Hebrew scriptures . . . in the form of a codex (and with an emphasis upon the discontinuous reading of the prophets rather than on the continuous reading of the Torah)" ("Books and Scrolls: Navigating the Bible," 43). See also Irven M. Resnick, "The Codex in Early Jewish and Christian Communities," *The Journal of Religious History* 17:1 (1992): 1–17; and Colin H. Roberts and T. C. Skeat, *The Birth of the Codex* (London, 1983).

57. Taylor, *Christ Revealed*, 208.

58. Luther, *Works*, vol. 27, 137.

59. Boyarin, " 'This We Know to Be the Carnal Israel' ": Circumcision and the Erotic Life of God and Israel," *Critical Inquiry* 18 (Spring 1992): 474–505, 490. For a fuller examination of these issues, see Boyarin's *Carnal Israel: Reading Sex in Talmudic Culture* (Berkeley, 1993).

60. Taylor, *Christ Revealed*, 208. Taylor's reading of Hebrew circumcision emphasizes its location in this world: "the Lord in this Sacrament tooke care that his people should carry upon their bodies the signe of sinne and death" (208).

61. Taylor, 206.

62. Taylor, 208, emphasis added.

63. Balachandra Rajan raises the issue of reading the poems together; see "To Which is Added *Samson Agonistes*," in *The Prison and the Pinnacle: Papers to Commemorate the Tercentenary of 'Paradise Regained' and 'Samson Agonistes,'* ed. Rajan (Toronto, 1973), 82–110. See also Wittreich, *Interpreting* Samson Agonistes; Rushdy, *The Empty Garden*; Wood, *Exiled from Light*; John T. Shawcross, "The Genres of *Paradise Regain'd* and *Samson Agonistes*: The Wisdom of their Joint Publication," in *Milton Studies* 17, ed. Richard S. Ide and Joseph Wittreich (Pittsburgh, 1983), 225–48; Daniel T. Lochman, "Conflicts of Authority: Interpretation of Events in *Paradise Regained* and *Samson Agonistes*," in *Spokesperson Milton: Voices in Contemporary Criticism*, 165–78; and Anne K. Krook, "The Hermeneutics of Opposition in *Paradise Regained* and *Samson Agonistes*," *Studies in English Literature* 36:1 (Winter 1996): 129–48. Grossman remarks that "the orthodox Christian reading of the Samson story points out that Samson's failure conduces to and explicates the glory of Jesus' success [but] Milton's volume complicates this facile typology, reversing the expected order and situating Samson, as it were, in the shadow of that unknown thing, which he cannot remember—because it has not yet occurred—and for which, in the exigence of his circumstances, he cannot wait" (*The Story of All Things: Writing the Self in English Renaissance Narrative Poetry*, 264–65).

RHETORIC, POLEMIC, MIMETIC:
THE DIALECTIC OF GENRES IN
TETRACHORDON AND *COLASTERION*

James Egan

I

THE MOST INFLUENTIAL recent treatments of Milton's divorce
pamphlets have recovered his ideology of divorce and, in particular, its
implications for gender study and self-construction.[1] The delineation of the
patriarchal Milton attempted by feminist critics has been complemented by
Stephen Fallon's analysis of the conflicting perspectives on sexuality in Milton's works on divorce and of the literal and metaphorical tensions between
dualism and monism.[2] Such ideological and hermeneutic readings as these
have surely addressed several prominent questions untreated by formalist
and new critical assessment, yet they have, simultaneously, led to a comparative neglect of the rhetorical and polemical details of the divorce tracts,
details that I argue require fuller consideration. Genre and stylistic criticism
have drawn several secure conclusions about Milton's writings on divorce,
beginning with Kester Svendsen's discussion of the relationship between
structure and imagery in *Doctrine and Discipline* and of the pamphlet's
recurring patterns of metaphor.[3] Importantly, Annabel Patterson has outlined a "concealed autobiographical novel" in *Doctrine and Discipline*, posi-
tioning the text between "psychobiography and a resurgent genre theory."[4]
Reuben Sanchez's stance on persona in Milton's prose has created room for
additional rhetorical and aesthetic study by locating in the prose a rhetoric of
"literary self-presentation."[5] The analysis I develop of the divorce tracts as an
evolving dialectic of genres derives several of its assumptions from those
posited by Svendsen, Patterson, and Sanchez, and from the pioneering work
of Michael Lieb and Joseph Anthony Wittreich, Jr. Wittreich has presented
the most thorough review of Milton's oratorical habits, while Lieb has treated
Of Reformation (1641) as a thematic and structural display of "fundamental
rhetorical principles" adapted to a specific occasion of theological controversy, and a dialectical exchange of "prevailing modes of discourse."[6]

Patterson's claim that *Doctrine and Discipline* "hovers on an undrawn
boundary between polemic and narrative," a claim that could easily be ex-

tended to *Tetrachordon* (1645) and *Colasterion* (1645), punctuates the rhetorical intricacy of the divorce writings.[7] I propose to read *Tetrachordon* and *Colasterion* as essentially polemics, as a sequence of nuanced arguments eliciting and then confuting the responses of others over the question of divorce. In order to recover the rhetorical context of these tracts, it is necessary to examine the details of their form, the sophisticated mechanics and processes of their polemic strategies. Such an examination reveals that a subtextual history exists, embedded in Milton's plea for divorce, of the interplay of several seventeenth-century prose idioms, including the disputation, the sermon, the jeremiad, the animadversion, and the protodramatic satire. To appreciate Milton's own rhetoric of counterpoint and the dialectic of forms in which he engages, one must survey the rhetorics and genre formats used against him from 1643 through 1645. The pamphlets of his opponents, in fact, constitute specialized prompts and challenges for Milton the controversialist, creating a shifting decorum of response.[8] What is more, the divorce tracts progress sequentially from discursive to aesthetic perspectives, so that they incorporate a record of genre and stylistic experimentation into their well-documented record of ideological evolution. If the divorce controversy can be read as a contest of genre and rhetoric in addition to its conventional interpretation as a doctrinal display, we can better appreciate its subtlety, its position on the "undrawn boundary" Patterson has alluded to.

II

Milton initiated the divorce controversy with two orations, the first (1643) and second (1644) editions of *Doctrine and Discipline*, perhaps anticipating an equally dignified oratorical response that would engage his startling doctrines fully and register objections with as much persuasive force as he had mustered in generating his own evidence.[9] Milton was to be disappointed: oratory was not the preferred medium of his detractors, whose mode of attack was diverse. William Riley Parker has described the "failure of anyone to offer a serious criticism or undertake a reply" and, more importantly, Milton's nearly desperate need to "argue with someone."[10] *Doctrine and Discipline* in both editions, of course, was widely "denounced as the work of a scandalous libertine."[11] Beyond the longstanding impression that Milton had provoked public outrage and gotten himself pilloried as a heretic, the actual rhetoric of response directed against him has not been examined. I suggest that he engaged the rhetorical and genre choices of his attackers very deliberately, very systematically, and that their rhetoric became a motive for his own in *Tetrachordon* and *Colasterion*.

In the preface to *Tetrachordon*, published with *Colasterion* on 4 March

1645, Milton singled out two of those who had blasted *Doctrine and Discipline*: Herbert Palmer, whose sermon *The Glasse of Gods Providence* was preached before both Houses of Parliament on 13 August 1644, and Daniel Featley, whose tract *The Dippers Dipt* was published in January 1645. In *Colasterion* Milton countered two more rebuttals, William Prynne's *Twelve Considerable Serious Questions Touching Church Government*, published in September 1644, and the anonymous *An Answer to a Book, Intituled, The Doctrine and Discipline of Divorce*, published in November 1644. Two additional sermons that appeared in time for Milton to have reckoned with them in *Tetrachordon* or *Colasterion* have also been identified: Thomas Young's *Hope's Incouragement* was preached before Commons on 28 February 1644, and Matthew Newcomen's *A Sermon, Tending to Set Forth*, was preached before both Houses on 13 September 1644.[12] The prevailing interpretation of Milton's reply to Palmer and Featley is that he vindicated himself literally, and in the preface to *Tetrachordon* only, by vigorously denouncing both men. As I demonstrate, his reaction is much more a matter of subtext and implication than a matter of direct assault.

Palmer's *The Glasse of Gods Providence* cautions against the civil perils of liberty of conscience and singles out Milton as a holder of *"pernicious and pestiferous . . . opinions"* in *Doctrine and Discipline* (56). Palmer's call for drastic measures against such heretical publications demands that God's *"Honour* requires still the same *Severity* against *such kind of Offendors"* (58). He catalogues the sins of the nation, targeting three primary offenses—sins of ignorance, of covetousness, and of profaneness—that cast a *"horrid mist of darknesse* over the land" (34). Milton's divorce writings would clearly be included among the *"Errors,* and *strange opinions"* Palmer censures (33). Young's *Hopes Incouragement* urges a stalwart patience among the faithful (9), equates lack of patience with lack of faith (7–9), and pleads with those who would effect Reformation not to "fall short of that heroicall disposition, whereupon all that wait on God ought to aspire" (22). Like Palmer, Young laments what he considers a "distracted Nation" (1) caught up in the "cloudy storm of . . . unnaturall troubles" (3). William Haller suggested that Young, a former Smectymnuan ally of Milton's, might have referred to Milton on several occasions: when he cautioned that "It is not courage, but presumption, for a man to adventure upon that work to which hee is not called of God" (11); when he advised against the "enacting of a Law that makes against God or his cause" (31); and when he indicted those who in their afflictions refuse to "wait upon him for his helpe . . ." (5).[13] Thomas Kranidas has recently found in *A Sermon, Tending To Set Forth,* by another Smectymnuan ally of Milton's, Thomas Newcomen, an additional disparaging allusion to the divorce tracts, an allusion magnified by virtue of its source.[14] Newcomen lashes out at the plague of heresy, schism, and "down-right Libertinisme" (36) afflicting England. Like Palmer and Young, he chronicles the signs of divine displeasure at a wayward nation, implying that the sins of the ministry may have offended the Almighty (29), that the army's setbacks might be attributed to the vices of Parliament (25), and that a general lukewarmness in religion might be impeding Reformation (26).

The works of Palmer, Young, and Newcomen partake of a widespread, familiar methodology, that of the Puritan sermon. In the sermon a scriptural text was divided, "opened" into as many relevant passages as the preacher chose to explicate. "Rules" or principles were then derived from the passages in question and generally linked to the sermon's topic. Rules were followed by "uses" or specific applications, normally historical and typological, to the moral circumstances of the sermon's occasion. Virtually all Puritan sermons, particularly those delivered before the Long Parliament and the Westminster Assembly, as were the sermons of Palmer, Young, and Newcomen, were composed in the plain style.[15] The fact that Parliament and the Assembly heard these sermons assail the divorce tracts constitutes a second element linking them. H. R. Trevor-Roper has discussed the vast political import of Fast Day Sermons in the 1640's, and James C. Spalding has compared the "special days for humiliation and thanksgiving to . . . nationally significant celebrations on the order of . . . Guy Fawkes' Day."[16] Because not all Fast Day sermons reached print, the fact that those of Palmer, Young, and Newcomen did intensifies their importance.[17] Spalding has emphasized the corporate character of these sermons, their tendency to provide a national moral measurement, one that was, because of its collective public quality, "quickly disseminated among the people."[18] Significantly, John F. Wilson describes sermons before the Long Parliament as part of a distinctive, institutionalized literary tradition.[19] Such a potent historical and political context suggests that Milton might have paid particular attention to Fast Day sermons; surely these attacks had demonized him, singled him out as an impediment to national piety, a disseminator of "false teaching [that] might alienate people, nation, and church from the promise of salvation."[20] A final connection among the works of Palmer, Young, and Newcomen is their membership in the category of the jeremiad, a localized seventeenth-century literary tradition that flourished during the Civil War and Interregnum. Formulaic lamentations over moral and political strife, jeremiads itemized moral decline and apostasy among those who had covenanted with God for Reformation.[21] Though sermons often assumed the features of jeremiads, the "prophetic lament over . . . apostasy" essential to the jeremiad also manifests itself in political documents of many other kinds, notably in "proclamations for fasting [and] letters to the army and the Parliament."[22] The cataloguing of national sins, which inevitably included heresy, "backsliding," a breakdown in church and family discipline, together with a rise in impatience and contentiousness, was the rhetorical backbone of the jeremiad.[23] Palmer, Young, and Newcomen either did not devote great attention to Milton's opinions on divorce, or attacked them only by implication, yet political and literary context multiplies the force of their diatribes. Because all three sermons qualified as jeremiads, their tone was morally strident. Milton was stigmatized as a favorite villain in the literature of the jeremiad—the heretic. The apocalyptic propensity of the genre was thus directed at Milton, and his divorce treatises were offered as stark evidence of one of the most notorious heresies imaginable. While none of these blasts added up to the studied exegetical response Milton may have expected, the sermons of Palmer, Young, and Newcomen nevertheless qualified as a weighty polemic challenge for him, one with distinctive rhetorical properties and mythologizing tendencies.

A long pamphlet that blended scholastic confutation with folklorish anecdotes about the erroneous ways of Anabaptists, Daniel Featley's *The Dippers Dipt* (1645) served up another stylized pattern of attack for Milton to address.[24] His dedicatory epistle indicts Milton: "Witnesse a Tractate of Divorce, in which the bonds of marriage are let loose to inordinate lust, and putting away wives for many other causes besides that which our Saviour only approveth, namely, in case of Adultery." Like Palmer, Newcomen, and Young, Featley considers Milton a personification of the most notorious errors afflicting the progress of Reformation, and implicitly links him in the preface to the reader with the lowly, despised Anabaptists, a baleful example of the "sorts of Heretiques and Schismatiques [who] breed and are exceedingly multiplyed" in a time of national tribulation. His dedicatory epistle threatens to use "Logicall and Theologicall weapons, weilded after a Scholasticall manner" against "every handy-craftsman" who, he warns in the preface, will be "*handling* the *pure* Word of God with *impure* and unwashed hands." In the body of the text, Featley painstakingly illustrates how disputation must be done:" . . . if you will dispute by Reason, you must conclude syllogistically in mood and figure, which I take to be out of your [Anabaptists'] Element" (2). He catalogues the doctrines of Anabaptists on child baptism, set forms of prayer, and the authority of the civil magistrate, and then rebuts them at length, repeatedly demonstrating the fallacies indulged in by particular Anabaptists along with the shortcomings of Anabaptism at large. Early on, *The Dippers Dipt* takes the form of a stage-managed mock disputation wherein a narrator challenges two Anabaptist "spokesmen" to disprove his claims against their doctrine, a task at which the Anabaptists prove incompetent. Chapter Six includes "Kicke-shoses" and a "variety of *strange fruits*," a compilation of folklorish anecdotes meant to illustrate the unsavory eccentricity and giddiness of the sect, thereby lending a measure of negative ethos to Featley's scholastic rebuttal of the systemic logic of Anabaptism.

Milton's response to Palmer, Young, Newcomen, and Featley suggests that he designed *Tetrachordon* as a deliberate exercise in counterpoint, one that would take the measure of the modes and genres opposing him and muster rhetorical and generic devices of his own as antidotes, the result being an orchestrated dialectic of forms between him and his attackers. The dedication to *Tetrachordon* angrily indicts both Palmer and Featley. Palmer, Milton charges, "having scarse read [*Doctrine and Discipline*], nor knowing him who writ it, or at least faining the latter, hath not forborn to scandalize him, unconferr'd with, unadmonisht, undealt with by any Pastorly or brotherly convincement, in the most open and invective manner, and at the most bitter opportunity that drift or set designe could have invented" (2:579). Milton assails *The Dippers Dipt* as a "late equivocating Treatise" that "mentions with ignominy the Tractate of Divorce; yet answers nothing . . ." (2:583). His reply to such complaints, however, goes well beyond these literal objections, extending into the structure, strategies of argument, language, and style of *Tetrachordon*.[25] Both Arnold Williams and Thomas Corns have characterized *Tetrachordon* structurally as an exegesis, and Williams has summarized Milton's tactics: "Just like scores of commentators, Milton takes up a passage of Scripture, divides it into phrases, sometimes divides the phrase into words, and discusses each detail fully . . ." (2:572).[26] This exegetical strategy, I argue, was chosen to evoke the format of the Parliamentary preachers who had attacked Milton and to surpass it. Clearly, several traditional structural arrangements, including the oration and the animadversion, were available to Milton as he prepared *Tetrachordon*, but only one would serve his purpose of besting the preachers at their own game.[27]

As a case in point, Milton's explication of Matthew 5:31–32 is essentially an "opening" of two lines crucial to his own case for divorce, an extraction of the text's meaning comprising six pages in all. He opens the passage according to the "rules of nature and eternal righteousnes, which no writt'n law extinguishes, and the Gospel least of all" (2:636). First, the line "It hath beene said" is deconstructed at length, and then "whosoever shall put away his wife." "Reasons" or justifications of the doctrines Milton has drawn out follow, and the exegesis concludes with several "uses" or applications, summarized here: "But what if the law of divorce be a morall law, as most certainly it is fundamentally, and hath been so prov'd in the reasons thereof. For though the giving of a bill may be judiciall, yet the act of divorce is altogether conversant in good or evill, and so absolutely moral"(2:642). Whether Milton opens literal or metaphorical meanings of passages in the four central scriptural texts that anchor *Tetrachordon*, the subdivisions and conclusions of his analysis inevitably parallel the reasons and applications of the Puritan sermon. The "Church-outed" Milton could certainly echo and evoke the rhetoric of those who had preached against him.

And he could do considerably more than evoke. While the attacks of Palmer, Young, and Newcomen were brief, Milton's defense of his thesis proves exhaustive, a triumph of quantity at the very least. One finds in the workings of his argument, moreover, a degree of clinical, technical precision rare in the sermons of the three preachers. The following dialectical exchange offers an illustration:

As for what they say we must bear with patience, to bear with patience, and to seek effectual remedies, implies no contradiction. It may no lesse be for our disobedience, our unfaithfulnes, and other sins against God, that wives becom adulterous to the bed, and questionles we ought to take the affliction as patiently, as christian prudence would wish; yet hereby is not lost the right of divorcing for adultery. No you say, because our Saviour excepted that only. But why, if he were so bent to punish our sins, and try our patience in binding on us a disastrous marriage, why did he except adultery. (2:590)

The quote and reply arrangement of the passage signifies a process of formal refutation absent from the sermons against Milton, a process reminiscent of the intricate, tightly focused dynamic of scholastic logic and disputation. Not only does Milton present his plea, he simultaneously anticipates and defends against several contingencies. This sophisticated mechanism, pervasive in *Tetrachordon*, acts as a display of transcendence, an assertion of mastery in the ways of debate. Crafted as a disputation, Milton's own biblical commentary trumps the sermons of his opponents. Finally, the very language of *Tetrachordon* communicates his formal expertise as a disputant. His repeated invocation of the terminology of scholastic logic and its appropriate usage (e.g., "*. . . Antecedent . . . Consequent; copulat axiom . . . compound axiom*" [2:676]; "*. . . discrete axiom*" [2:685]), and, most tellingly, the framing of his definition of marriage according to the Aristotelian doctrine of the four causes (2:608–9) all connote the clinical, learned expertise of the practiced logician, an expertise certified by one of the most frequently invoked criteria of the seventeenth century, the venerable *modus operandi* of scholasticism.

Milton's scholastic stratagems, then, add up to a strict methodology of greater precision and detail than any of the relatively elementary arrangements of opening, application, and use favored by Palmer, Young, or Newcomen: an exegetical disputation becomes the ideal generic antidote to its less rigorous relative, the sermon. Equally important, scholastic methodology doubles as a comprehensive exercise in *ethos* to offset Featley's charge that Milton, as a kindred of unlearned Anabaptists, did not know the rules of

debate, could not cite the relevant texts of logic, could not formulate coherent syllogisms or pursue refutational cross-examination. *Tetrachordon* is a
masterpiece of analytical critique that dispels any suggestion that in *Doctrine
and Discipline* Milton was a mere "handy-craftsman . . . *handling* the *pure*
Word of God.*" The tract's exegetical framework qualifies as a structural
version of testimony directed at the three ministers who had chastised Milton
as well as at Featley. Not only does *Tetrachordon* rebut Featley's implication that the divorce tracts smacked of Anabaptist ignorance, but Milton's
dependence upon David Paraeus, his incorporation of the tactics of a renowned exegete into his own argument, simultaneously invokes a more durable, wide-ranging theological credibility than the occasional sermons of
Palmer, Young, and Newcomen, three momentarily fashionable preachers
before the Long Parliament, could plausibly claim.[28] The style of Milton's
exegesis offers additional instances of the ways in which he tried to counter
the strategies used against *Doctrine and Discipline*. The majority of Fast Day
sermons were composed in a plain style, those of Palmer, Young, and Newcomen being no exception. The following selection from Palmer's *The Glasse
of Gods Providence* typifies the style of Milton's attackers:

And so you have the Story of the Text set before you; and the Doctrines observed out
of it, confirmed (each of them) by this Historicall Exemplification, of their Behaviours
and GODS Dealings.
I come now to a more generall handling of them; And the I. of them is this. *That even
the Faithfull Servants of God may so provoke Him, that they may neede His pardon,
and even give Him Occasion to Take Vengeance on their Inventions and Practices.* (11)

Palmer shuns the distractions of figurative language, relying upon a
simple vocabulary and short, coordinate sentence members. He intends to
be analytical, not evocative, to review his previous argument and to announce the first general doctrine to be derived from the scriptural text he has
opened. With few exceptions, Featley makes his case against Anabaptists in
essentially the same style. The plain mode of Puritan sermon and tract writing posed a specific challenge for Milton. Even the relatively austere first
edition of *Doctrine and Discipline* caused one detractor to accuse him of
being "apt to speake very high language," language that was occasionally "too
sublime and Angelicall for mortail creatures to comprehend it."[29] In *Tetrachordon* Milton would need to reckon with the plainness brought against
him and to counter charges that he wrote above the comprehension of his
audience.

He did so by adapting the low style first developed in *Doctrine and
Discipline* to the task of exegesis. Milton's stylistic habits in *Tetrachordon* can
be exemplified in the following refutation:

Hemingius, an approved Author, *Melanchtons* Scholler, and who next to *Bucer* and *Erasmus* writes of divorce most like a Divine, thus comprises, *Mariage is a conjunction of one man and one woman lawfully consenting, into one flesh, for mutual helps sake, ordain'd of God.* And in his explanation stands punctually upon the conditions of consent, that it be not in any main matter deluded, as beeing the life of wedloc, and no true marriage without a true consent. *Into one flesh* he expounds into one minde, as well as one body, and makes it the formal cause: Heerin only missing, while he puts the effect into his definition instead of the cause which the Text affords him. For *one flesh* is not the formal essence of wedloc, but one end, or one effect of *a meet help;* The end oft times beeing the effect and fruit of the form, as Logic teaches: Els many aged and holy matrimonies, and more eminently that of *Joseph* and *Mary,* would bee no true mariage. And that *maxim* generally receiv'd, would be fals, that *consent alone, though copulation never follow, makes the mariage.* Therefore to consent lawfully into one flesh, is not the formal cause of Matrimony, but only one of the effects. (2:610–11).

Milton the exegete writes technically rather than tropally or affectively, carefully attentive to the strict conceptual framework of Aristotelian causality. He achieves a clinical precision by deriving his position syllogistically, from the opening phrase through the conclusion, avoiding figurative digression or intense schematic amplification; short, bare sentences, particularly in the crucial closing lines, predominate. Like that of the ministers he countered, his tone is rigorously expository. His incorporation of a scholastic frame of reference, in this passage and throughout the treatise, represents a conversion of the low style of *Doctrine and Discipline* into a specialized analytical instrument at least comparable in its severity to the unadorned modes used against him: the language of *Tetrachordon* is anything but "sugred."[30]

III

In *Colasterion* Milton responded primarily to two tracts issued in 1644: William Prynne's *Twelve Considerable Serious Questions,* probably published in September, and the anonymous *An Answer to a Book, Intituled, The Doctrine and Discipline of Divorce,* likely published in November. Prynne attacks *"Independency,"* which he labels a "very Seminary of Schismes," a malaise of "unsociablenesse and coldnesse of brotherly affection" (7), and in so doing settles upon Milton as a cause of the "sad effects whereof we have already experimentally felt, by the late dangerous increase of many *Anabaptisticall, Antinomian, Hereticall, Atheisticall opinions, as of the soules mortality, divorce at pleasure,* [etc.] lately . . . printed in this famous City" (7). Prynne justifies a national church by invoking precedent and tradition as principles not to be abandoned. If unity is "Gods own precept" (8), divorce would naturally register as an aberration, a signal example of *"Independency's"* errors. Prynne stigmatizes Milton as one of the "common Enemyes" of natural order and just Reformation (1), continuing the apocalyptic metaphors of the preachers and thus magnifying, almost mythologizing, the importance of Milton's position. A quote-and-reply animadversion combining argumentation with assault on Milton's prose style, language, and sensibility, *An Answer* constitutes the only full-length reply to the divorce tracts. The Answerer indicts Milton's "high language" (31) and amplification (". . . we shal be driven to contract or shorten your arguments for brevity sake," 13), designating *Doctrine and Discipline* as no more than "frothie discourse," appalling ideas "sugred over with a little neat language"(41). These aesthetic charges, along with Prynne's mythmaking agenda, establish a decorum for the carefully crafted countermeasure of *Colasterion*.

Because *Colasterion* takes the form of a point-by-point, *seriatim* rebuttal of *An Answer*, Milton's primary concern seems to be argument, yet an examination of the particulars of his case suggests otherwise. Since the Answerer had ignored the second edition of *Doctrine and Discipline*, confining himself to the 1643 text, Milton could not engage in a fully valid confutation, a fact he acknowledges (2:726). Moreover, even the arguments he does offer are frequently less than exhaustive. New evidence proves rare, and exegetical detailing such as that which had dominated *Tetrachordon* seldom occurs. Instead, Milton typically contents himself with raising challenges to the Answerer's procedures of debate (2:730, 755), correcting the Answerer's misreadings of passages at issue (2:731), or referring the reader back to the original discussion in *Doctrine and Discipline* (2:732, 733). Milton's prose style in *Colasterion*, a plain style of argument absent the scholastic qualities found in *Tetrachordon*, is as unemphatic and ordinary as the Answerer's had been.

In *Colasterion*, I propose that Milton contests his opponents not primarily with a structural or stylistic rejoinder, as he had done in *Tetrachordon*, but with an aesthetic mechanism aimed at Prynne and *An Answer* as well as the preachers who had rebuked him earlier. The historical origin of his stratagem can be located in the Marprelate paradigm, an ingenious satiric device that converted the conventional formulas of literal quote and reply into weapons that mocked scholastic conventions.[31] Milton responds to the literal animadversion of the Answerer and its challenges to his style and sensibility with a strategy of counterpoint designed to accomplish several goals, one of which is to assert his mastery and transcendence of the very genre used against him. His tactic is dramatic in nature. Because the adversarial dialogue of the Marprelate tradition was itself implicitly theatrical, the paradigm within which Milton's satiric instruments originated offered considerable potential for additional dramatic development, or at least improvisation. A pattern of allusions and references pervasive in *Colasterion* clarifies and reinforces its dramatic design. Early on, Milton describes his opponent as the "lowest person of an interlude" (2:726), referring to the tradition of medieval farce, and midway through the tract alludes to the scheming servant of Jonsonian comedy with his characterization of the Answerer as "this Brainworm against all the Laws of Dispute" (2:743). Milton also compares one of the Answerer's arguments to the plot of *Andria*, the classical low comedy of Terence,[32] urges that his foe be "blanketed" as characters in medieval farces occasionally were (2:754, n. 142), and finally regrets that polemic occasion had forced him to deal with "*Clowns and Vices*" (2:756–57). This pattern of allusions points to a mimetic tactic in *Colasterion*: Milton devises a mock-debate, a fictional substitute for the public hearing on divorce he had desired but that he now realized would not be allowed to him. The fundamental Aristotelian sense of mimesis controls *Colasterion*. As Aristotle defined mimesis in the *Poetics*, the process produced and maintained an illusion, one that could comprehend both the possible and the universal.[33] Mimesis, according to Aristotle, generated a fable or plot, a fiction that would differentiate the writing of poetry from the writing of history.[34] Broadly considered, Milton's mimesis qualifies as dramatic, adapted from the debate framework of the Marprelate tradition and contoured by the allusions I have identified. Specifically, he formulates a proto-drama by fusing the literal rhetorical ingredients supplied by *An Answer* with elements of dialogic interaction, character, and plot, the result being a farce intended to lower and mock his enemies. Dramatic mimesis would grant him greater freedom to maneuver against these enemies and ultimately to trump them than the rhetorical arrangements of *Tetrachordon* had.

The dramatic trope governing *Colasterion* manifests itself most evidently in Milton's process of characterization. The fact that the Answerer hid behind anonymity allowed Milton to identify him through a series of creative deductions based on the evidence of the Answerer's own text, deductions that constitute a systematic development of character. Milton's creative license shapes a fictive identity composed of several distinct layers, the first of which is that of a lawyer. His opponent, Milton charges, must be a "hacney of the Law" (2:748) or a "tradsman of the Law" (2:756), a surmise reinforced by a substantial body of information and implication meant to detail it. For example, in an allusion to Sir Thomas Littleton's *Les Tenures*, upon which Coke's legal *Commentary* was based, Milton sneers that his antagonist "knew not" the body of precedent available in the "ancient civil Law . . . for it was not in his Tenures" (2:735, n. 56). A second fictive inference can be found in the following jibe at the Answerer as "a meer Servingman, a meer and arrant petti-fogger, who lately was so hardy, as to lay aside his buckram wallet, and make himself a fool in Print, with confuting books, which are above him" (2:743).[35] Again, a grouping of references and allusions provides decorous particulars for the servingman inference. Milton draws from divinity a third component of the Answerer's identity. The Answerer, he speculates, has "convers'd much with a stripling Divine or two of those newly fledge *Probationers*, that usually come scouting from the University" (2:727). Worse, the Answerer may have been selected for the task of confuting *Doctrine and Discipline* by his "ghostly Patrons," (2:751), a probable allusion to his preference for popish canon law. Even if he does not personally aspire to be a divine, the Answerer has been "set on by plot and consultation with a *Junto* of Clergymen and Licensers, commended also and rejoyc't in by those whose partiality cannot yet forgoe old papisticall principles" (2:757).

Milton refines the Answerer's identity by linking it with another character type, one consistent with the tract's controlling dramatic trope—the Vice. As mentioned earlier, he laments having to deal with "*Clowns and Vices*" (2:756–57) and makes regular reference to the literary context of medieval and Renaissance drama. Collectively, these references recall the salient features of the Vice, the primary comic character of medieval farces and interludes, a jester, fool, or buffoon given to raucous, taunting, physical humor, slapstick, and bawdry.[36] The Vice was a skilled intriguer and manipulator as well, with a threatening quality and obvious associations of evil.[37] By labeling the Answerer as "this Brain-worm against all the Laws of Dispute" (2:743) and urging that he be "blanketed" (2:754), Milton not only evokes such familiar Vices as Mak from the *Second Shepherd's Play*, but the Vice tradition as a whole. That Milton expected readers to equate the Answerer's antics with those of the stage Vice is further suggested by several additional associations. The Vice of stage tradition was typically vulgar and crude, while Milton's Answerer is compared to "this Pork, who never read [Philosophy]" (2:737) as well as to someone whose "doctrin" came out "of som School, or som stie" (2:739), and described as being offended that "rankest should signify ought, but his own smell" (2:743). The humor of the stage Vice was often obscene and scatological, and imagery surrounding Milton's foe has similar connotations, for example, the suggestion that the Answerer "leavs the noysome stench of his rude *slot* behind him (2:751), and Milton's paraphrase of the wisdom the Answerer offers to his friends: "I send them by his advice to sit upon the stool and strain" (2:738).[38] Just as the Vice of stage tradition was often crude, bestial, or scatological, so is Milton's adversary. Just as the Vice was the rowdy mocker of virtue in the morality plays, the Answerer mimics, distorts, and schemes against Milton's idealism. Milton transforms the connotations of vulgarity and coarseness that often had literal, physical manifestations for the stage Vice into the vulgarity of spirit and intellect he considers the signature of the Answerer. The Answerer has devolved, in Milton's hands, into the low, degrading enemy of the high spirituality Milton had argued for in the divorce tracts.

The plotlike series of conflicts that make up *Colasterion* embeds more evidence of the central trope as Milton connects his antagonist with a specific type of medieval drama, the interlude. The Answerer, he speculates early in *Colasterion*, could be described as "the lowest person of an interlude" (2:726). Though the term "interlude" has been attached to "every kind of drama known to the Middle Ages," and therefore cannot be restricted to a single form, interludes were invariably short (sometimes confined to a single episode), and typically light or farcical.[39] The dramatic "combat" of the interlude becomes a rudimentary plot in *Colasterion* when Milton parades the fictionalized Answerer through a series of scenes in which his arguments against *Doctrine and Discipline* are recast as low-comic physical actions connoting clumsiness or ineptitude, as the following passages illustrate:

Now hee comes to the Position, which I sett down whole; and like an able text man slits it into fowr, that hee may the better come at it with his Barbar Surgery.... (2:736–37)

His next attempt is upon the Arguments which I brought to prove the position. And for the first, not finding it of that structure, as to bee scal'd with his short ladder, hee retreats with a bravado, that it deservs no answer. (2:740)

In short, *Colasterion* exhibits a consistent movement, the metamorphosis of the Answerer's intellectual activity into barbaric or ridiculous gestures of physical futility through Milton's selective arrangement. While Milton avoids fictionalizing his own position (it remains that of the aggrieved victim and outraged spiritual idealist), he systematically transforms the Answerer's objections into a series of combats and encounters akin to the scheming plot machinations of the stage Vice, and strengthens the connotation of an interludic structure by the brevity of *Colasterion*, the shortest of the divorce tracts, shorter even than *An Answer*. Finally, *Colasterion* has a sort of dénouement consistent with that of an interlude. As Stanley J. Kahrl and others have shown, the Vices are ultimately held up to scorn, becoming the butt of jokes and the recipients of dismissal and thwarting in the final scene.[40] Harsh dismissal stands out on the last few pages of the pamphlet, where Milton sneers contemptuously at the "reprobate ignorance" (2:754) of his rival, chiding his "penury of Soul" (2:757). Having become "this caitif . . . now not seasonable for my jest" (2:753), the Answerer must endure a scornful, direct chastisement, the intensity of Milton's attack recalling satire's folkloric quality as a lethal weapon.

Colasterion does not contain a literal dramatic setting, though Lowell Coolidge has proposed *"a place . . . of punishment"* as a likely reading of the title (2:722, n. 1), and the text surely qualifies as a metaphorical location for the addressing of Milton's grievances. The trope that organizes the attack stops short of providing a literal stage, yet sophisticated mimetic effects may be found if the overall intention of Milton's mockery is allowed for, effects that render *Colasterion* a masterful transcendence of the forms and voices clamoring out against him. Milton molds the Answerer into a composite character who represents a mimetic universal, the sum total of his opponents.[41] The Answerer had written a conventional animadversion against *Doctrine and Discipline*, introducing aesthetic considerations by ridiculing Milton's language and its affective qualities. *Colasterion* silences *An Answer* by redefining its author as a buffoon, a pretentious lackey whose literality merely generates raw material for Milton's creative inference: the dramatic dialogue of *Colasterion* evokes the commonplace genre format of animadversion even as it mocks and surpasses that genre. Prynne was also a target, and the Answerer was portrayed as a pedantic solicitor whose Prynnean penchant for tedious, legalistic inquiry was relentlessly parodied—that Milton's caricature of the Answerer invokes the infamous Prynne seems manifest at every turn. It will be remembered as well that the Answerer was described as a novice divine who had colluded with other divines, a characterization that recalls Palmer, Young, and Newcomen. The same association can be extended to Joseph Caryl, the Long Parliament licenser who had authorized the printing of *An Answer* and who was the object of Milton's derision early in the pamphlet; as John F. Wilson has shown, Caryl was a prominent contributor to the Fast Day tradition.[42] The cultural prominence and collective moral authority of the preachers who had demonized Milton are thereby shrunken to those of a "stripling," an amateur whose lack of training ill equips him to comprehend the theology of *Doctrine and Discipline*. The ministers, and to a lesser extent Prynne, had also turned the rhetoric of the jeremiad, a moral declamation with an apocalyptic tenor, against Milton. Milton's reaction to what he likely considered the heroic posturing of such a strategy was to shape *Colasterion* as a *reductio ad absurdum*, an exercise in mock-heroic deflation aimed at insensitive literalists, "common-expositors," and the morally pretentious among his accusers. Against the mythological magnifications of the jeremiad, he set an appropriate antimythic debunker, the interlude, a mimetic form with rich historical connotations of low comedy. In effect, *Colasterion* reads as an exercise in satirical comeuppance and counterpoint that not only levels individuals, but blunts their weapons of choice.

These claims for mimesis require some stipulation. *Colasterion* cannot be explained as a typical animadversion, nor does it qualify as fully developed mimesis, but rather as a protodrama prevented from reaching aesthetic completion by its utilitarian nature as a polemic. If Milton's stated aims in composing the pamphlet are taken into account, additional evidence of its departure from literal argument emerges. He observes early on that, "as soon as leisure granted [him] the recreation" (2:727), he elected to reply to his anonymous tormentor, and the closing paragraph explains his effort as a "talent of sport" (2:757). This commentary implies that Milton saw the creation of *Colasterion* as a form of pleasure and entertainment. The rationale of pleasure links the text again with the Aristotelian notion of mimesis—Aristotle considered pleasure as the aim of mimesis.[43] The reading of *The Readie and Easie Way* as a jeremiad by Laura Lunger Knoppers provides some illustrative analogies.[44] She shows that Milton's jeremiad "takes on a distinctly literary aim, to provide a myth of the nation, a story by which the English under the restored monarchy can interpret their tragedy"; his reasons for writing cannot be resolved as an attempt to "change the immediate situation."[45] Like *The Readie Way*, *Colasterion* seems intended not to "change the immediate situation" as a specimen of polemic debate might, but rather to accomplish the primary goal of besting Milton's detractors at their own game, a goal that could be met effectively and pleasurably if he were to select a medium capable of being shaped imaginatively by his creative sensibility. The Marprelate paradigm, itself implicitly literary, would have offered him the same latitude in *Colasterion* that the jeremiad provided in *The Readie Way*. The "literary aim" Knoppers locates in *The Readie Way* broadly parallels the dramatic, mock-heroic agenda of *Colasterion*.[46] Moreover, the aesthetic coda Milton presents in the tract's final pages, his measured assessment of the reasons for his attack on the Answerer, and other countermeasures he might have taken resemble literary theory and deliberation a great deal more than they do routine polemic persuasion.[47]

IV

Pamphlet campaigns against Milton's notorious heresies continued throughout the 1640's and even resurfaced in the debate over freedom of conscience for nonconformists between Samuel Parker and Andrew Marvell in 1672–73. William Riley Parker identified Milton as the "spokesman for a heretical sect, the Divorcers, in the second edition of Ephraim Pagitt's *Heresiography, or a Description of the Heretics and Sectaries of These Latter Times* (1645)."[48] Ernest Sirluck and Christopher Hill found three other broadsides: the anonymous *Little Non-Such* (1646), a sermon before Commons by Thomas Case (1647), and the anonymous *A Glasse for the Times* (1648).[49] No evidence exists of Miltonic replies to any of these. Only the *Defensio Secunda*, in its

intellectual autobiography of Milton's early career, refers directly to the divorce controversy (4, Pt. 1: 609–10, 624–25). Milton did, of course, compose
two sonnets on divorce, Sonnet Eleven: "I did but prompt the age" and
Sonnet Twelve: "A Book was writ of late call'd *Tetrachordon.*"[50] The order of
these sonnets is less important for considerations of genre and form than the
fact that Milton resolved to address the topic of divorce in poetry rather than
in another pamphlet, despite the "provocation" of his detractors to do so. The
closing statement of *Colasterion* lets us contextualize that choice. There,
Milton assesses his strategies as a pamphleteer and confronts several hypo-
thetical situations in which he might need to defend himself. His remarks
include this description of the possible fate that might still await the Answerer: "Nay perhaps, as the provocation may bee, I may bee driv'n to curle
up this gliding prose into a rough *Sotadic*, that shall rime him into such a
condition, as instead of judging good Books to bee burn't by the executioner,
hee shall be readier to be his own hangman. Thus much to this *Nuisance*"
(2:757). Lowell Coolidge traced Milton's allusion to Sotades, a third-century
Greek poet renowned for scurrilous satires (2:757, n. 158). This reference to
a poetic text and an earlier one to the *Battle of the Frogs and Mice*, a mock-
heroic poem attributed to Homer (2:757, n. 155), suggests that Milton had
chosen how to proceed in the divorce controversy, a choice anticipated by the
protodramatic structure of *Colasterion.* The "rough *Sotadic*" he envisions did
not materialize, but his two divorce sonnets culminate the literary dynamic
initiated in *Colasterion.*

William Riley Parker summarized Milton's plan of argument in the divorce tracts as follows: [Milton achieved objectivity] " by scrupulously avoiding references to specific cases, by limiting his argument to broad statements
of principle."[51] When, in Sonnets Eleven and Twelve, he completed the
mimetic movement of *Colasterion*, Milton achieved a similar result. Poetic
statement allowed him to dignify the question of divorce by turning it from a
controversial rhetorical proposition into a literary construct, and thus to legit-
imate a topic that many had decried as merely an expression of licentiousness
or, worse, had refused to consider a decorous matter for public debate. By
disengaging from pamphleteering, he could secure the control and closure
that a time-bound context denied him as well as a catharsis unavailable in the
unstable, negotiable medium of polemic. To replace disputations and proto-
dramas with poetry would be to achieve the permanence inherent in poetry.
This construction of Milton's rationales for writing sonnets instead of additional tracts complements Reuben A. Sanchez's persuasive estimate of Milton's motives for prose composition generally: ". . . in the course of his prose
writing career, Milton becomes less and less concerned with his immediate
audience and more and more concerned with how posterity will read his

autobiography . . . the 'in time' aspect of context becomes less a concern for Milton than the 'timeless' aspect of context . . . Although Milton responds to immediate events and hence participates in the history he creates, he also wishes to ensure that his work will survive beyond the immediate historical moment."[52] The 1673 date of publication of Sonnets Eleven and Twelve frees Milton from the charge that the poems are utilitarian, designed as agents of change in a specific situation. They are, rather, attempts to rise above the polemic partisanship of 1643–45, literary artifacts accomplishing what sonnets typically accomplish, the sonneteer's self-examination with a degree of detachment provided by retrospect.

Reconstructing the polemical context of Milton's divorce tracts allows for several primary conclusions about the workings of genre, structure, and style in them. The dialectic of genres embedded in *Tetrachordon* and *Colasterion* suggests that Milton's engagement with those who had vilified *Doctrine and Discipline* extends well beyond his literal denunciation of them in the preface to each pamphlet. Milton reads the attacks of opponents as rhetorical and genre challenges that he attempts to answer with more sophisticated, authoritative countermeasures of his own. The divorce controversy as a whole displays a range of seventeenth-century prose forms, including the sermon, the jeremiad, the animadversion, the exegesis, and the Marprelate satire, so that the controversy proves to be as much a contest of genres and styles as it is a contest of hermeneutics over the scriptural meaning of divorce. Moreover, if Milton's pamphlets are examined in their most probable order of composition, a progression from dialectical to mimetic modes appears. His discursive analysis of the topic of divorce evolves into a literary representation of an artist treating the theme of writing about divorce. The sonnets become, therefore, the natural aesthetic consequences of the mimetic movement initiated in *Colasterion*, a process that implies a closer linkage of polemic and poetry than is generally assumed.

The interplay of genres and modes considered here parallels several other prominent groupings and templates in the Milton canon, and may be an early expression of a pervasive paradigm. Annabel Patterson has pointed to the sophisticated interface of literature and history in seventeenth-century texts, notably those of Milton and Marvell, a position supported by the evidence of this essay.[53] Joseph Wittreich established that Milton's *Defenses* take their "various structures" from the tracts of antagonists, particularly *Defensio Regia*, *Regii Sanguinis Clamor*, and *Fides Publica*.[54] What Wittreich claims for the *Defenses* is clearly anticipated in *Tetrachordon* and *Colasterion*. In the influential reading of *Of Reformation* referred to earlier, Michael Lieb confirmed that Milton drew upon prevailing modes of discourse, especially polemical strategies, in order to transcend them.[55] Again, similar instances of one genre designed to trump another occur in both *Tetrachordon* and *Colasterion*. Recently, Lieb has examined how, in *Defensio Secunda*, Milton counters two poems written against him in the *Clamor*, which Milton attributed to Alexander More, with devices of low comedy that Lieb interprets as a "theater of assault."[56] Milton's mock-heroic *reductio* in *Colasterion*, his proto-drama of "assault" not only against the aspersions cast upon him by *An Answer*, but also against the public stigmatizing of his position and character by preachers before the Long Parliament, matches Lieb's description. Finally, current studies by Reuben Sanchez and Stephen Fallon have directed attention, respectively, to the evolution of Milton's "literary self-presentation" in the prose and to the mechanics of his "self-construction" in the divorce tracts.[57] Milton's "literary self-presentation" grows more pronounced and more nuanced as the divorce controversy evolves from literal, discursive exegesis in *Tetrachordon*, through protodrama in *Colasterion*, and then into poetry. To Fallon's evidence for Milton's "explicit self-representation" in *Doctrine and Discipline* and *Tetrachordon* should be added the claim made in this essay for a Miltonic self-representation, in *Tetrachordon* and *Colasterion*, that is implicit, responsive to genre considerations, and typically polemical.

The University of Akron

NOTES

1. See, for example, Charles Hatten, "The Politics of Marital Reform and the Rationalization of Romance in The Doctrine and Discipline of Divorce," *Milton Studies* 27, ed. James D. Simmonds (Pittsburgh, 1991), 95–113; Olga Lucia Valbuena, "Milton's 'Divorsive' Interpretation and the Gendered Reader," *Milton Studies* 27, 115–37; Mary Nyquist, "The Genesis of Gendered Subjectivity in the Divorce Tracts and in *Paradise Lost*," in *Re-Membering Milton: Essays on the Texts and Traditions*, ed. Mary Nyquist and Margaret W. Ferguson (London, 1988), 99–127. Along with those of Hatten, Valbuena, and Nyquist, the following studies represent the range of interpretations presently in play: John Halkett, *Milton and the Idea of Matrimony: A Study of the Divorce Tracts and Paradise Lost* (New Haven, 1970); Gladys J. Willis, *The Penalty of Eve: John Milton and Divorce* (New York, 1984); James Grantham Turner, *One Flesh: Paradisal Marriage and Sexual Relations in the Age of Milton* (Oxford, 1987); Thomas N. Corns, *John Milton: The Prose Works* (New York, 1998), chap. 4.

2. Stephen M. Fallon, "The Metaphysics of Milton's Divorce Tracts," in *Politics, Poetics, and Hermeneutics in Milton's Prose*, ed. David Loewenstein and James Grantham Turner (Cambridge, 1990), 69–83.

3. Kester Svendsen, "Science and Structure in Milton's *Doctrine of Divorce*," *PMLA* 67(1952): 435–45.

4. Annabel Patterson, "No Meer Amatorious Novel?," in *Politics, Poetics, and Hermeneutics in Milton's Prose*, 85–87. This essay is the starting point for contemporary genre study of the divorce tracts.

5. Reuben Sanchez, Jr., *Persona and Decorum in Milton's Prose* (Madison, N.J., 1997), 33–42.

6. Joseph Anthony Wittreich, Jr., "'The Crown of Eloquence': The Figure of the Orator in Milton's Prose Works," in *Achievements of the Left Hand: Essays on the Prose of John Milton*, ed. Michael Lieb and John T. Shawcross (Amherst, 1974), 3–54; Michael Lieb, "Milton's *Of Reformation* and the Dynamics of Controversy," in *Achievements of the Left Hand*, 56–62. A current example of methodologies akin to those of Wittreich and Lieb is Jameela Lares, *Milton and the Preaching Arts* (Cambridge, 2001).

7. Patterson, "No Meer Amatorious Novel?," 85.

8. Cf. Thomas Kranidas, *The Fierce Equation: A Study of Milton's Decorum* (The Hague, 1965), 77. Kranidas has documented Milton's habit of defining himself by opposites, a habit that can be likened to some of the rhetorical movements I will examine. In the divorce tracts, however, Milton defines himself primarily by extrapolations or intensifications of an opponent's mode rather than by reversals of it. My analysis will feature *Tetrachordon* and *Colasterion* because in these two pamphlets the dialectic and adaptation of genres seem most evident. The same dialectic does not occur in either the first or second edition of *Doctrine and Discipline* or in *The Judgement of Martin Bucer* (1644).

9. Cf. Wittreich, "The Crown of Eloquence," 4–42. Wittreich's analysis works broadly across Milton's prose, the divorce tracts included, with particular attention to the *Defenses*. See also James Egan, *The Inward Teacher: Milton's Rhetoric of Christian Liberty* (University Park, Pa., 1980), chap. 2. That both editions of *Doctrine and Discipline* are structured as orations has been noted by many, but close analysis of prose style has been rare.

10. William Riley Parker, *Milton: A Biography* (Oxford, 1968), 244, 260.

11. Turner, *One Flesh,* 190.

12. William Haller, *Liberty and Reformation in the Puritan Revolution* (New York, 1955), 123; Thomas Kranidas, "The *Colasterion*: Milton's Plural Adversary," *Prose Studies* 19 (December 1996): 275–81.

13. Haller, 123–24. My examples differ somewhat from Haller's, though they support his conclusion. See also Christopher Hill, *Milton and the English Revolution* (New York, 1977), 131. Hill notes that Young warns against digamy in the sermon. Hill's position reinforces Haller's.

14. Kranidas, "Milton's Plural Adversary," 279–81.

15. John F. Wilson, *Pulpit in Parliament: Puritanism during the English Civil Wars 1640–1648* (Princeton, 1969), 141.

16. H. R. Trevor-Roper, *The Crisis of the Seventeenth Century: Religion, the Reformation and Social Change* (New York, 1956), 296; James C. Spalding, "Sermons before Parliament (1640–1649) as a Public Puritan Diary," *Church History* 36 (March 1967): 35.

17. Trevor-Roper, *The Crisis of the Seventeenth Century*, chap. 6.

18. Spalding, "Sermons before Parliament," 25.

19. Wilson, *Pulpit in Parliament*, ix.

20. Ibid., 177.

21. Laura Lunger Knoppers, "Milton's *The Readie and Easie Way* and the English Jeremiad," in *Politics, Poetics, and Hermeneutics in Milton's Prose*, 213. See also David Minter, "The Puritan Jeremiad as a Literary Form," in *The American Puritan Imagination: Essays in Revaluation*, ed. Sacvan Bercovitch (Cambridge, 1974), 45–55.

22. Knoppers, "Milton's *The Readie and Easie Way*," 213–14.

23. Perry Miller, *The New England Mind: From Colony to Province* (Boston, 1961), 27–39. Miller's discussion remains comprehensive and accurate.

24. All quotations from Milton's prose are from *The Complete Prose Works of John Milton*, 8

vols., ed. Don M. Wolfe, et. al. (New Haven, 1953–82), vol. 2, 144, hereafter cited parenthetically in the text by volume and page number and abbreviated as YP.

25. Cf. Egan, *The Inward Teacher*, 59–66. In *The Inward Teacher* I traced in *Tetrachordon*
an overall movement from logic to evocation. Now I consider the pamphlet as a participant in a
contest of rhetoric between Milton and his antagonists.

26. See also Corns, *John Milton*, 50.

27. Cf. Lawrence A. Sasek, *The Literary Temper of the English Puritans* (1961; rpt. New
York, 1969), 39. Sasek has claimed that the "structure of a puritan sermon could be duplicated in
a commentary on the Bible, but hardly elsewhere." Milton's mode of exegesis implies his awareness of this basic structural relationship.

28. See YP 2:572. Williams notes Milton's "extensive" use of the commentaries of Paraeus,
especially those on Genesis and Matthew.

29. *An Answer to a Book, Intituled, The Doctrine and Discipline of Divorce*, in William
Riley Parker, *Milton's Contemporary Reputation* (1940; rpt. New York, 1971), 31, 41.

30. Stylistic analysis of *Tetrachordon* has been infrequent. See Corns, *John Milton*, chap. 4,
and Sanchez, *Persona and Decorum in Milton's Prose*, chap. 5. Corns records that *Tetrachordon*
is written in the "less figurative style" Milton had experimented with in the first edition of
Doctrine and Discipline (50). Sanchez has called attention to "sound design" and to what he
designates as "Euphuistic" elements in *Tetrachordon*; he describes the style of the tract as
generally "oratorical" (81–82). My claim is more specific than those of Corns and Sanchez,
though broadly congruent with Corns's position. I stress that the low style of *Tetrachordon*
functions as one part of a deliberate exercise in counterpoint. Milton's plainness seems compati-
ble with the characterization of the low style of argument found in Cicero's *Orator*: "[One] must
avoid all the figures that I described above, such as clauses of equal length, with similar endings
or identical cadences, and the studied charm produced by the change of a letter, lest the
elaborate symmetry and a certain grasping after a pleasant effect be too obvious . . . Other figures
of speech [the orator] will be able to use freely, provided only he breaks up and divides the
periodic structure and uses the commonest of words and the mildest of metaphors." See *Orator*,
in *Brutus and Orator*, trans. G. L. Hendrickson and H. M. Hubbell, Loeb Classical Library
(Cambridge, Mass., 1952), 367–69. Although other deployments are both suggested and implied in Cicero's treatises on rhetoric, in Quintilian's *Institutio Oratoria*, and in the *Rhetorica ad
Herennium* (of debated authorship), the low style's most appropriate location in an oration would
be in the confirmation and refutation, the body of the argument.

31. James Egan, "Milton and the Marprelate Tradition," *Milton Studies* 8, ed. James D.
Simmonds (Pittsburgh, 1975), 103–21, and Kranidas, "Milton's Plural Adversary," 275. In the
first essay I reviewed the Marprelate tradition in the seventeenth century and Milton's indebtedness to it. Kranidas contends that *Colasterion* is the "least persuasive ideologically of Milton's
early prose tracts." I would agree for two reasons, the first of which is that Milton develops little
fresh evidence beyond that which he had presented in *Doctrine and Discipline* and *Tetrachordon*. Secondly, as I shall demonstrate, *Colasterion* is not fundamentally an ideological
persuasion at all, but rather an aesthetic statement.

32. YP 2:748, n. 115.

33. Robert Alter, *Motives For Fiction* (Cambridge, Mass., 1984), 12; Gunter Gebauer and
Christoph Wulf, *Mimesis: Culture, Art, and Society*, trans. Don Reneau (Berkeley, 1995), 54.

34. Gebauer and Wulf, *Mimesis*, 55.

35. Cf. Corns, *John Milton*, 52–55, and Egan, "Milton and the Marprelate Tradition," 115–
16. Corns addresses the implications of class in this image. I propose an alternative reading of
Milton's characterization. In the 1975 essay, I treated the servingman-lawyer image as the core of

a comic genealogy adapted from the Marprelate tradition. Here I examine the larger mimetic processes at work in *Colasterion*.

36. Alan C. Dessen, *Shakespeare and the Late Moral Plays* (Lincoln, 1986), 18; Edgar T. Schell and J. D. Schuchter, eds., *English Morality Plays and Moral Interludes* (New York, 1969), ix.

37. F. P. Wilson, *The English Drama 1485–1585* (Oxford, 1969), 59–66; Dessen, *Shakespeare and the Late Moral Plays*, 19; J. M. R. Margeson, *The Origins of English Tragedy* (Oxford, 1967), 45.

38. David M. Bevington, *From Mankind to Marlowe: Growth of Structure in the Popular Drama of Tudor England* (Cambridge, Mass., 1962), 16.

39. Wilson, *The English Drama*, 10; Phyllis Hartnoll, ed., *The Oxford Companion to the Theater*, 4th ed. (Oxford, 1983), 416–17; Glynne Wickham, *The Medieval Theater*, 3rd ed. (London, 1987), 106. Wickham has portrayed the moral interludes as "combats . . . far more deeply concerned with argument and debate than with narrative or the portrayal of character."

40. Stanley J. Kahrl, *Traditions of Medieval English Drama* (Pittsburgh, 1975), 105. See also Martha Tuck Rozett, *The Doctrine of Election and the Emergence of Elizabethan Tragedy* (Princeton, 1984), 91; Wilson, *The English Drama*, 63; Schell and Schuchter, *English Morality Plays and Moral Interludes*, ix.

41. Cf. Wittreich, "The Crown of Eloquence," 26. Wittreich points out that *Defensio Secunda* is directed as much against a type as an individual.

42. Wilson, *Pulpit in Parliament*, 110.

43. John D. Boyd, S. J., *The Function of Mimesis and Its Decline* (New York, 1980), 28. See also Kranidas, "Milton's Plural Adversary," 277–80. Kranidas has noticed plaintive elements in the pamphlet—Milton's expressions of "significant passion," his anger over being betrayed by his former Smectymnuan allies. Occasionally, as the examples Kranidas includes reveal, these powerful expressions spill over the dramatic-mimetic boundaries I have illustrated. Earlier, Kranidas showed that Milton was able to "objectify his frustration in his elaborate contempt for the servingman" (*The Fierce Equation*, 81). My position is closer to this early claim, conceding the plaintive qualities Kranidas notices, yet emphasizing the frequent objectification of Milton's dismay into the mimetic of satire.

44. Knoppers, "Milton's *The Readie and Easie Way*," 213–25.

45. Ibid., 224, 217.

46. Ibid., 224.

47. Cf. John M. Perlette, "Milton, Ascham, and the Rhetoric of the Divorce Controversy," *Milton Studies* 10, ed. James D. Simmonds (Pittsburgh, 1977), 195–215. Perlette identifies similar motives for composition in Anthony Ascham's "Of Marriage" (1647–48).

48. Parker, *Milton*, 287.

49. Sirluck, YP 2:800–7; Hill, *Milton and the English Revolution*, 131.

50. *A Milton Encyclopedia*, 9 vols., ed. William B. Hunter, Jr., et. al. (Lewisburg, 1978–83), vol. 8, 22–23. The consensus of modern editors dates "I did but prompt" before "A Book was writ of late," which was probably composed in 1647. The order of the two sonnets is much debated, primarily because Milton reversed the numbering of Eleven and Twelve in the 1673 edition of his poetry.

51. Parker, *Milton*, 237.

52. Sanchez, *Persona and Decorum in Milton's Prose*, 33, 45.

53. Annabel Patterson, *Early Modern Liberalism* (Cambridge, 1997), chap. 2. Patterson offers Milton's sonnets as one example of her thesis.

54. Wittreich, "The Crown of Eloquence," 37.

55. Lieb, "Milton's *Of Reformation* and the Dynamics of Controversy," 56.

56. Michael Lieb, *Milton and the Culture of Violence* (Ithaca, 1994), 201–20.

57. Sanchez, *Persona and Decorum in Milton's Prose*, 33; Stephen M. Fallon, "The Spur of Self-Concernment: Milton in His Divorce Tracts," *Milton Studies* 38, ed. Albert C. Labriola (Pittsburgh, 2000), 220–42.

CHARLES'S GRANDMOTHER,
MILTON'S SPENSER, AND
THE RHETORIC OF REVOLUTION

John D. Staines

JOHN DRYDEN WAS the first to inform his readers that "Milton has acknowledg'd to me, that Spencer was his Original."[1] Annabel Patterson has rightly questioned Dryden's formulation of influence as a simple patrilineal structure of imitation and, in the process, questioned the tendency of modern literary criticism to overstate how much Milton owed to Spenser.[2] In *Eikonoklastes*, however, Milton does invoke family inheritance, in this case matrilineal, in order to denigrate Charles I.[3] Milton describes the king's book *Eikon Basilike* as stemming from the Stuart legacy and accuses Charles of "imitating therin not our Saviour, but his Grand-mother *Mary* Queen of Scots, as also in the most of his other scruples, exceptions and evasions" (3.597).[4] Instead of imitating the truth of Christ, Charles has imitated Mary's rhetorical evasions; she is the original of *Eikon Basilike*.

The debt Milton does not acknowledge here, however, is his own—to Spenser's earlier analysis of Mary Stuart as Duessa in the Legend of Justice, Book Five of *The Faerie Queene*. *Eikonoklastes* thus becomes a test case in a new and more complex theory of influence than those to which we have become accustomed, one in which the line of descent occurs not only from text to text but from one historical context to later, often distant and dissimilar, sequences of events. The focus on producing genealogies of poetic influence, by contrast, frequently overlooks the contingencies that generate these literary borrowings and distortions. I thus caution against the erection of coherent monuments in the literary tradition and argue in favor of more complicated figures who are constantly reacting to the pressures of their historical moments.

In his attack upon Charles I in *Eikonoklastes*, Milton figures "Spenser" as an image for the voice of truth; he uses this Spenser to sweep away the contingencies and lies of political rhetoric that he claims Charles learned from his grandmother. But he does not acknowledge his memory of Spenser's Duessa, the allegorical representation of Mary's rhetoric. Instead, he summons Spenser's Talus, Book Five's iron agent of justice, as a model for his own impatience with Stuart deceptions. This is a very partial reading of *The Faerie Queene*. Whereas Spenser has Talus impatiently destroy debate whenever he appears, as when he solves Artegall's rhetorical impasse with the egalitarian Giant by throwing him off a cliff (5.2.49–50),[5] Spenser uses Duessa and her trial to dismantle the rhetorical strategies of both Mary *and* her accusers. Spenser is concerned less with slandering Mary than with showing how all political rhetoric works. By avoiding Duessa's trial and Spenser's unveiling of the machinery of political rhetoric, Milton manipulates Spenser's text for his own rhetorical ends.

At issue in *Eikonoklastes*, then, are Milton's conflicting attitudes toward rhetoric.[6] On one hand, rhetoric is the art of persuasion, the goal of all his poetry and prose: "Give me the liberty to know, to utter, and to argue freely according to conscience, above all liberties" (*Areopagitica*, 2.560). It is one of the arts that "inable men to discourse and write perspicuously, elegantly, and according to the fitted stile of lofty, mean, or lowly" (*Of Education*, 2.401). Using rhetoric, the writer leads readers to find and recognize the truth. On the other hand, rhetoric also represents all the subtle, deceptive entanglings of misused language, the serpent's "persuasive words, impregn'd / With Reason, to [Eve] seeming, and with Truth" (*PL* 9.737–38).[7] As Aristotle sets out the problem, "one person will be [called] *rhetor* on the basis of his knowledge [of what is truly persuasive] and another on the basis of his deliberate choice [to say what is only apparently persuasive.]"[8] That is, when one says that a text is *rhetoric*, one may be referring either to the writer's knowledge and skill or to the writer's dubious ethical and moral intention. Milton believes that he possesses a rhetoric of truth, that he can express the truth persuasively, yet he recognizes the danger of rhetoric "replete with guile" that seems truthful and reasonable but deceives by appealing to the "heart," the seat of the passions (*PL* 9.733, 734). For instance, when he raises his doubts about whether Charles actually wrote the book that bears his name, *Eikon Basilike. The Povrtraictvre of His Sacred Maiestie in His Solitvdes and Svfferings*, Milton calls the forger the king's "Houshold *Rhetorician*" (*Eikonoklastes*, 3.383), evoking Aristotle's second definition of *rhetor*, the orator who will say anything that sounds persuasive, no matter how false and untrue.[9] This division between true and false rhetoric, moreover, parallels a division between the theory and practice of rhetoric. Aristotle gives a definition of a theory of rhetoric, whose "function is not to persuade but to see the available means of persuasion in each case" (1.14.1355b); it observes how persuasion should work, rather than seeking to engage and persuade a real audience. A practice of rhetoric, by contrast, will always be implicated in the contingencies of historical experience, in the accidents and demands of occasions and events.[10] Whether there can be a truly ethical practice of rhetoric in the fallen world of history is a question that Milton's polemics and poetry frequently address but never fully resolve.

This essay will begin by showing the polemical background that can account for Milton's use of Mary Queen of Scots to attack the Stuart monarchy. Mary was Charles's grandmother and, like him, fell from power in a rebellion and was finally executed. The parallels in the political and historical events were obvious and would lead some writers (Milton included) to turn to political tracts from the 1570s and 1580s, especially George Buchanan's *De iure regni apud scotos* and *Historia rerum scoticarum*, both of which develop a theory of political resistance and tyrannicide. Less immediately obvious but still recognized by many writers, the rhetoric used by the queen and her grandson are parallel in numerous ways. Both presented themselves and were represented by others as martyrs whose pathetic speeches and "tragic" fates appealed to the emotions of their audiences. The first part of this essay thus demonstrates the importance of Mary's life and story to the literary prehistory of *Eikon Basilike*, the great royalist bestseller that attempted to make Charles's execution into a tragedy of injustice by presenting the king as a man of integrity and passion. The second part examines Milton's use of both Mary and Spenser in his response to *Eikon Basilike*. Milton turns Mary into a figure of rhetorical and emotional manipulation, to which he replies by creating out of Spenser a figure for absolute truth. Both the queen and the poet, nonetheless, are rhetorical figures contingent upon Milton's local, historical ends.

I. Two Tragic Scaffolds

The most familiar expression of the conflicting emotions generated by the sight of Charles's execution is surely Andrew Marvell's couplet in the "Horatian Ode": "That thence the *Royal Actor* born / The *Tragick Scaffold* might adorn." The poem's evasive irony manages to celebrate the king's theatrical performance in the midst of a celebration of his conqueror. The tragedy of a king produces in the audience a pathetic response made only stronger by the sublime terror of Cromwell's historical power, "the force of angry Heavens flame" that stands behind the one man's "forced Pow'r."[11] The famous ambivalence of this "tragick scaffold" revisits a problem raised a century earlier by Mary's execution. As soon as a writer represents the death of king or queen, even a tyrant, he or she introduces sympathy into the political equation. In Marvell's poem, pity and fear generate paralytic awe; political action seems circumscribed by the forces of history, and readers are left to puzzle out their political choices. Other Commonwealth representations of the tragic scaffold, by contrast, struggle to turn this sense of awe into an immediate choice of allegiance, to channel those passions towards political action.

Marvell, of course, is responding to the common and popular conception of the death of this king—or indeed any king—as a tragedy. For example, in his biography of Charles I, included in some of the lengthy expanded editions of *Eikon Basilike* that were published the late 1650s, Peter Heylyn narrates the king's final moment in conformity to this familiar plot:

No sooner had he done his Devotions, but he is hurried to *White-hall*, out of the Banqueting-house, whereof a way was forced to a *Scaffold* on which he was to act the last part of his *Tragedy* in the sight of the people. Having declared that he died a Martyr for the Lawes of this Kingdome, and the Liberties of the Subjects, he made a Confession of his Faith, insinuating that he died a true Son of the Church of *England*, he betook himself to his private Devotions, and patiently submitted that Royall Head to an Executioner, which had before beene crowned with so much outward Pomp and Splendour.[12]

Heylyn, who was once Laud's chaplain but found a new career as a royalist and Anglican polemicist, lacks any of Marvell's ambivalence: the public tragedy of the martyred king is a sign of his devotion to the kingdom and, especially, the Church of England. Milton, for one, recognizes that such versions of the king's life take the form of a "Tragedie, wherein the Poet us'd not much licence in departing from the truth of History" (*Eikonoklastes*, 3.362). Milton urges his readers to recognize that the tragic plot imposes a shape—an untruthful shape—upon the events of history, a narrative that moves the reader to a release of emotional sympathy, which in turn becomes political sympathy.

Crucial in the prehistory of *Eikon Basilike* is the martyrdom of Charles's grandmother. The literary accounts of her death help to make the king's tragedy an intelligible experience for their readers.[13] In formulating the icon of what Roy Strong suggestively calls the Church of England's "Counter-Reformation Baroque royal saint,"[14] seventeenth-century royalists harness the pathos of Mary's tragic scaffold into a royalist aesthetic where passion and pity bring loyalty. The regicides respond by attempting to project an image of absolute divine justice overwhelming the human image of the king, just as Mary, too, was destroyed by Scottish and English justice. They ultimately fail, however, to counter the seductive emotional power of this royal saint and his book.

The origins of this rhetorical failure are rooted in the events of January 1649. In their zeal to hold a public trial and execution, the regicides do not appear to have looked back and studied the lessons of Mary's execution, lessons that Charles himself appears to have learned well.[15] Elizabeth and her councilors carefully saw that Mary's trial followed all legal forms. Mary at first refused to participate in the trial, but the Lord Treasurer Burghley threatened to prosecute her whether or not she appeared before the court.

Under this pressure, she relented, listening to Christopher Hatton's advice that she should try to clear her name. She was deceived, however: by appearing before the court, she gave the proceedings legitimacy despite her protests. As the trial and sentencing progressed, Mary was never able to gain a tactical advantage. Most importantly, the English persisted in denying her requests to state her case in London. Elizabeth wisely recognized the dangers of allowing her charismatic cousin to address Parliament or appear before the London crowds. Finally, although Mary's death was not performed in secret—Elizabeth's agents refused her requests to murder Mary and instead beheaded her before a crowd of select witnesses—the scaffold was set up indoors, inside the great hall of Fotheringhay Castle, far from the urban crowds. Only a handful of Mary's supporters were admitted as witnesses, and all potential relics, from her dress to her little dog, were cleansed of blood or burned. Her friends were not allowed to touch the body, which was immediately encased in a lead coffin. Although Mary's public performance—her speeches and actions—assured that she would hold a place in the history of Catholic martyrs to the Reformation, her body left no cache of holy relics to join those of Thomas More and Edmund Campion.

In following this course of action, Elizabeth's government avoided the problems that embroiled the republican regicides, while Charles made none of the mistakes that undermined his grandmother's cause.[16] Unlike Mary, Charles steadfastly refused to participate in his trial. He stood before the High Court of Justice and rejected its right to judge him; the court's awkward attempt to silence his protests merely exposed to their critics the insecurity of their position. Charles's defenders would immediately print *His Majesties Reasons against the pretended Jurisdiction of the High Court of Justice* (London, 1649), giving prominent attention to the fact that the regicides refused to let him complete the speech; the pamphlet would also appear in many editions of *Eikon Basilike*. Charles's refusal to enter a plea even frustrated the attempt to maintain the form of a complete trial. Although Lord President Bradshaw threatened to take his silence *pro confessio*, Charles did not panic as his grandmother did; he maintained throughout the integrity of his stance. Without a plea from the defendant, the trial could not progress; the court met in private and was forced to enter a summary verdict of guilty.[17] Although technically the correct procedure to follow,[18] the swift verdict exposed the basic unfairness of the trial. Indeed, Charles's refusal to answer the charges and thereby recognize the authority of the High Court of Justice created a serious challenge to the legitimacy of revolutionary justice. Because of this debate over the legality of the judicial process, both regicides and royalists printed strikingly similar trial documents as evidence of the justice of their causes. For example, the republican treatise, *King Charls His Tryal* (London,

1649), publishes much of the same material from the trial as *Reliquiae Sacrae Carolinae* (London, 1650) and other expanded editions of *Eikon Basilike*. The regicides soon found themselves vulnerable to *Eikon Basilike's* derision of their legal process:

those greater formalities, whereby My Enemies (being more solemnly cruell) will, it may be, seeke to adde (as those did, who Crucified Christ) the mockery of Justice, to the cruelty of Malice: That I may be destroyed, as with greater pomp and artifice, so with lesse pity, it will be but a necessary policy to make My death appeare as an act of Justice, done by Subjects upon their Soveraigne; who know that no Law of God or Man invests them with any power of Judicature without Me, much lesse against Me: and who, being sworn and bound by all that is sacred before God and man, to endeavour My preservation, must pretend Justice to cover their Perjury. (256)[19]

Here Charles predicts that his accusers will "pretend Justice" and put on a show of "pomp and artifice" to hide their lack of authority. Readers of *Eikon Basilike* look back at the trial—or at the documents from the trial included in the later editions—and see not a proclamation of justice but a botched theatrical performance. The king's book reveals that the regicides themselves are just actors in a theatre of power—actors, moreover, far less skilled than Charles.

In the end, the regicides were not just poor actors; they were poor producers who failed to control the crowd's response to the theatre of the execution. In theory, the public execution of the tyrant would proclaim the people's justice. The people, however, responded with what can best be termed ambivalence. The reports of a great groan rising from the crowd would serve royalist propagandists for centuries: the emotions generated by the execution undermined the new government. Performing the execution in front of such a hostile audience made it impossible to secure the body as effectively as Elizabeth's agents had done in the case of Mary Stuart. Soon relics of Charles's body were circulating throughout the country.

The control of Elizabeth's government is well represented by a response from the opposing side, the engraving of Mary's execution at the end of Richard Verstegan's Catholic martyrology, *Theatrvm Crudelitatum Haereticorum Nostri Temporis* (*The Theatre of the Cruelties of the Heretics of Our Times*, Antwerp, 1587). The scene is one of order, emphasized by the straight lines of the room's classical architecture; only the rumpled cloth covering the scaffold, flowing as if from the folds of Mary's dress, breaks the severity (Figure 1).[20] Only one pious woman responds to the emotion of the scaffold; the other witnesses stand impassively, displaying no emotion. The crowd outside, cruel Protestants all, do not flinch as they view Mary's head. Verstegan places his martyrology of Mary as the final and climactic showpiece of

Perſecutiones aduerſus Catholicos à Prote-
ſtantibus Caluiniſtis excitæ in Anglia.

Poſt varias clades miſerorum, & cædis aceruos
Inſontum, comes exornat ſpectacula mater
Supplicio, & regum ſoror & fidiſſima coniux.
Illa Caledonijs diademate claruit oris,
Sed micat in cœlo fulgentior, inde corona
Sanguinis, infandæꝗ manet vindicta ſecuris.

Figure 1. Richard Vestegan. *Theatrvm Crudelitatem Haerecorum Nostri Temporis [The Theater of the Cruelties Inflicted by the Heretics of Our Times]* (Antwerp, 1587).

Figure 2. *The Execution of Charles I* (artist unknown).

Protestant persecution. The heretics, he implies, are calculating men of politics, men incapable of responding with passion to a scene of suffering. His attack upon the political heartlessness of the Protestants is powerful propaganda, but expresses one important truth: Elizabeth and her council kept control over the scaffold and thus controlled and limited the unstable emotions of the crowd.

By contrast, a royalist painting of Charles's execution shows the crowd in disorder. While some Puritans, dressed in dark colors, respond without emotion—once again taking the role of the calculating politicians—others have bloodlust on their faces (Figure 2). The painting soon draws the viewer's eye to the woman in light colored dress who has collapsed from the pity of the scene. We can see the regicides losing control over the scaffold and over the emotions of the crowd. The English scaffold is notoriously difficult to control, a carnival site, in Thomas Lacqueur's account, where the crowd frequently challenges the state's ritualized performance of justice.²¹ Charles's execution was certainly not festive, but even the solemn rituals of the event failed to move significant portions of the crowd to embrace the image of justice on display. Before the army's two troops of horse could charge and disperse the crowd, the king's supporters were grasping at the scaffold to collect relics of his body and blood, as shown in the lower right panel of the royalist painting. The regicides were battling the "Image-doting rabble" (*Eikonoklastes*, 3.601) even before they had read *Eikon Basilike*.²²

In short, Charles succeeded in doing what Mary had failed to do: he undermined the court that tried him by exposing the political nature of his opponents' "justice." The king's book then goes further by using passionate rhetoric to transcend politics. *Eikon Basilike* pulls away from political battles and invites the reader into the conscience of the man who was king. In place of the abstract defenses of divine right and royal prerogative, texts that served both James and Charles so poorly during their reigns, *Eikon Basilike* personalizes the face of monarchy. The appeal is direct, sympathetic, passionate. Although the title of the first chapter, "Vpon His Majesties calling this last Parliament," might suggest an official style, the text opens not with the royal we but with an intimate first-person singular voice: "This last Parliament I called, not more by others advise, and necessity of My affaires, then by My owne choice and inclination; who have alwaies thought the right way of Parliaments most safe for My Crowne, and best pleasing to My People" (1). The king does not answer Parliament's projects for "the new modelling of Soveraignty and Kingship" (68); rather, he passively protests that "yet they cannot deprive me of my own innocency, or Gods mercy, nor obstruct my way to Heaven" (72–73). In keeping with the rhetorical tactics of the King's book, the documents that different editors add to the basic text of the *Eikon*

Basilike are almost all personal or religious, not official or political: his prayers, letters and addresses to his children, and private letters to his wife.[23]

Elizabeth Skerpan Wheeler, in her provocative reading of *Eikon Basilike*, shows the ways in which the king's book invites readers to "collaborate" in its creation, to enter into intimate sympathy with Charles's text and even become co-creators who add material to it. She calls this process the "democratization" of the king's image, though we should not let this term mislead us.[24] It is important not to confuse the *popularization* of the king's image with *democratization*. *Eikon Basilike*, like the crowd's response to the execution, does not "democratize" politics or even rhetoric. Quite the contrary, the reader's intimate sympathy with the king's suffering effaces the power of the people. This popularizing of the king encourages a fetishization of his relics and thereby a submission to his charisma—and thus submission to his authoritarian heirs. The royalist re-creation of the king's trial and execution answers abstract, "democratic" justice with personalized, "popular" pity.

Eikon Basilike thus opens a debate over the king's character while challenging the republicans to control its emotional power. Significantly, in the propaganda of the 1650s, writers return repeatedly to the theme, "Qui nescit dissimulare nescit regnare," "He (or she) who does not know how to dissimulate, does not know how to reign." For example, Anthony Weldon's notorious slander against the Stuarts, *The Court and Character of King James* (London, 1650), and its sequel, *The Court and Character of King Charles* (London, 1651), both print the motto on their title pages and return to the phrase again and again as a touchstone.[25] The anonymous *Life and Reigne of King Charls, Or the Pseudo-Martyr discovered* (London, 1651) then uses the motto specifically to attack the king's book as the product of "the subtilest Disciple of *Machavill*" (159):

'Tis most true, that they which look on the first face of things, and heed only the outside of objects, without an intentive eye on their in-sides, are easily deceived; but such as will narrowly look into all his Expresses, compared with his deeds, shall doutlesse soon finde, that this unhappy King was one of the deepest and boldest dissemblers, of any one Prince which the last Century hath produced; and I am prone to beleeve, that he took too much of the patterne of *Lews* th'eleventh of *France*, who was wont to say, that he desired to leave his Sonne no other Learning, than *Qui nescit dissimulare, nescit regnare,* he that knows not to dissemble, knowes not how to play the King; and it hath been feared, and by those which wisht him well, that he was too much verst in the principles of *Machiavill*. (174)

The author goes on to link Charles to various "ITALIAN Politicians" (174), calling on a familiar popular prejudice by linking Charles to the machiavellian politics of the Catholic powers: *Eikon Basilike* is a continuation of the popish plot.[26] What was for King Louis XI a political prescription, a description of how to use language in the political world, thus becomes a warning against popish political deception.[27] It is, moreover, a lesson in political hermeneutics: *Eikon Basilike* can only be defeated by a suspicious reader, an "intentive eye" that can uncover the dissembling rhetoric of the king.[28] By contrast, royalist readers of *Eikon Basilike* made special claims for the relationship that the text builds with them:

> He that can spel a Sigh, or reade a Tear;
> Pronounce amazement, or Accent wilde Fear:
> Having All Grief by Heart, He, onely He
> Is fit to write and read thy Elegy
> Unvalued CHARLS: Thou art so hard a Text,
> Writ in one Age, not understood i'th' next.[29]

This royalist responds to the king's text by proclaiming that only the sensitive reader—the man who reads through feeling, who reads feelingly—can understand Charles; the new age, he further claims, is emptied of such passion and thus cannot understand or value the dead king. The author of *The Pseudo-Martyr discovered* counters that it is not passion but *suspicion* that provides the correct key to interpreting Charles's text. Charles's claim to be unveiling his conscience to his people, he urges, is merely another rhetorical deception.

This criticism is astute, for in *Eikon Basilike* the king counters his persecutors with the fantasy that his book will transcend language:

Yet since providence will have it so, I am content so much of My heart (which I study to approve to Gods omniscience) should be discovered to the world, without any of those dresses, or popular capatations, which some men use in their Speeches, and Expresses; I wish My Subjects had yet a clearer sight into My most retired thoughts:

Where they might discover, how they are divided between the love and care I have, not more to preserve My owne Rights, than to procure their peace and happinesse, and that extreame grief to see them both deceived and destroyed. (190)

The King here is responding to the printing of the cabinet of his letters, which were published as evidence of his wicked intents, much as his grandmother's "casket letters" were printed by Elizabeth's government to discredit Mary.[30] He does not disavow the letters as fakes but counters that his private thoughts, taken out of context, have not been given a fair reading. In the wish that his subjects could see into his private thoughts and secret grief, the king's book proclaims its liberation from the dissimulation of politics.

This claim of transparent access to truth and passion suggests to the reader that his or her emotional response is direct and natural rather than the result of rhetorical manipulation. This pathos is given a visual form by William Marshall's frontispiece to *Eikon Basilike* (Figure 3). Marshall's

Figure 3. William Marshall. Frontispiece to *Eikon Basilike, The Povrtraictvre of His Sacred Maiestie in His Solitvdes and Svfferings* (London, 1648/49).

engraving is the first reading of the martyred king's rhetorical performance, one sanctioned by his supporters and one that develops subtly through the various editions. The focal point of all versions of the frontispiece is the figure of Charles at prayer in his closet. The king lets fall the crown of temporal power (*vanitas*) to take up Christ's crown of thorns (*gratia*); he sets his sights on the blessed crown (*gloria*). His left hand, beating his chest in penitence and grief, triangulates with the beam from heaven (*clarior è tenebris*) and the beam from his eye (*caeli specto*), thereby drawing the viewer's eyes to the king's eyes. In the first version, the reader only sees the king in profile; his one visible eye is set firmly and even stoically upon the crown of glory. Notice, however, that Marshall changes the king's eyes in his second version of the engraving (Figure 4). Here we see a three-quarter view of the king's face, and his two eyes visible now seem sunken and sorrowful under the furrowed brow. This new view opens the king's face, and thus his passions, to the

The Explanation of the EMBLEME.

Ponderibus *genus omne mali, probris, gravatus,*
(V'ixq, ferenda ferens, Palma *ut* Depressa, *resurgo.*

Ac, velut undarum Fluctûs Ventiq, *furorem*
Irati Populi Rupes immota *repello .*
Clarior è tenebris, *cœlestis stella, corusco.*
(Victor et æternùm-felici pace triumpho.

Auro Fulgentem *rutilo gemmisq, micantem,*
At curis Gravidam *spernendo* calco Coronam.

Spinosam, *at ferri facilem, quo* Spes mea, Christi
Auxilio, Nobis non est tractare molestum .

Æternam, *fixis fidei, sempérq,*—beatam
In Cœlos oculis Specto, *Nobísq, paratam.*

Quod Vanum *est, sperno; quod* Christi *Gratia fænebet*
Amplecti studium est: Virtutis Gloria merces.

Though clogg'd with weights of miseries
Palm-like Depress'd, I higher rise .

And as th'unmoved Rock out-brave's
The boistrous Windes and rageing waves:
So triumph I. And shine more bright
In sad Affliction's Darksom night .

That Splendid, but yet toilsom Crown
Regardlesly I trample down .

With joie I take this Crown of thorn,
Though sharp, yet easie to be born .

That heav'nlie Crown, already mine,
I View with eies. of Faith divine .

I slight vain things; and do embrace
Glorie, the just reward of Grace .

Τῷ Χρ ὐδὲν ἠδίκησε τὴν πόλιν, ὐδὲ τὸ Κάτωα .

G.D.

Figure 4. William Marshall. Frontispiece to *Eikon Basilike, The Povrtraictvre of His Sacred Maiestie in His Solitvdes and Svfferings, Whereunto are annexed His Praiers and Apophthegms* (London, 1649).

reader's gaze. Marshall thus emphasizes the pathetic power of the king's passion and sets the new reader on a search into the private emotions of the king's closet and conscience. Charles's eyes, weighed down by his miseries, are the windows (like the two windows above him) into the grief of the royal conscience. The book, the frontispiece implies, will allow the reader to understand, value, and finally join in the king's tearful devotional experience.

The text of the king's book lives up to the promise of the frontispiece and succeeds in producing an emotional response from its readers. This passion is above all a religious experience. As other critics have noticed, Marshall's portrait of Charles at prayer puts him in the role of Christ in the Garden of Gethsemene.[31] One sympathetic reader responds:

> If that [the Crucifixion] go first in horrour, this [the regicide] comes next,
> A pregnant Comment on that gastly Text.
> The Heav'ns nere saw, but in that Tragick howre,
> Slaughter'd so great an *Innocence* and *Power.*[32]

First Christ was killed, then Charles. They both have been "Slaughter'd," offered as sacrifices. This sacrificial violence becomes sacred text of "gastly" power. The anonymous royalist thus observes that *Eikon Basilike*, like the frontispiece, has placed the king in a history of textual representations, a typology of tragic pity read backwards from today to the gospel.

This eclipsing of the political issues makes the work difficult to argue against *except* on the grounds that it is false rhetoric. The regicide thus attempts to disrupt the chain of "Comment" by uncovering the text's Catholic and idolatrous roots; indeed, that Charles's enemies chose iconoclasm as the method of attack reflects their recognition of the Catholic subtext of the pity of The Passion.[33] *The Pseudo-Martyr discovered* complains that the frontispiece is "the meer jugling devise of some hypocriticall or Mahometean Imposter, the better to stir up the People and vaine beholders to pitty him" (178–79). This pamphleteer builds upon Milton's charge of plagiarism and fraud against Charles and his ghostwriter by charging Marshall with fabricating false emotion. The phrase "Mahometean Imposter" evokes apostasy and false religion; it identifies the source of the frontispiece's power in its appeals to Catholic, sacred iconography. This is a powerful charge, since, to the Puritan, the frontispiece, if tainted with associations with Catholic iconography, is *ipso facto* hypocritical, deceptive, false, and idolatrous.[34] Meditative reflections where the poet envisions himself or herself witnessing or participating in a scene from the life of Christ are not, of course, alien to English Protestantism, witnessed by Milton's own "Upon the Morning of Christ's Nativity." Zealous Protestants, however, have great difficulty reconciling the "sacrificial pathos" of Christ's Passion with their iconoclastic religiosity, as

Florence Sandler has noted.[35] Milton thus abandons his early poem on "The Passion," and after 1649, when the *Eikon Basilike* forever taints the pity of the crucifixion with political and religious manipulation, he never again attempts to represent Christ's Passion.

Through the Marshall frontispiece, the pity of the sacrificial Passion becomes part of Royalist mythology; here again, however, Charles's followers are merely replicating the work of Mary's defenders. While Verstegan was placing Mary at the head of the ranks of Catholic martyrs, others were placing her with Christ on Golgotha. In some editions of Adam Blackwood's martyrology, *La Mort de la Royne d'Escosse* (*The Death of the Queen of Scots*, [Paris?], 1588), a woodcut portrays Mary in the role of either the Virgin Mary or Mary Magdalene, kneeling in adoration before the crucified Christ, kissing his feet (Figure 5). Other versions of the same portrait show Constantine's motto scrolled across the Cross, "IN HOC SIGNO VINCES," in this sign you will triumph.[36] Mary herself consciously assumed the role of Christ at her death. Reports agree that as she was waiting for the stroke to fall, she repeated several times, "In Manus tuas, Domine, commendo Spiritum meum"—Into your hands, Lord, I commend my Spirit—Christ's final words on the cross.[37] The paradox of this passive triumphant stance is the logic of the royal martyrology: the pathos the reader feels for the murdered king will translate some day into a resurrected monarchy.

Charles himself seems to have been too circumspect to allude directly to his grandmother's tragic end, probably because of her role in English Catholic propaganda. Indeed, Catholic royalist writers were among the first to draw direct parallels between their deaths. In 1650, for example, Mary's life and death took a prominent role in Robert Codrington's new English translation of *The Holy Court*, a lengthy exposition of Catholic piety and politics by the French Jesuit Nicolas Caussin.[38] To present Caussin's Mary Stuart to a wide English audience for the first time, Codrington lifted this life out of its placement in the French text, where it stands with other lives of eminent queens and ladies,[39] and put it at the end of the entire work, paired with a life of Cardinal Poole. Its publication within a few months of Charles's execution suggests the prominent place that Mary's and Charles's executions were taking in Catholic royalist propaganda: a history that was written in the 1630s to remind Charles of his faithful Catholic ancestor now links them in martyrdom. This revision turns the book into a recusant commentary on the execution of Charles. Without altering Caussin's text, the editor adds new significance to the life's zealous appeals for Charles I to convert Britain back to the true church:

It is in your veins, most mighty Monarch of *Great Brittain*, where still her bloud doth run. That cruel Axe which made three Crowns to fall with one head, hath not yet poured it all out, it doth preserve itself in your body, and in the body of your Posterity, animated with the Spirit of *Marie*, and imprinted with the image of her goodness. (5.312)

Mary's blood, once spilled at Fotheringhay, was preserved in Charles's blood, now spilled at Whitehall. The events of the years since Caussin penned these lines give an eerie, almost prescient irony to the comment, "That cruel Axe . . . hath not yet poured it all out." Caussin's account is steeped in blood, which he gives a sacramental nature. As she lies bleeding, "The bloud was collected in silver Basons"; it is, Caussin assures us, "the bloud of [a] Martyr," which is why the Protestants are so careful to destroy it (5.311). The reader in 1650 would certainly hear in Caussin the language that was producing royalist texts like Peter Du Moulin's *Regii sanguinis clamor ad coelum adversus parricidas anglicanos* (*The Shout to Heaven of the Royal Blood Against the English Parricides*, Hague, 1652). Indeed, Caussin's final exhortation for Charles to convert to Catholicism—"Establish that which your Grandmother of ever-lasting memory, hath practised by her Virtues, demonstrated by her Examples, honoured by her Constancy, and sealed with her Bloud" (5.313)— becomes an even more urgent declaration of blood libel. The text encourages the readers of 1650 to conclude that once more the British heretics have killed their prince.

Not surprisingly, Anglican clergymen, expelled from their livings and often from their country, took up the rhetorical strategies of Catholic recu-sants and exiles.[40] In *A Compleat History of The Lives and Reigns of Mary Queen of Scotland, And of Her Son and Successor, James* (London, 1656) and the companion volume, *A Compleat History of the Life and Reign of King Charles* (London, 1658), William Sanderson follows the editor of *The Holy Court* by explicitly linking the death of Mary to the sufferings of her son and grandson. He uses this tragic narrative to make a defense of the Protestant monarchy of England: the Anglican, faithful to king and bishop, embraces Mary as the first martyr of the long-suffering Stuart line. The high-point of this renovation of Mary as Charles's original comes in the work of the exiled Anglican royalist Richard Watson, whose *Historicall Collections of Eccle-siastick Affairs in Scotland And Politick related to them* (London, 1657) is a lengthy history critical of the Scottish Reformation and the deposition and eventual execution of Queen Mary.[41] He refutes the histories of Knox and Buchanan for the express purpose of discrediting the reformed revolution, which he portrays as a Scottish provocation begun under Mary and imported to England under Charles. To reform the Scots of their rebelliousness, Wat-son turns to their original sin: "If, by pourtraiting the horrid actions of their Ancestours, I can excite their guilty consciences to compare the *copy* with the

Figure 5. [Adam Blackwood], *La Mort de la Royne d'Escosse* (Paris[?], 1588).

original, and repent *effectually* for the transcendencie of their own rebellions, I shall have great complacency in the assurance that I have outrun, or outwrit my hopes."[42] The rebellion against Mary is the *"original,"* while that against Charles is but the *"copy."* Although Watson claims that he is aiming his moral and political reading of history at the "guily consciences" of the Scots, his challenge to the Commonwealth is clear: just as, in Milton's tracts, Charles is the heir to Mary's rhetoric and politics, so, in Watson's, are the Commonwealthsmen the heirs to the rebels against Mary.[43]

Although Marshall likely never saw Blackwood's or Caussin's books, in putting Charles in a passive, even feminized position, he is drawing on this same tradition of recuperative, transformative, defiant pathos. For the Catholic, these tears announce a conversion experience. As in the Blackwood frontispiece, Christ's arms embrace the world, while the martyr falls into submission. For the Anglican royalist, these tears announce political defiance. In Marshall's frontispiece, the Catholic crucifix has been replaced with a crown of thorns, which symbolizes suffering but also reminds the reader of the king's dominion over church and state. Such a passion promises to fit the subject, whether Mary or Charles, into a narrative of victory; suffering will lead to rebirth, resurrection, and restoration. The original sin, they promise, will be redeemed through the suffering of the king. To prevent the triumph of this pathetic icon, however, Milton and the regicides work to unveil the literary history of the king's rhetoric, to reveal its origin in Stuart and Catholic deception.

II. ORIGINALS: MARY AND SPENSER IN MILTON'S RHETORIC OF JUSTICE

King James himself had recognized that the legitimacy of the Stuart line was threatened by attacks upon his mother's character. In *Basilikon Doron,* he shows extreme sensitivity toward this subject, repeatedly telling Prince Henry, "sith yee are come of as honourable Predecessours as anie Prince liuing, represse the insolence of such, as vnder pretence to taxe a vice in the person, seekes craftily *to staine the race,* and to steale the affection of the people from their posteritie." Elsewhere he charges his son, "sen yee are the lawfull magistrate, suffer not both your Princes and your Parents to be dishonoured by any."[44] James followed his own advice. As soon as he was old enough to exercise authority in Scotland, he banned Buchanan's anti-Marian works.[45] Then, when he took the throne of England, he tried to pressure the French *politique* historian Jacques Auguste de Thou to exonerate Mary of the charges of adultery, murder, and treason; he had Sir Robert Cotten and William Camden send to France his version of events, which shifted blame for the deposition and execution onto her Scottish and English enemies.[46]

After witnessing James's anger when de Thou failed to provide a flattering account of Mary's life, Camden set out to write a carefully balanced and extremely tactful version of events which portrays Mary as the tragic victim of historical circumstances. Mary is innocent of the worst of Buchanan's libels, he writes, while Puritan zealots and duplicitous, ambitious courtiers trick Elizabeth into executing Mary. This version of Mary's fall becomes central to James's sense of his own legitimacy. Not coincidentally, the first part of Camden's *Annales* to appear in English was William Udall's translation of *The Historie of the Life and Death of Mary Stuart Qveene of Scotland* (London, 1624). Published first under James and then at the height of Charles's personal rule (1636), Udall's history popularizes a version of events that aids Stuart claims to legitimacy. The celebration of Mary's life belongs to James and Charles's official story, the official legend of Stuart legitimacy. Until the outbreak of the Civil War and the breakdown of the Stuart censorship regime, it was the only story in print. As Charles mounted the scaffold, however, his grandmother's own execution, as well as her complicity (real or alleged) in murder and treason, made her, as James might have predicted, a convenient tool with which to justify the destruction of the Stuarts.

Milton is the first republican after the regicide to attack Mary in print as a stain upon the Stuart race. But he does not introduce her into the polemic of the revolution, as such attacks arise briefly during her grandson's trial. Faced with Charles's repudiation of the High Court of Justice's authority to try him, Lord President Bradshaw answers by citing "one of your [Scottish] Authors"—that is, Buchanan—and noting, "It is not far to go for an example neer you, your Grandmother set aside, and your Father an Infant crowned."[47] Buchanan's account of Mary's reign and the revolt that overthrew her thus becomes one of the primary precedents for the new court. In *The Tenure of Kings and Magistrates*, Milton will make just such a use of Buchanan. He defines the Scottish revolution of the 1550s and 1560s as a battle for "libertie of conscience" (3.223) and then paraphrases the Scottish justification for the deposition of the tyrant Mary: "the Scots were a free Nation, made King whom they freely chose, and with the same freedom unkingd him if they saw cause, by right of ancient laws and Ceremonies yet remaining" (3.225–26).[48] Mary's fate is an example of the just punishment of tyrants—specifically, tyrants over conscience and religion—and thus helps to bolster a theory of resistance and tyrannicide.

Some replies to *Eikon Basilike* do take such an approach and attack Charles on the grounds of political theory. For example, *The Pseudo-Martyr discovered* cites the "divers presidents" of the Scots deposing and executing their rulers, "when they found them perverse and intractable to any reason" (sig. A7). In *Eikonoklastes*, by contrast, Milton recognizes that the power of the king's book is not its political theories but its (apparently) persuasive rhetoric. He does not, therefore, provide any abstract or theoretical defense of the regicide (as he would in *Tenure*), preferring to stay consistent to his strategy of unraveling the rhetoric sustaining his opponent. Thomas Corns also notes the absence of political theory in *Eikonoklastes*, concluding that "Kingship as such is not the issue: this king and the punishment of this king are."[49] In this treatise, however, Milton, does take issue with kingship, with its rhetorical, iconic power.

Milton uses the example of Mary to make a specific point: Charles's *Eikon Basilike* is not a sincere expression of belief but an exercise of rhetorical manipulation that employs skills he learned from his grandmother. Milton writes, "*It is a sad fate*, he [Charles] saith, *to have his Enemies both accusers, Parties, and Judges*. Sad indeed, but no sufficient Plea to acquitt him from being so judg'd. For what Malefactor might not sometimes plead the like?" (3.597). Milton attacks Charles's appeal to pity—his "sad fate"—and his appeal to a legal technicality. Ignore Charles's plea to emotion and to right of law, Milton tells his readers; such complaints—standard practices in forensic rhetoric—distract us from the charges against him.

When Mary was tried by Elizabeth's government for treason, she had offered the same two defenses. First, she attacked the legal jurisdiction of the English court, denying not only that an English court had the right to try a Scottish sovereign but that *any* court had the right to try a sovereign. Second, she presented a pathetic portrait, appealing to pity for the sad fate of the beautiful woman, a former queen of Scotland and France. The Catholic propaganda in her favor produced elaborate martyrologies celebrating these themes.[50] With this similarity in mind, Milton identifies Charles's "evasions" as tricks learned from his grandmother, "from whom he seems to have learnt, as it were by heart, or els by kind, that which is thought by his admirers to be the most vertuous, most manly, most Christian, most Martyr-like both of his words and speeches heer, and of his answers and behaviour at his Tryall" (3.597). Alluding to Mary's own attempts to stage-manage her execution so that she would appear to be a martyr to the Catholic faith,[51] Milton claims that Charles is merely an actor playing a role he learned from his manipulative and image-conscious grandmother.[52] Neither manly, Christian, nor martyr-like, Charles imitates a feminine, Catholic idol.[53] Mary is the queen of pity and tricky legal rhetoric, and, either through their shared character or their shared blood, Charles has learned these skills: it is his literary inheritance.[54]

In his response to Charles's arguments, Milton appeals directly to a higher law. He tries to take Charles's case out of the human courtroom, where forensic rhetoric determines the outcome through appeals to pathos and to legal niceties, and place it in an ideal courtroom: "For what Malefactor might

not somtimes plead the like? If his own crimes have made all men his Enemies, who els can judge him? . . . Nay at the Resurrection it may as well be
pleaded, that the Saints who then shall judge the World, are *both Enemies,
Judges, Parties, and Accusers*" (3.597). This move is itself a rhetorical trick.
Milton covers the ruthless political maneuvering that produced the verdict
against Charles with an appeal to an abstract ideal of higher justice. Instead
of answering the attack upon parliamentary justice with a detailed defense
of the Rump, he attacks Charles's protest as nothing more than an attempt
to draw attention away from his crimes. Drawing attention away from the
charge, of course, is precisely Milton's own rhetorical strategy here.

Milton's evasion of Charles's complaint does not easily reconcile with his
attempts to theorize the trial in *The Tenure of Kings and Magistrates*. In that
pamphlet, he is careful to prove that although "the right of choosing, yea of
changing thir own Government is by the grant of God himself in the People"
(3.207), this power resides only in the magistrate as a representative of the
people: "to doe justice on a lawless King is to a privat man unlawful, to
an inferior Magistrate lawfull" (3.257). His theory, though, cannot answer
Charles's complaint about the dubious constitutional authority and legality of
that inferior magistrate. Although in *Tenure* Milton states that the trial by
Parliament proves that "Justice, is the onely true sovran and supreme Majesty upon earth" (3.237), in *Eikonoklastes* he avoids reconciling his rhetoric
of ideal justice with the compromised political reality of the magistrate who
has executed that ideal. When pressed by *Eikon Basilike* to make such a
defense, he dismisses the gap between the ideal and real: "For what Malefactor might not sometimes plead the like?"⁵⁵

Earlier in *Eikonoklastes*, however, Milton does offer one unlikely solution to the conflict between the ideals of justice and the ruthless workings of
politics: a reading of Book Five of Spenser's *Faerie Queene*, the Legend of
Justice. Milton responds to Charles's complaint about the illegality of Parliament's actions against him by citing Spenser as an authority on justice:

If there were a man of iron, such as *Talus*, by our Poet *Spencer*, is fain'd to be the page
of Justice, who with his iron flaile could doe all this, and expeditiously, without those
deceitfull formes and circumstances of Law, worse then ceremonies in Religion; I say
God send it don, whether by one *Talus*, or by a thousand. (3.390)

Milton rejects not the Law—the ideal behind true justice—but the "deceitfull
formes and circumstances of Law," the conventions, language, and false
rhetoric that mediate between human beings and the truth of God's Law.
Drawing on a powerful concept from his theology, Milton equates the ceremonies of the law with the ceremonies of religion, those practices that separate individuals from the immediate experience of the divine. Talus makes

possible immediate access to the true Law. Milton's Spenser here embodies one seductive aspect of the Book of Justice. In Milton's version, Spenser is a poet who sweeps away the difficult negotiations between political ideals and political realities with the iron flail of righteousness.

Milton's memory of Spenser's Legend of Justice, however, is very selective. He draws upon the absolute, easy justice of Talus's iron flail, figuring Spenser as the poet of absolute truth. This characterization of Spenser ignores the bulk of Book Five, including the allegory of the trial of Mary Queen of Scots, much as when *Areopagitica* incorrectly remembers the Palmer joining Guyon in the Cave of Mammon.[56] Although Milton undoubtedly would have recalled Spenser's allegory of Mary as Duessa when making his equation between Charles and Mary, his attacks upon Charles make no allusion to Duessa's trial at Mercilla's Court. One might think that Milton has missed an opportunity to follow Spenser in slandering Mary, and hence Charles, as the Catholic archvillainess Duessa; however, Milton *must* avoid Duessa's trial if he is going to continue to press his attack upon Charles. His omission does not point so much to an ethical difference between Spenser and Milton as to the different rhetorical aims of their two works.[57]

The trial of Duessa uses a highly self-conscious exercise in both forensic rhetoric and state propaganda to explore the rhetoric that the state uses to produce justice.[58] Zele the prosecutor is an orator "[t]hat well could charme his tongue, and time his speach / To all assayes" (5.9.39.3–4). *Charm* is a charged word in *The Faerie Queene*, most often applied to Archimago, Duessa, and their tricky Catholic rhetoric; this echo invites the reader to examine the orator with some suspicion.[59] The canto, moreover, emphasizes the superficial appearances of the court and its courtiers. Arthur and Artegall come to Mercilla's court to "see her rich array" (5.9.Argument.4), to experience the rhetorical array set out by Mercilla and her courtiers; likewise, they come to see and hear the rhetoric of her enemy Duessa, who is herself described as being "royally arayd" (5.9.40.2). These rhetorical performances echo beyond the courtroom into the world of public relations. Zele's prosecution, in fact, does not draw upon the trial records but instead closely follows the government's propaganda pamphlets, especially *The Copie of a Letter to the Right Honorable the Earle of Leycester* (London, 1586), which was published under the direction of the Privy Council.[60] Indeed, Arthur and Artegall's experience comprises an allegory of how to read the rhetoric and propaganda produced by both sides of a conflict. Artegall and Arthur must make sense of their responses to Duessa's "wretched semblant" (5.9.38.8), a figure who produces sympathy in all who see her. At the same time, they must learn to judge the rhetoric of Queen Mercilla or, more to the point, Queen Elizabeth, her original. Mercilla demonstrates great concern with the public presentation of her justice: " . . . that gratious Queene: / Who sate on high, that she might all men see, / And might of all men royally be seene" (5.9.27.3–5). She wants to observe all men and overwhelm their senses with her rhetorical displays. In a world where every person is putting on a public show and using rhetoric to shape other people's responses to him or her, the process of making a just decision, of telling the truth from the mere appearance of truth, becomes extremely difficult, if not impossible.

Significantly, Spenser's Talus does not appear at Mercilla's court; once he has performed his function by capturing and executing Malengin or Guile, he disappears, receiving no mention at all for the rest of the canto. Talus has no role to play in Duessa's trial; indeed, his victory over Guile is a fleeting illusion. Spenser suggests that to believe that the scourge of justice can easily destroy Guile is to believe a fantasy. Only guileful rhetoric and all the compromised ideals implied by such dissimulation can counter a guileful, dissembling enemy. Likewise, whereas in Book One Arthur simply strips Duessa of her scarlet and purple robes in order to reveal her true hideous nature (1.7.46), here she remains a beautiful and piteous figure that only forensic rhetoric can defeat and expose. Indeed, the entire canto is told as a battle between two enemies, each skilled at using the guile of rhetoric. Duessa's attractive figure makes a rhetorical defense—the appeal to pathos—that Zele must answer with his own emotional manipulation. When Zele perceives that Duessa has touched Arthur's "tender hart," "He gan his earnest feruour to augment, / And many fearefull obiects to them to present" (5.9.46). His presentation manages to turn sympathy into fear and anger, a transformation that requires not a heavy club but a light tongue.

The success of this rhetorical performance, however, does not result in the return of Talus and his gratuitous displays of public punishment. Even when Zele has proven his case, Mercilla hides her own decision from public eyes with a display of crocodile tears performed to win over the sympathy of her audience. Duessa dies in the space between canto nine and canto ten, away from the public eye. In its account of the trial, the state distances itself from the piteous scene of the scaffold. Spenser's account thus accurately represents the English propaganda campaign, which was aimed at raising sympathy for Elizabeth and choking off pity for Mary. Numerous defenses of the trial and sentence issued from English presses, several under the direction of Elizabeth's chief minister, Lord Burghley, and they all combine legal defenses with celebrations of Elizabeth's merciful feelings. Nonetheless, no official English account of the execution survives in print, probably because any narration of the events must confront the image of Mary as pathetic martyr. Spenser's account unveils how politicians, orators, and propagandists construct images of justice and move their audiences to believe in and act upon those images. He does not, by contrast, concern himself with defending some abstract and inflexible ideal of justice. Had Talus been present at this trial, he would have executed Duessa when the first tears fell for her, and readers would never have witnessed the subtle workings of justice in the real world.

Talus is an image of absolute justice cutting through all the contingencies of real-world rhetoric and politics. To silence Charles and Mary—these figures of pathos—Milton needs his own Talus, a mechanical man who feels no pity. When Milton can find no support for his position beyond his conviction of the transcendent truth of his beliefs, he calls on Talus's iron flail to silence the opposition. Talus thus embodies not simply "rough justice" (to quote Patterson) but the dismissal of the appeals to emotion and legal conventions.[61] The justice of *lex talionis* puts an end to politics and its rhetoric; as recast by Milton, Talus's image of divinely sanctioned violence overcomes the failure of conventional laws, conventional language, and conventional rhetoric. Identifying Spenser's justice solely with Talus, nonetheless, seriously distorts Spenser's views. Such an account omits the political manifestations of justice that occupy most of Book Five, namely equity and rhetoric.[62] Indeed, the Spenser who wrote this legend of justice is far too realistic to believe in the efficacy of a Talus in the world of modern politics, that "stonie age" in which he finds himself living (5.proem.2).

Milton surely would have recognized this complicated aspect of the Legend of Justice, and he may even have thought of Duessa's appeals to "Pittie," "Regard of womanhead," "Nobilitie," and "Griefe" when attacking Charles's speeches (5.9.45). Spenser, however, published his allegory a decade after the propaganda campaign it describes. Free from the urgency of polemics, Spenser has the luxury to cast a skeptical eye upon the practices of both sides. His suspicious attitude toward the rhetoric of both parties makes the episode useless for Milton's attack upon Charles's appeals to pity and conventional laws. As a writer engaged in rhetorical combat, Milton needs to find the best supporting evidence and ignore what does not help his case. In just this way, Quintilian describes the preparation for a forensic oration as "judging what should be said, what concealed [*dissimulandum*], what avoided, altered, and even invented."[63] Milton has therefore neither misread nor revised Spenser, at least not in the way that Harold Bloom and others formulate the concept. Milton is not battling and overworking his literary forefather but twisting another writer's words and views to serve a local rhetorical or persuasive end.[64]

If we follow Milton's partial account, however, we are liable to fall into such an unconscious misreading by replicating his rhetorical distortion. Edwin Greenlaw, for example, echoed Milton's version of the absolute unflinching Spenser nearly a century ago when he portrayed Spenser as a "high-souled" idealist confronting the Machiavellian politics of Lord Burghley.[65] This version of Spenser remains with us today, as in Richard McCabe's interpretation of Duessa's trial: "[Although] Expediency rather than principle secured the Elizabethan peace . . . Spenser's moral universe allows no such compromise."[66] Nonetheless, it is important to remember that for Spenser, *zeal* was a rhetorical construct, one implicated in the pragmatic language of politics—the language from which *Eikonoklastes* proclaims its freedom.[67] Spenser observes how language works in the compromised political universe, though he does not claim to stand above it. At the same time, although *Eikonoklastes* tries to efface its rhetorical nature, it remains a work of political rhetoric. Its "Spenser" is a rhetorical response to a specific debate, and we should not allow it to distort our understandings of Spenser's *Faerie Queene*.

The value in recognizing Milton's return here to Spenser, however, is that it helps us to see Milton's sharp attention to the problems of political rhetoric. The concluding paragraph to *Eikonoklastes* reminds Milton's readers that both Charles and Mary speak a language of compassion that hides evil intentions:

He glories much in the forgivness of his Enemies; *so did his Grandmother at her death*. Wise men would sooner have beleev'd him had he not so oft'n told us so. But he hopes to erect the Trophies of his charity over us. And Trophies of Charity no doubt will be as glorious as Trumpets before the almes of Hypocrites; and more especially the Trophies of such an aspiring charitie as offers in his Prayer to share Victory with Gods compassion, which is over all his works. Such Prayers as these may happly catch the People, as was intended: but how they please God, is to be much doubted, though pray'd in secret, much less writt'n to be divulg'd. (3.600–601, emphasis added)

Milton's sarcasm is blunt here, as is his pessimistic assessment of whether the people can see through the king's rhetoric. His fear of rhetorical manipulation collapses into a fear of the people whom the orator controls. Nonetheless, Milton is rejecting neither practical politics, as Keith Stavely argues, nor poetics, as Stephen Zwicker argues, nor even rhetoric per se.[68] If we examine this final paragraph as a self-consciously rhetorical attack upon Charles's false rhetoric, the issue becomes not truth versus politics, poetry, or rhetoric, but true rhetoric versus false rhetoric. Milton is challenging his readers to learn to read the king rightly, to unveil the intentions behind his words; he is telling his readers to reject the king's rhetoric because it conceals untruths, not because his appeals are poetic. For Milton's own oration to control Charles's infernal parody of divine charity, he must let loose an onslaught of violent language himself, issuing forth as a Talus to chastise the "inconstant, irrational, Image-doting rabble" (3.601). Reform demands that violent and truthful rhetoric uncover the violence hiding behind the name and image of compassion, to read the deception that truly "was intended." Milton thus does not reject the beautiful and moving "Trophies" and "Trumpets" of rhetoric, any more than he rejects poetry or language. Rather, he challenges his readers to learn to read such language skeptically, to become readers alert to how rhetoric is "intended" to "catch" them.

It is important to remember that Milton's figure of talionic justice is only one of his responses to the contingencies of rhetorical occasions. There is another strain in his imagery that figures rhetoric in the language of the equitable, merciful, and charitable interpretation.[69] This Milton tries to teach the Parliament of England not only about divorce but about the interpretation of Scripture:

Yet when I remember the little that our Saviour could prevail about this doctrine of Charity against the crabbed textuists of his time, I make no wonder, but rest confident that who so preferrs either Matrimony, or other Ordinance before the good of man and the plain exigence of Charity, . . . he is no better than a Pharise, and understands not the Gospel. (*Doctrine and Discipline of Divorce*, 2.233)

This charity toward the human and toward the text is the justice that Milton's later poetry will teach. For that Milton—as distinct from the Milton engaged in the demands of rhetorical combat—the goal of living is to search through the dark rhetoric of the world in an attempt to see the hidden God and the hidden Justice. It is not accidental that all Milton's allusions to the Spenser of the *lex talionis* occur before the fall of the Commonwealth. The world after the Fall—post-Eden, post-Commonwealth—is a world that has denied itself access to Talus's easy justice.[70] For Adam and Eve and for Milton's readers, there is no Talus to destroy Satan's seductive rhetoric. They—and we—must seek out a less easy politics, determining the justice of the world's trials without a Talus. This family inheritance begins as a curse but ends as a blessing: "And what he brings, what needs he elsewhere seek" (*Paradise Regain'd*, 4.325).

Earlham College

NOTES

    Richard Vestegan's *Theatrvm Crudelitatem Haerecorum Nostri Temporis* [*The Theater of the Cruelties Inflicted by the Heretics of Our Times*]; *Eikon Basilike, The Povrtraictvre of His Sacred Maiestie in His Solitvdes and Svfferings;* and *Eikon Basilike, The Povrtraictvre of His Sacred Maiestie in His Solitvdes and Svfferings, Whereunto are annexed His Praiers and Apophthegms* are used by courtesy of the Beinecke Rare Book and Manuscript Library, Yale

University. *The Execution of Charles I* from the Scottish National Portrait Gallery, Edinburgh, is used by permission of Lord Dalmeny. *La Mort de la Royne d'Escosse*, sig. Aiiijv, is reproduced by permission of the Trustees of the National Library of Scotland.

1. *Fables Ancient and Modern* (1700), in *The Poems*, ed. John Kinsley, vol. 4 (Oxford, 1958), 1445.

Maureen Quilligan, too, takes this quotation as her starting point in *Milton's Spenser: The Politics of Reading* (Ithaca, 1983), 19. My title echoes hers, but in a general rather than specific sense. That is, I am implicitly critiquing traditional literary histories of which hers is just one.

2. Annabel Patterson, *Reading Between the Lines* (Madison, 1993), 36–56.

3. *Eikonoklastes* was once dismissed as one of the embarrassing and even dull subliterary products of Milton's political career, but it has recently begun to receive attention for its poetic imagination. In the process, the pamphlet has begun to take a central place in readings of Milton's literary career. This reevaluation began slowly with the essays in *The Achievements of the Left Hand*, ed. Michael Lieb and John T. Shawcross (Amherst, 1974) and reached maturity with the volume *Politics, Poetics, and Hermeneutics in Milton's Prose*, ed. David Loewenstein and James Grantham Turner (Cambridge, 1990). Several recent works—including Thomas Corns, *Uncloistered Virtue: English Political Literature, 1640–1660* (Oxford, 1992); Stephen Zwicker, *Lines of Authority: Politics and English Literary Culture, 1649–1689* (Ithaca, N.Y., 1993); and Laura Lunger Knoppers, *Historicizing Milton: Spectacle, Power, and Poetry in Restoration England* (Athens, Ga., 1994)—have identified *Eikonoklastes* as a formative moment in Milton's poetic and intellectual development.

4. All quotations from Milton's prose are from *Complete Prose Works of John Milton*, 8 vols., ed. Don M. Wolfe et al. (New Haven, 1953–82), hereafter designated as YP and cited parenthetically by volume and page number in the text.

5. All quotations from Spenser's *Faerie Queene* are from A. C. Hamilton's edition (London, 1980).

6. Milton's ambivalent attitudes toward rhetoric have been the subject of several important works, notably Stanley Fish, *Surprised by Sin: The Reader in "Paradise Lost"* (London, 1967); Fish, *Self-Consuming Artifacts: The Experience of Seventeenth-Century Literature* (Berkeley and Los Angeles, 1972), 265–302; Thomas O. Sloane, *Donne, Milton, and the End of Humanist Rhetoric* (Berkeley, 1985), 209–78. Both Fish and Sloane insist that Milton's writing is, at heart, antirhetorical, antipersuasive, and even irrational, at least in the way that the Renaissance humanist usually understood the terms. More congenial to my approach are Joseph Anthony Wittreich, " 'The Crown of Eloquence': The Figure of the Orator in Milton's Prose Works," in *Achievements of the Left Hand*, 3–54; and, especially, Victoria Kahn, *Machiavellian Rhetoric: From the Counter-Reformation to Milton* (Princeton, 1994), 167–241.

7. All quotations from Milton's poetry are cited parenthetically from, *John Milton: Complete Poems and Major Prose*, ed. Merritt Y. Hughes (New York, 1957).

8. Aristotle, *On Rhetoric: A Theory of Civic Discourse*, trans. George A. Kennedy (Oxford, 1991), 1.14:1355b.

9. Milton was among the first to charge that *Eikon Basilike* was a forgery, and the debate raged throughout the seventeenth and eighteenth centuries. Francis F. Madan has shown definitively that John Gauden, later Bishop of Exeter and then of Worcester, composed *Eikon Basilike* from a collection of Charles's papers (*A New Bibliography of the Eikon Basilike* [Oxford, 1950], 126–63). The question of the authenticity of the book is not at issue in this essay, which will treat the author King Charles as a figure created by the rhetoric of the book.

10. Sharon Achinstein describes such moments as "Milton's rhetorical opportunism, that is, the political choices he made at different times during the course of a terrifying turbulent period" (*Milton and the Revolutionary Reader* [Princeton, 1994], 225). Her phrase, "rhetorical

opportunism," has unfortunate negative overtones, but her suggestion that we acknowledge the political contingencies that produced Milton's works coincides with my argument here.

11. Marvell, "An Horatian Ode upon Cromwel's Return from Ireland,"*The Poems and Letters of Andrew Marvell*, ed. H. M. Margoliouth, 3d ed., vol. 1 (Oxford, 1971), 91–94, ll. 53–54, 26, 66.

12. [Peter Heylyn,] *A Short View of the Life and Reign of King Charles (The second Monarch of Great Britain) from his Birth to his Burial*, printed in *Reliquiae Sacrae Carolinae. The Workes of that Great Monarch and Glorious Martyr King Charles the Ist. both Civil and Sacred. With A short view of the Life and Reign of that most blessed Prince from his Birth to his Buriall* (The Hague, 1648 [i.e., London, 1658]), 89–90. *A Short View* was also published separately in London in 1658. *Reliquiae Sacrae Carolinae* is one of the expanded editions of *Eikon Basilike* and appeared in several, often markedly different, versions beginning in 1650 (though some editions also carry a false imprint of 1648). The ninety-six page *Short View*, which covers events through 1654, is a late addition and reflects the tendency of the editions of the late 1650s to outweigh the text of *Eikon Basilike* with supporting material; the book becomes a fetishized reliquary of the king's remains. See Madan, 69–78.

13. Critics have rightly seen the influence of Foxe's *Acts and Monuments* in the literary prehistory of the king's book, though I suggest that the life of Mary Queen of Scots supplements the Foxean tradition and enables the imagination of a truly *royal* tragedy for the house of Stuart. See Elizabeth Skerpan Wheeler, "*Eikon Basilike* and the rhetoric of self-representation," in *The Royal Image: Representations of Charles I*, ed. Thomas N. Corns (Cambridge, 1999), 130–31, 136; and Skerpan [Wheeler], *The Rhetoric of Politics in the English Revolution, 1642–1660* (Columbia, Mo., 1992), 103–4. For Knoppers, defeating Charles's claims to the Foxean martyrological tradition is the goal of *Eikonoklastes* (*Historicizing Milton*, 17–28).

14. Roy Strong, *Van Dyck: Charles I on Horseback* (New York, 1972), 29.

15. The following account of the trial and execution of Mary Queen of Scots is derived from T. B. Howell, ed., *Complete Collection of State Trials*, vol. 1 (London, 1816), 1161–1228; and Robert Wyngfield, "An Account of the Execution of Mary, Queen of Scots," *The Clarendon Historical Society's Reprints*, Series II (Edinburgh, 1884–86), 251–62.

16. The following account of the trial and execution of Charles I is derived from C. V. Wedgewood, *A Coffin for King Charles: The Trial and Execution of Charles I* (New York: Macmillan, 1964).

17. For the king's refusal to recognize the Court and their subsequent summary verdict, see Roger Lockyer, ed., *The Trial of Charles I* (London, 1974), 86–91. The best and fullest account of the political maneuvers that paved the way to the king's execution is David Underdown, *Pride's Purge: Politics in the Puritan Revolution* (Oxford, 1971).

18. Under the act 33 Hen. VIII c. 12, a refusal to enter a plea in a treason case was treated as if the accused had answered "guilty." John Bellamy, *The Tudor Law of Treason: An Introduction* (London, 1979), 139–40.

19. Quotations are taken from *Eikon Basilike. The Povrtraictvre of His Sacred Maiestie in His Solitvdes and Svfferings* (London, 1648/49), the first edition, second issue.

20. The text to the engraving follows (my translation):

"THE PERSECUTIONS AGAINST CATHOLICS AROUSED BY
THE CALVINIST PROTESTANTS IN ENGLAND."
After various misfortunes of wretches and heaps of innocent victims,
The companion, mother, sister, and most faithful wife of kings
Tops off the spectacle with her martyrdom.
In her crown, she once shone brightly from the Scottish shores,

But in heaven she shines brighter: from now on a crown
Of blood is hers forever, and vengeance for the abominable ax.

21. "Crowds, Carnival, and the State in English Executions, 1604–1868," in *The First Modern Society: Essays in English History in Honour of Lawrence Stone*, ed. A. L. Beier, David Cannadine, and James M. Rosenheim (Cambridge, 1989).

22. Tellingly, today in Edinburgh's Holyrood Palace, still an odd monument to Stuart loyalism, a room is arranged to display "Relics" of Mary Queen of Scots and King Charles. The dedicated royalists who first put the display together featured jewel-encrusted reliquaries containing handkerchiefs soaked in Charles's martyred blood; for Mary, they had to settle for a few pieces of her embroidery. Works of her hands are the only traces left of her body.

23. For example, many editions omit "His Majesties Reasons against the pretended Jurisdiction of the high Court of Justice." As a theoretical assault upon the court, this stirring challenge is superfluous, though some editors may have chosen to include it as part of the *Eikon Basilike* because it portrays Charles as a man of conscience, courage, and integrity. The publication of the Henderson papers, letters giving Charles's defense of an episcopal Protestant church, might appear to be another exception to this emphasis on the private character of Charles. Nonetheless, those letters fit the Anglican polemicists' attempt to create in Charles their own image of a martyr. They are assimilating his devotion to the episcopacy to his general religious character, making the two inseparable. Likewise, although the later editions of the *Reliquiae Sacrae* give a somewhat fuller representation of Charles as a king, most of the texts chosen for inclusion demonstrate either his private character or his devotion to the episcopal church.

24. Wheeler, *"Eikon Basilike," The Royal Image*, 122–40.

25. See, for example, A[nthony] W[eldon], *The Court and Character of King James* (London, 1650), 103. The commendatory poem to the sequel, *The Court and Character of King James. Whereunto is now added The Court of King Charles* (London, 1651), uses phrases like "Tricks of State" to epitomize the book's theme of *nescit dissimulare*.

26. On the influence of popish plot theories on the development of the conflict between King and Parliament, see Caroline M. Hibbard, *Charles I and the Popish Plot* (Chapel Hill, 1983), especially the suggestions in her appendix, "The Plot Tradition and Civil War Historiography," 239–47. Peter Lake has confirmed the importance of the logic of antipopery in producing the Civil War in "Anti-Popery: the Structure of a Prejudice," in *Conflict in Early Stuart England: Studies in Religion and Politics 1603–1642*, ed. Richard Cust and Ann Hughes (London and New York, 1989), 72–106. Using these findings, Sharon Achinstein has outlined the importance of the popish-plot interpretation of history and Charles's identification with Counter-Reformation politics to Milton's portrayals of the King, in "Milton and King Charles," *The Royal Image*, ed. Corns, 141–61.

27. David Loewenstein has shown that whatever the accuracy of revisionist accounts of King Charles, radical writers of the 1640s and 1650s believed him to be "a master of political dissimulation, prevarication and treachery . . . a manifestation of treacherous Machiavellian designs to subvert fundamental laws, to destroy parliaments as well as the liberties and rights of his subjects, and to introduce arbitrary government and unlimited power in church and state." They then used this imagery to radically question the structure of Commonwealth society and government. ("The King among the Radicals: Godly Republicans, Levellers, Diggers and Fifth Monarchists," *The Royal Image*, ed. Corns, 97).

28. As Alison Shell demonstrates, the English Protestant imagination makes the unveiling of Papist dissembling and dissimulation the basis of anti-Catholic writing. *Catholicism, Controversy and the English Literary Imagination, 1558–1660* (Cambridge, 1999), 23–55.

29. "Several Verses made by diverse Persons upon His Majesties Death," in *Reliquiae Sacrae Carolinae*, 2 vols. (Hague [i.e., London], 1650), 2: 353.

30. To counter Catholic campaigns in Mary's favor, William Cecil, Elizabeth's chief minister, oversaw the publication of her letters in the pamphlet, [George Buchanan], *Ane Detectiovn of the duinges of Marie Quene of Scottes* ([London], 1572). He also prepared editions in Latin and French. On the publication of these pamphlets and the Elizabethan propaganda campaign against Mary, see James E. Phillips, *Images of a Queen: Mary Stuart in Sixteenth-Century Literature* (Berkeley and Los Angeles, 1964), 61–68.

On the letter and the epistolary genre as both private expression and public evidence, see Patterson, *Censorship and Interpretation: The Conditions of Writing and Reading in Early Modern England* (Madison, 1984), 9, 203–32; on the publication of Charles's letters as a formative moment in the development of royalist coded writing, see Lois Potter, *Secret Rites and Secret Writing: Royalist Literature, 1641–1660* (Cambridge, 1989), 57–71.

31. Strong, *Van Dyck*, 29–31.

32. "A Deep Groan at the Funeral of the Incomparable and glorious Monarch CHARLS the first," *Reliquiae Sacrae Carolinae* (The Hague [London], 1650), 2: 357. Potter argues that seeing Christ in Marshall's frontispiece is a modern misreading popularized by Roy Strong, among others (*Secret Rites*, 160–61); however, this poem, as well as numerous others, shows that contemporary readers were looking for Christ in the image of Charles. Sermons like Richard Watson's *Regicidium Judaicum, or A Discourse, about the Jewes crucifying Christ, their King. With An Appendix, or supplement, upon the late murder of Ovr Blessed Soveraigne Charles The First* (The Hague, 1649) encouraged such interpretations by reading *Eikon Basilike* alongside the life of Christ.

33. As Loewenstein argues, *Eikon Basilike* presents history as unchanging, which encourages Milton to attack it by positing a vision of history with radical, iconoclastic breaks (Loewenstein, *Milton and the Drama of History: Historical Vision, Iconoclasm, and the Literary Imagination* [Cambridge, 1990], 51–73). See also Florence Sandler, "Icon & Iconoclast," in *Achievements of the Left Hand*, 160–84; Lana Cable, "Milton's Iconoclastic Truth," in *Politics, Poetics, and Hermeneutics*, 135–51.

34. On the link Puritan writing makes between Catholicism and idolatry, see Shell, *Catholicism, Controversy*, especially 32–36.

35. Sandler, "Icon," 172, 183.

36. Blackwood, *Histoire et Matryre de la Royne d'Escosse* (Paris, 1589), sig. Aiiijv.

37. See, for example, Wyngfield, "Account," 11; Nicolas Caussin, *The Holy Court in Five Tomes* (London, 1650), 5: 311.

38. Thomas Hawkins, the translator of the early volumes of *The Holy Court*, died in 1640. Robert Codrington, who was imprisoned in 1641 for publishing an elegy for the Earl of Strafford, is credited with completing this edition. See *Dictionary of National Biography*, ed. Leslie Stephen and Sidney Lee, 22 vols. (London, 1885–1901), s.v., hereafter designated as *DNB*.

39. See Caussin, *La Cour Sainte du R. Pere Nicolas Caussin, de la Compagnie de Jesus* (Brussels, 1664).

40. See Shell, *Catholicism, Controversy*, 168–87.

41. Watson served the royal court in exile and gave the sermon *Regicidium Judaicum* to Charles II shortly after the execution of his father (see *DNB*). He signs his *Historicall Collections* from Caen.

42. Richard Watson, *Historicall Collections Of Ecclesiastick Affairs In Scotland And Politick related to them, Including the Murder of the Cardinal of St. Andrews, And the Beheading of their Queen Mary in England* (London, 1657), sigs. A4v–A5.

43. Since the Scots shifted allegiances so often in the civil war, both regicides and royalists

virulently attack them for causing the civil war and revolution. While royalists like Sanderson and Watson blame them for being the original of Presbyterian radicalism, regicides and Independents frequently attack the Scots for being the homeland and origin of the tyrannical Stuarts. Anthony Weldon, for instance, ends his *Cat May look upon a King* (London, 1652) with an attack upon the Union of the two crowns and an exhortation to reduce Scotland to an English province.

44. *Basilikon Doron. Or His Maiesties Instructions to His Dearest Sonne, Henry the Prince* (London, 1603), 33, 32, emphasis mine.

45. P. Hume-Brown, *George Buchanan: Humanist and Reformer* (Edinburgh, 1890), 269, 325–26; I. D. MacFarlane, *Buchanan* (London, 1981), 436–37.

46. D. R. Woolf gives the best recent account of the controversy in *The Idea of History in Early Stuart England: Erudition, Ideology, and "The Light of Truth" from the Accession of James I to the Civil War* (Toronto, 1990), 117–25. See also Hugh Trevor-Roper, *Queen Elizabeth's First Historian: William Camden and the Beginnings of English "Civil History"* (London, 1971); Kevin Sharpe, *Sir Robert Cotton 1586–1631: History and Politics in Early Modern England* (Oxford 1979), 84–110; and Wallace T. MacCaffrey, introduction to *The History of the Most Renowned and Victorious Princess Elizabeth, Late Queen of England [Selected Chapters]* by William Camden (Chicago, 1960), xxxv–xxxviii.

47. *The Tryall of Charles the I. King of England, In the Great Hall at Westm. Jan. 20. 1648*, in *Reliquiae Sacrae Carolinae* (Hague, 1648 [i.e., London, 1658]), 70, 71.

48. As Merritt Hughes notes, Milton is paraphrasing Buchanan's account in *Rerum Scoticarum Historia* of a speech that the Earl of Morton, regent for the infant James VI, gave to Elizabeth in 1571 (*YP* 3:226). This defense of the deposition shares many of the ideas of Buchanan's *De Iure regni apud Scotos*. As Hugh Trevor-Roper has shown, Buchanan himself probably wrote the speech, making it one of the earliest formulations of his political theories (*George Buchanan and the Ancient Scottish Constitution* [London, 1966], 1–16).

49. Corns, *Uncloistered Virtue*, 208.

50. See Mary's self-defense as recorded in Howell, *State Trials*, 1161–228. These arguments reappear in the main Catholic defenses of the executed queen such as Adam Blackwood, *Martyre De La Royne D'Escosse* . . . (Edinburgh [i.e., Paris], 1587), Robert Turner, *Maria Stuarta, Regina Scotia* . . . (Ingolstadt, 1588), and Romoaldus Scotus, *Svmmarivm Rationvm* . . . (Ingolstadt, 1588). The latter two pamphlets were republished together in 1627 as companion pieces to Peter Hennigan's *Vera et Sincera Historia Schismatis Anglicani* (Cologne, 1628), part of a German Catholic propaganda campaign during the Thirty Years' War. This suggests the enduring resonance of Mary's story during the religious conflicts of the seventeenth century, as well as the continued activity of Scottish Catholic exiles.

51. According to the report of the execution sent by Robert Wyngfield to Lord Burghley, Mary demanded that her servants witness the execution so "that their Eyes and Harts maye see witness how patiently their Queen and Mistriss would endure hir Execution, and so make Relation when they came into their Country, that shee dyed a trewe constant Catholique to hir Religion" (Wyngfield, 257).

52. On the relationship between antitheatricality and iconoclasm in *Eikonoklastes*, see Loewenstein, *Milton and the Drama of History*, 51–73. Knoppers also reads *Eikonoklastes* as an attack upon Charles's "false, theatrical martyrdom" (*Historicizing Milton*, 27). As Wayne A. Rebhorn has shown, early modern rhetoricians and their critics both equated false rhetoric with the theatrical. *The Emperor of Men's Minds: Literature and the Renaissance Discourse of Rhetoric* (Ithaca, 1995), 208–9.

53. John R. Knott sees Milton attacking a theatrical and hence false martyrdom in this allusion to Mary Queen of Scots ("'Suffering for Truths sake': Milton and martyrdom," in *Politics, Poetics, and Hermeneutics*, 162). Potter makes a similar point by pairing Milton's attack

upon Mary Queen of Scots with his attack upon Pamela's prayer. She concludes that Milton labels Charles as "an actor in three senses; a hypocrite, whose actions contradicted his pious words; a mere formal mouthpiece of rituals and words which he had not made truly his own; and an effeminate puppet, not only controlled by women but modelling his language and behaviour on theirs" (Potter, 183–84).

54. As Thomas N. Corns has shown, *Eikonoklastes* answers the rich language and imagery of the king's book with a comparatively "leaner style" (*The Development of Milton's Prose Style* [Oxford, 1982], 87–88). I would add that this is a style that *seems* less rhetorical, but in fitting style to matter, Milton is doing exactly what his study of rhetoric has taught him to do.

55. As Kahn notes, Milton and the republicans struggled to protect their belief that success was a sign of divine favor from a cynical conclusion that would justify any successful use of force. They do so in part by turning to a distinction between true persuasion and coercion. Kahn, *Machiavellian Rhetoric*, 148–56.

56. In *Areopagitica*, Milton has Guyon's Palmer accompany him during the temptation in the Cave of Mammon, "that he might see and know, and yet abstain" (*YP* 2:516). His argument in the revised allegory is that you need to carry your knowledge with you as you encounter trials of your temperance. Spenser, however, requires that one experience temptation on one's own, relying on educational experience and habit (*Faerie Queene* 2.7.2).

57. On the ethical differences between the two poets as demonstrated by *Areopagitica*'s rewriting of Spenser's Cave of Mammon, see Ernest Sirluck, "Milton Revises *The Faerie Queene*," *Modern Philology* 48 (1950): 90–96.

58. See John D. Staines, "Elizabeth, Mercilla, and the Rhetoric of Propaganda in Spenser's *Faerie Queene*," *Journal of Medieval and Early Modern Studies* 31 (2001): 283–312.

59. In Book One, for example, Spenser describes Archimago's "charmes and hidden artes" (1.45.1) and Duessa's "charmes and magicke might" (2.42.4). On Archimago as the figure of the diabolic, charming artist, see James Nohrnberg, *The Analogy of "The Faerie Queene"* (Princeton, 1976), 103 and passim.

60. R[obert] C[ecil], *The Copie of a Letter to the Right Honorable the Earle of Leycester* (London, 1586). On Lord Burghley's role in the editing and publication of *The Copie of a Letter*, see J. E. Neale, *Elizabeth I and Her Parliaments*, 2 vols. (New York, 1966), 2:129–31. For a full account of Spenser's ironic use of Elizabethan propaganda, see Staines, "Elizabeth, Mercilla, and the Rhetoric of Propaganda."

61. Patterson, *Reading Between the Lines*, 43–46.

62. Critics agree that *equity* (Aristotle's *epieikeia*) is the central unifying concept of the moral allegory of Book Five. See James E. Phillips, "Renaissance Concepts of Justice and the Structure of *The Faerie Queene*, Book V," *The Huntington Library Quarterly* 33 (1970), 103–20; Frank Kermode, *Shakespeare, Spenser, Donne*, (London, 1971), 50–59; W. Nicholas Knight, "The Narrative Unity of Book V of *The Faerie Queene*: 'That Part of Justice Which Is Equity,'" *Review of English Studies*, New Series 21 (1970), 267–94; Jane Aptekar, *Icons of Justice: Iconography and Thematic Imagery in Book V of "The Faerie Queene"* (New York, 1969), 87–124; Angus Fletcher, *The Prophetic Moment: An Essay on Spenser* (Chicago, 1971), 276–87; and Andrew Hadfield, *Edmund Spenser's Irish Experience: Wilde Fruit and Salvage Soyl* (Oxford, 1997), 146–84. As a corrective to this received opinion, I argue that Spenser repeatedly draws attention to the rhetorical construction of equity.

63. ". . . iudicare, quid dicendum, quid dissimulandum, quid declinandum, mutandum, fingendum etiam sit." *Institutio Oratoria*, trans. H. E. Butler, Loeb Classical Library (London, 1923), 12.8.5.

64. I would extend this criticism to Bloom's reading of the Palmer revision, a mistake that is surely not the result of an Oepidal conflict but of Milton's rhetorical needs subtly twisting his

memory (*A Map of Misreading* [Oxford, 1975], 128). Bloom's work sets the terms in which recent literary historians have approached Milton and his tradition. Other innovative contributions that follow Bloom's lead include Quilligan's *Milton's Spenser* and John Guillory's *Poetic Authority: Spenser, Milton, and Literary History* (New York, 1983).

65. "Spenser and British Imperialism," rpt. in *The Works of Edmund Spenser, A Variorum Edition*, ed. Edwin Greenlaw et al., 11 vols. (Baltimore, 1932–57), 5.303–10. It is important to note that this version of Lord Burghley, which derives from Conyers Read's biography, has been tempered by recent attention to Burghley's sincere religious beliefs. See Malcolm R. Thorp, "Catholic Conspiracy in Early Elizabethan Foreign Policy," *Sixteenth Century Journal* 15 (1984): 433; Michael A. R. Graves, *Burghley: William Cecil, Lord Burghley* (London, 1998), 169–88.

66. "The Masks of Duessa: Spenser, Mary Queen of Scots, and James VI," *ELR* 17 (1987): 242.

67. Even the figure Zele who greets Redcross at the entrance to the House of Holiness is a sort of orator, albeit one who manages to match his speech to his inner convictions: "His name was *Zele*, that him right well became, / For in his speeches and behauiour hee / Did labour liuely to expresse the same . . . " (I.x.6.7–8).

68. Stavely, *The Politics of Milton's Prose Styles* (New Haven, 1975), 84–92; Zwicker, *Lines of Authority: Politics and English Literary Culture, 1649–1689* (Ithaca, 1993), 39–59.

69. For a brief overview of this rhetorical tradition, with its roots in both Pauline and Aristotelian thought, see Kathy Eden, *Hermeneutics and the Rhetorical Tradition: Chapters in the Ancient Legacy & Its Humanist Reception* (New Haven, 1997).

70. Most of the allusions to a talionic Spenser seem to come from the early 1640s, including a reference to *The Shepheardes Calender* in *Animadversions* (1641), two references to *A View of the Present State of Ireland* in the *Commonplace Book* (dated 1642–44 by Ruth Mohl [*YP* 1:465, 496]), and a reference to a bloody scene from *The Faerie Queene* in Book One of *The History of Britain* (probably written before 1645). Cf. Patterson's accounting (*Reading Between the Lines*, 41–6).

DE DOCTRINA CHRISTIANA AND
THE QUESTION OF AUTHORSHIP

Michael Lieb
for Lauren

I

E VER SINCE WILLIAM B. HUNTER challenged the notion of Milton's authorship of the *De Doctrina Christiana*, charges and countercharges have been the order of the day. Those siding with Hunter—and there are not many—maintain that either the authorship is that of another individual entirely or that Milton's role in the production of the treatise is minimal at best. Those in the opposing camp maintain unequivocally that Milton did indeed author the work and that to question its canonicity is at the very least a distraction and at most an errancy amounting to something like heresy. As much as these Miltonic faithful might wish to dismiss Hunter's findings with remarkably little fuss, he keeps coming back to haunt the world of Milton scholarship like the little man who wasn't there.[1] Whatever can be "proven" about the nature of Milton's participation in the production of the *De Doctrina Christiana*, Hunter has performed an invaluable service by reopening the whole issue of authorship. Like it or not, scholars will be obliged to engage the issue anew for generations to come. My take on the issue is to argue that the attempt to prove or disprove Miltonic authorship is misguided. Given the information currently at our disposal, I do not think we shall ever know conclusively whether or not Milton authored all of the *De Doctrina Christiana*, part of it, or none of it.[2] That uncertainty suits me just fine, for it leaves open the possibility of speculating not only on the whole question of what it means to have "authored" a work such as the theological treatise in the first place, but also on the way in which the phenomenon of authorship is to be understood as the result of considering the genesis, recovery, and publication of this so-called posthumous work.[3]

To address the question of authorship, I pursue how the perception of "the author" is shaped by those who demand that a single great figure be responsible for the theological treatise, a figure forged in the imaginations of the Miltonic faithful. By rehearsing the genesis, recovery, and publication of the *De Doctrina Christiana* I consider the treatise as a distinctly physical document, the nature of which is deeply implicated in the assumptions about authorship that its readers bring to it. The issue of whether the ideas evinced in the treatise are consistent with or antipathetic to those evinced in Milton's other works is not of immediate concern.[4] Rather, I am interested in how the treatise became the focus of what might be called "narratives of authorship" from the point of its alleged production to the point of its discovery and subsequent publication. These narratives represent a means of understanding the way in which the identity of the author resides as much in those people who are responsible for producing the document that has come down to us as it does in the individual whose name appears to be inscribed on the document as the signature of authorship but whose actual identity remains ultimately elusive.

As scholars have come to realize, nothing about the *De Doctrina Christiana* can be taken for granted. This fact proves significant as a reflection of the problems with which one is faced in a consideration of the many issues that beset the treatise, among them the presence of the author's name. Anyone who consults only the published versions of the treatise (as opposed to the manuscript itself) is already in trouble, for these versions lead the reader immediately to believe that the author is clearly and indisputably the individual whose name appears in large bold print both in the Latin original and in the English translation. Thus, in the published versions, we encounter "IOANNES MILTONVS ANGLVS" (for the Latin original) and "JOHN MILTON ENGLISHMAN" (for the English translation). This is the form that appears as a heading to the prefatory epistle, which concludes with the initials "I. M." (in the Latin) and "J. M." (in the English). As a heading to the opening of the first book of the treatise, the name is reiterated in its genitival form, "IOANNIS MILTONI ANGLI."[5] In response to these bold declarations of authorship in the published versions, we are prompted to ask whether there can be any doubt whose treatise this is. The answer is most definitely yes. One needs only to examine the manuscript of the *De Doctrina Christiana* (designated hereafter as SP 9/61) to gain a sense of just how uncertain are the circumstances surrounding the presence of the name as it is transcribed both as a heading to the prefatory epistle and as a heading to the opening of book one.

Even a cursory glance at SP 9/61 confirms that the name (in both occurrences) was almost certainly not part of the manuscript as originally transcribed.[6] For the small block capitals in which the name is written are (not to put too fine a point on it) "squeezed in above what would otherwise be the top line of the text."[7] Such signatory evidence strongly suggests that the manuscript in its present form had been transcribed *before* the name was inserted. By whom, at what time, and under what circumstances are facts that are simply not known. One might think of the name almost as an interlineation (a prominent feature of much of the manuscript itself). The less that is known about who inserted the name in small block characters, the more heated the debate becomes.[8] The point is that the insertion of the name represents what might be called "author-creation," a "forging" (in both senses of that term) of identity by an individual determined that the treatise not be dismissed as anonymous, or, more accurately, that it be construed as authored by John Milton, a name that enjoys universal recognition. Whether or not the name "IOANNES MILTONVS ANGLVS" is in fact a stamp that proclaims the true identity of the author is of little moment here. What is important is the way in which that stamp makes its presence known. In the manuscript, it does so in a manner that immediately raises a suspicion of its genuineness. If it were a coin, one would be inclined to bite it to make certain it is legal tender. I suggest not only that the manuscript as originally transcribed was anonymous, but that the name forged to designate its authorship must be viewed as a supplement to a text that otherwise is nameless.[9] The very signatures of authorship prompt us to question precisely what that concept means when applied to the *De Doctrina Christiana*. Unlike the manuscript, the published editions preclude any possibility that the presence of the name gives rise to such considerations. By virtue of the way in which the name appears on the printed page, they affirm that there is but one author: JOHN MILTON ENGLISHMAN.

In keeping with the uncertainties surrounding the presence of the author's name in the manuscript, there is an additional factor to be considered. This factor is an extension of the second, genitival reference to the author's name as "IOANNIS MILTONI ANGLI." Genitival of what? The answer, of course, is that which has customarily been conceived as the title proper, transcribed as a heading to the first book of the treatise: "*De Doctrina Christiana ex sacris duntaxat libris petita disquisitionum libri duo posthumi*" (CM 14:16; SP 9/61, 7).[10] The use of *posthumi* in the title (particularly its placement as the final word) brings to the fore an issue of major import to an understanding of the question of authorship. This is the issue of provenance, an issue already destabilized by the so-called posthumous nature of the production of the treatise. The word *posthumi* begins to tell the tale. By definition, that which is posthumi (also *postumus*, "coming after, next") refers to those born after the death of their father.[11] According to an erroneus (but telling) etymology, "posthumous" is also that which is "unearthed" after it has been buried (post-humus).[12] There are fascinating stories of Milton's own disinterment more than a century after his death.[13] The theological treatise was also "unearthed" many years after its interment. It too, then, is posthumous in the sense of being post-humus. Whether as posthumus or as posthumus, the *De Doctrina Christiana* is a work that calls attention to its posthumous identity in the very title through which it makes itself known. Implicit in this self-identification is the fact of its belatedness (its "coming after") and what will be its disinterment in the centuries following its burial.

The ironies that arise from this act of self-identification serve to heighten an already problematic situation. This situation is further compounded by the explanation that Charles R. Sumner, the first translator of the treatise, provides in his "Preliminary Observations" to the *De Doctrina Christiana* in 1825. According to Sumner, this treatise "was originally intended" by its author "to be a posthumous publication." "The reproaches to which its author had been exposed in consequence of opinions contained in his early controversial writings have induced him to avoid attracting the notice of the public, during the ascendancy of his political opponents, by a frank avowal of his religious sentiments."[14] The implications of Sumner's explanation are fascinating: they suggest that the author has inscribed the fact of his own impending death in the very title of his work. It is perfectly acceptable to have authored a work that is designated by others as posthumous, but it is quite another thing for a living author to declare his or her own work as posthumous. To do so is to proclaim one's demise as a defining characteristic of authorship.

Although I do not concur with this idea, I think it important to note that the work was viewed in this manner from the very outset. The idea appears to have proven rather unsettling to John Carey and Maurice Kelley (the translator and the editor, respectively, of the Yale University Press edition of the treatise). In their edition, they respond to the dilemma by omitting the term *posthumi* from the title altogether. When in doubt, leave it out. To justify what amounts to an unjustifiable omission, they explain that *posthumi* is not part of the original title. They contend that a discernible punctuation mark in the manuscript—specifically, a period—after the term *duo* provides evidence that the title concludes with that term. "*Posthumi* is a later addition to the title (YP 6:124, n. 1)."[15] William B. Hunter concurs in a reading based not on the presence of a punctuation mark after the term *duo* but on the spacing (or lack of it) after *duo*."[16] If Milton's name is "squeezed in above" the text as a heading to the prefatory epistle and to book one, *posthumi* is "squeezed in beside" the text of the inscribed title. Clearly, the presence of *posthumi* needs to be explained somehow. The complications wrought by *posthumi*, then, compound an already problematic situation.[17] For this is a work that not only registers the death of its author as a fact of its production but, as we have seen, ultimately implies that the name of the author has been inserted marginally in a document that is otherwise anonymous. This is a work in which its posthumous state is further underscored by the fact of its anonymity. Posthumous and anonymous: I can think of no better way than that of considering the question of authorship in a work that has come to be known as the *De Doctrina Christiana*.

I say come to be known as because there are those who argue that the very title *De Doctrina Christiana* may have been imposed upon the treatise by someone other than the original author.[18] Whether or not there is evidence to support this contenton, one must note that, shortly after its discovery, the work was known not as the *De Doctrina Christiana* but as the *De Dei Cultu*, which appears to be the title of the second book of the treatise.[19] The Parliament under George IV used this title in its deliberations over whether the treatise should be published in the first place.[20] Had the work not been published with the title by which it is presently known, *De Dei Cultu* is the name we might have been calling the treatise to this day. It is entirely understandable that the "mistake" of calling the work *De Dei Cultu* might have occurred, for one must acknowledge that the manuscript itself does not immediately indicate precisely what the title is.

To discover the title (assuming that it is the title), one must take the trouble to move beyond the prefatory epistle to the heading of the first book, which, as indicated, is *De Doctrina Christiana ex sacris duntaxat libris petita disquisitionum libri duo posthumi*, a phrase preceded by the cramped insertion IOANNIS MILTONI ANGLI. This, one assumes, is clearly the title of the work as a whole; on the other hand, the first book (designated *Liber primus*) of the treatise lacks its own title, in contrast to the second book (designated *Liber secundus*), which is assigned the title *Dei cultu*.[21] To discover the title of the first book, we must consult the first chapter, which informs us that Christian doctrine is divided into two parts: faith, or the knowledge of God, and charity, or the worship of God ("Partes doctrinae Christianae duae sunt: Fides seu Cognitio Dei, et charitas seu Dei cultu") (SP 9/61, 8; cf. 462).[22] If the title of the second book is *Dei cultu*, then, might the title of *Cognitio Dei* be assigned to the first book (which otherwise lacks a title)? It is not immediately clear, then, how nomenclature functions in the manuscript. These circumstances are totally at odds with the published versions, which set titles in a manner that precludes any possibility of uncertainty. The point of all this is that we think we know the title of the work as much as we think we know the author of the work. In both instances perhaps we do, but we must also be aware that behind this knowledge lurks the unsettling specter of assumption. At some deep level "title" and "author" are constructed from a reader's presuppositions, a process having profound implications for an understanding of the work we have come to know as the *De Doctrina Christiana*.[23] A posthumous work by a posthumous author, the theological treatise invites us to address the whole question of authorship with a renewed sense of mission, one that takes into account both the profound uncertainties and complexities of the text.[24]

Whoever the author is, one fact is clear: he certainly takes the trouble to make his presence known in the prefatory epistle. What emerges is a figure whose sense of self and whose voice are distinctly "Miltonic." The discourse of selfhood in which the author engages is one with which we are all familiar. Almost as if dutifully recounting "in strictest measure eev'n"[25] the process by which the treatise took shape, the author provides an account of the journey (with both its advances and retreats) he undertook to produce the treatise. There appear to be three stages that follow upon an initial or formative stage of preparation, one that involves the childhood study of Scriptures in their original languages. With that under his belt, he first methodically examined the shorter theological systems available to him. Doing so, he compiled a series of commonplaces (the so-called locos communes), comprised of the appropriate biblical texts that would serve to support his beliefs. This was the first stage. As he gained confidence, he then took account of the various complex arguments that distinguished more diffuse volumes of divinity. This was perhaps the second stage. He abandoned that enterprise as unproductive because it relied on the views of those who (for him) were themselves misguided. Nonetheless, he was entirely convinced of the necessity of having at his disposal "a systematic exposition of Christian teaching" as an aid to both faith and memory. Accordingly, he made "a fresh start" and, as the result of assiduous study, next compiled his systematic exposition for his own sake. In this way, he "laid up provision" for that time of judgment when he would be called upon to provide an "account" of his "beliefs" (YP 6:119–21). This was the third stage. I hedge my bets in the enumeration of these stages, because it is quite possible to conceive them differently.

No matter: at issue is not the number of stages but the manner in which they are presented. In the author's account of orderly proceeding, there emerges a sense of a life kept in check by one who controls his destiny, who has everything well in hand. It is a narrative we have heard many times (in fact, repeatedly) in Milton's works, ranging from the antiprelatical tracts to the defenses. Here, as elsewhere, the main features of the narrative are growth, maturation, and a coming to wisdom through which one gains renewed insight into his vocation. Laying up provision for the final judgment resonates in Milton's ever-present concern with "all-judging *Jove* / As he pronounces lastly on each deed."[26] A studious pursuit of the highest truths from one's earliest years is a hallmark of the Miltonic personality, one through which the author portrays himself driven by a fierce independence, unencumbered by secondary aids. Accompanying this development is a compulsion to recount the events of his life, to "justify" himself before those who might otherwise view him critically. His fit audience, moreover, is made up of his peers: "learned," as well as "strong-minded men who thoroughly understand the teaching of the gospel" (YP 6:122). To know Milton's works is indisputably to hear him addressing his reader in this epistle.

It is precisely this strong personality, however, that proceeds to erase itself in its account of the methodology it has adopted to conduct the argument. Thus, the author of the epistle makes it clear that his citations of biblical texts will not relegate the word of God to the margins (as is the case with so many other treatises of this type). Rather, the divine biblical word will be featured in the body of the text to speak for itself as the ultimate authority. What is conventionally conceived as the "proof-text," then, will be reconceived as "*the* text," that is, the core or primary text. Accordingly, the author maintains that he has "striven to cram [his] pages even to overflowing [ingerentibus redundare], with quotations drawn from all parts of the Bible and to leave as little space as possible for [his] own words" (YP 6:122; CM 14:10; SP 9/61, 3–4). This act of cramming one's pages to overflowing is one that gives new meaning to the notion of authorship, for in the very assertion of the authorial self, that entity is then paradoxically obliterated, erased, in order to give voice to the "overflowingness" (redundare) of the One True Author.

In the service of this ultimate authority, the author of the treatise conceives himself as a kind of amanuensis. He acts as God's scribe, one who is more than willing to leave as little space as possible for his own words so that the words of God-as-Author shall have their say. The author of the treatise, then, would have his own presence conceived as subsumed within the word of God and reinscribed in the text of God's great abundance. It goes without saying that the primacy of the biblical text is of paramount importance to such a conception, one that confirms the author's account of moving from an early reliance upon the authority of others to a realization of what he has known all along, that is, the efficacy of Scriptures as the true source of God's teachings and as the wellspring of His theology. This privileging of the biblical text is germane to everything that the author of the treatise holds dear. It is the foundation of his credo and the means by which he conducts his argument. At the same time, it underscores the notion of authorship as one in which the presence of the author becomes the means of embodying the presence of God Himself. The author is, in effect, the bearer, custodian, and interpreter of the word of God.[27] Under these circumstances, the prefatory epistle provides the opportunity for the author to offer a telling narrative of his own spiritual growth and maturation, to delineate the nature of his methodology, and to put forward his conception of authorship in the context of the One True Author whose word is made known through the citations that permeate the text. The author's regard for his accomplishment could not be greater. It is, he says, his "best," indeed, his "most precious" (qvibus melius aut pretiosius) possession (SP 9/61, 3).[28]

I examine the prefatory epistle in this manner because all the fuss that is being made about the question of authorship begins to be answered here. It is almost as if the author (whom I construe as at once the persona of John Milton and the anonymous figure who deliberately erases his name from the text by privileging the text of God) is responding implicitly to the debate. Embodied in the voice and in the presence of the author, the signature "IOANNES MILTONVS ANGLVS" is there, and then it is not. Now you see it; now you don't. It strikes us as authentic but then is erased by an examination of its own provenance, an examination that in itself raises more questions than it answers, as the author all but disappears from the text and replaces his presence with God's. The act of self-obliteration and of self-erasure speaks urgently to the question of authorship. It anticipates all those later arguments that were to arise (inevitably, I would say) from the disinterment of the body of the text from its hidden resting place. Is the corpus that of John Milton? The question was destined to be answered with a challenge, indeed, a series of challenges, because of the very dynamics of the text, one in which the author is first at pains to presence himself, only then to disappear. This is most certainly a text that teases us with its disappearing acts, a text riddled with conundrums and uncertainties, a text the canonicity of which calls itself into question in the very act of declaring who produced it and how it was produced. This is a declaration intimately bound up with the narratives of authorship surrounding the production, discovery, and transmission of the text. I propose here to examine those narratives as a way of gaining greater insight into how authorship is construed in them, what they imply about the idea of the author and his work, and the extent to which they highlight even further the essentially mysterious nature of the text that has come down to us. Accordingly, the manuscript itself (particularly in relation to the versions that have appeared in published form) will be a concern as an object that reinforces still further the sense of mystery with which the text known as the *De Doctrina Christiana* is imbued.

II

To some extent, we have already examined one narrative of authorship that addresses the issue of how the *De Doctrina Christiana* came into being, the author's own act of self-fashioning in the prefatory epistle to the treatise. Just as I have sought to divide that narrative into stages of various sorts, others have approached the narrative in a similar manner. The idea of stages is part

of the lore surrounding the genesis of the *De Doctrina Christiana*, a work
that already "stages" itself in its own opening narrative. In response to Arthur
Sewell's contention that there are three stages of composition, then, Maurice
Kelley confidently opts for two.[29] As an aspect of those two stages, it is
perfectly clear for Kelley that the *locos communes* of which the author speaks
in the prefatory epistle has its source in Milton's *Commonplace Book*, with its
cross-references to a "Theological Index" *(Indicem Theologicum)* now unfortunately lost (YP 6:16).[30] What results is the presencing of a lost work to
provide a basis for the rationale of "staging" the genesis of a work ultimately
anonymous. The act of staging through self-portrayal invites the pursuit of
corroboration wherever evidence can be found as scholars devise their own
narratives to connect two lives: that portrayed in the prefatory epistle with
that of Milton himself. This is not necessarily a misguided pursuit, but it is
one nonetheless that finds corroboration in documents (such as the *Indicem
Theologicum*) that do not exist. All this is in keeping with the sense of confidence provided by the "strictest measure eev'n" school of composition that
the author of the prefatory epistle fosters. It is from such a perspective that
scholars venture a chronology of the stages of composition. These range from
a period before 1641 to a variety of periods, including 1643–45, 1655–58,
1658–60, 1660 or later. In short, it is really not known precisely when (or
under what circumstances) the theological treatise was composed, that is,
assuming that Milton was in any sense the "author." What is known is that
Miltonists, even those entirely confident of Miltonic authorship, have dis-
agreed strongly in their assessment not only of the stages but the dates of
composition.[31]

Implicit in the process of ordering the production of the treatise is the
pervasive assumption that the name (and therefore the identity) of the author
is a matter of record. With that assumption intact, one may then find additional corroborative evidence in the narratives provided by the early biographies (or "lives") of Milton. These biographies are crucial to the cause of
Miltonic authorship of the *De Doctrina Christiana*. They include the "Minutes" of John Aubrey (1681); the *Anonymous Life* (probably early 1680s,
attributed to Milton's pupil and friend Cyriack Skinner); and the biographies
of Anthony à Wood (1691), Edward Phillips (1694), John Toland (1698),
and Jonathan Richardson (1734). Derived from interviews, from first-hand
knowledge, and from information that makes its way from one biography to
the next, these crucial (although at times flawed) accounts attest to the belief
that some sort of theological treatise occupied Milton at various times during
his career. Although the names that the biographies apply to this treatise
differ, the nature of the undertaking remains fairly consistent in the various
accounts. Accordingly, the biographies conceive the treatise under such di-

verse headings as an "Idea Theologiae" (Aubrey, Wood), a *"Body of Divinity out of the Bible"* (Anonymous Biographer, Wood, Richardson), and a "perfect System of Divinity" (Phillips, Toland).[32]

The extent to which each of these biographies is authoritative in its portrayal of Milton and his works depends upon the evidence employed.[33] One is inclined perhaps to lend greater credence to a biography that grounds its conclusions in first-hand experience than to one that derives its conclusions primarily from earlier biographies. Even conclusions drawn from first-hand experience, however, can be faulty if the biographer's memory is inaccurate or perhaps predisposed to recall events in a particular way. In dealing with each of the biographies, one must therefore be sensitive to the nature of its evidence and to its predilections. In the context of the theological treatise, the references in Wood, Toland, and Richardson are, according to William B. Hunter, of less moment than those of Aubrey, the Anonymous Biographer, and Phillips.[34] Each of the biographies, however, is important in its own right, and for each the existence of some sort of theological treatise in Milton's body of writings is a given.

Among the early biographies that allude to such a treatise, Edward Phillips's is perhaps the most germane. Arising from first-hand knowledge, his account of the period when a theological undertaking of some sort was to have actively engaged Milton has the ring of immediacy and even intimacy about it.[35] This is an account derived not from the observations of others but from the record of his personal memories of how he was tutored by his uncle shortly after Milton's return from his continental journey to France and Italy (1638–39).[36] John Phillips (Edward's younger brother) had already become part of Milton's household, and Edward followed after. Having begun his tutoring with only his two nephews, Milton was sufficiently successful to have his little school grow larger over time. It should come as no surprise that Phillips's account of the kind of schooling he received is reminiscent of the curriculum that Milton himself proposed in *Of Education* (1644). Phillips clearly takes a good deal of pride in his having read "the many Authors both of the Latin and the Greek" to which his uncle exposed him during his years as a student. Ranging from Cato, Varro, and Pliny (among the Latin authors) to Hesiod, Aratus, and Xenophon (among the Greek authors), this is indeed a formidable regimen.

For Phillips, the recitation of the regimen functions almost as a means to establish his authority to hold forth on the life of so learned a man as his uncle. In the establishment of that authority, Phillips goes so far as to suggest that in the very act of undertaking such a regimen for the benefit of his students, Milton as a teacher actually bettered himself: "Thus by teaching he in some measure increased his own knowledge, having the reading of all these Authors as if it were by Proxy."[37] This is a remarkable assertion, one that suggests the extent to which Phillips felt himself empowered by his uncle, who not only increased his own knowledge by teaching his students but who bestowed upon his students the honor and responsibility of acting as a "proxy" for their learned teacher. That is, the students assumed the responsibility of reading texts (aloud, it would seem) to those assembled for the sake of discussion and instruction. The use of the term "proxy" here is of particular moment, because it implies that the student has been elevated to the level of agent or procurator for one of higher office.[38] To extend this sense of authority still further, Phillips maintains that his uncle taught his students as warriors of sorts to "conquer" not only "the *Greek* and *Latin* Tongues" but the "chief Oriental Languages," including *"Hebrew, Chaldee,* and *Syriac"* as well. This undertaking provided students the wherewithal to read the biblical texts in the original. After glancing at the modern languages and texts that the students also studied, Phillips returns to the subject of the regimen involving mastery of the biblical languages. Here, he reconstructs his experience of reading Scriptures on Sunday and listening as his uncle engaged in a "Learned Exposition" of the particular text that was the subject of their reading for that day.[39] I have made a point carefully to follow Phillips's account, because the subtext of what he says has as much to do with his own empowerment as it does with the life of his uncle. One finds a climactic movement in the account, one in which the student is authorized to assume something of the role of teacher himself.

It is only at this pivotal point of learning and of power that Phillips turns to the matter of a theological treatise. His reflections on this work give rise to some issues of great moment: "The next work after this, was the writing from his own dictation, some part, from time to time, of a Tractate which he thought fit to collect from the ablest of Divines, who had written of that Subject; *Amesius, Wollebius,* &c. *viz.* A perfect System of Divinity, of which more hereafter."[40] The statement must be seen in the context of the discourse on the educational curriculum that Phillips outlines. That is, the reference to the treatise is framed by the regimen of mastering languages and authors both classical and modern and of becoming adept at interpreting the biblical text. From a reference to hearing Milton's "Learned Exposition" on Scriptures, the account moves to "the next work after this." This is the so-called "perfect System of Divinity," a treatise that must be seen as an integral part of Milton's curriculum. The method here apparently required students to transcribe what was dictated to them by their teacher. On the other hand, the production of the treatise must be viewed in light of the educational experience Milton's nephews sustained in their role as students.

The text (or texts) that these students produced in response to the dictation of their teacher must be conceived not simply as the result of verbatim transcription. Rather, what was transcribed by the students must be seen as the product of a knowledge in the making. That knowledge arose from the interchange between teacher and student, an interchange that was no doubt crucial to the curriculum from the very outset. This, I take it, is what Phillips means in his reference to reading "by Proxy." Assuming the function of procurator, the student not only reads by proxy but writes or transcribes by proxy. What is true of reading is true of writing: the student becomes the means by which the teacher increases his own knowledge. Phillips does not hesitate to make grand claims for the procuratorial role of the student. He maintains that a student fully engaged in the enterprise of learning with the same industry and thirst after knowledge as that of the teacher might very well "come near to the equalling of the Master."[41] To be sure, such an esti-mate idealizes the situation. The process of undergoing so ambitious a regi-men by young men "from Ten to Fifteen or Sixteen Years of Age" is "not a bow for every man to shoot" with who counts himself a student, and, at a tender age, one has far to go before acquiring the sinews of Ulysses with which to handle that bow.[42] Nonetheless, the view of empowerment as the result of such an educational experience has a lot to recommend it.

I emphasize what I have called the procuratorial dimensions of Phillips's account, because they are crucial to an understanding of his reference to Milton's "perfect System of Divinity." On the assumption that this "system" represents in some form a basis for the *De Doctrina Christiana*, it is clear that the theological treatise owes its production to what in effect began not only as a text for the instruction of students but as something of a collaborative undertaking between author and scribe. It is an undertaking that has been ably noted by Stephen B. Dobranski. Responding to the ongoing controversy concerning the authorship of the *De Doctrina Christiana*, Dobranski ob-serves that the controversy "has betrayed how little attention critics have de-voted to Milton's collaborative practice of writing." Those who argue either "for or against attributing the work to Milton have sometimes been impaired by too strict adherence to a post-Romantic conception of the author."[43] Al-though the phrase "post-Romantic conception of the author" might give one pause, Dobranski is no doubt correct in calling attention to Milton's mode of authoring texts as a distinctly collaborative enterprise. That enterprise was already in evidence when Milton had his sight. This is not to suggest that he produced works only through collaboration. In the very account in which he speaks of Milton's method of having his students transcribe his texts, Phillips claims (on reflection) that his uncle might have preserved his "Eye-sight" had he adopted this method of composition even beyond the classroom. For Milton, as both a reader and a writer, "had been perpetually busied in his own

Laborious Undertaking of the Book or Pen," quite aside from the responsibilities he assumed as a teacher.[44] In short, not all is by collaboration and not all is by proxy. If the "perfect System of Divinity" is in any sense an early stage of what has come to be known as the *De Doctrina Christiana*, then these considerations must be taken into account in addressing the question of authorship.

The precise relationship between the "perfect System of Divinity" and the *De Doctrina Christiana* is, of course, a matter of conjecture. Having alluded to the tractate Milton dictated to his students "from time to time," Phillips promises to say "more hereafter," but, in what is no doubt among the most frustrating occurrences in all of literary history, he fails to deliver on his promise. The rest is silence: the nature of the hereafter must be taken on faith. Short of possessing any additional evidence of the link between the Miltonic "perfect System of Divinity" and the *De Doctrina Christiana*, one might well be prompted to bring closure to the uncertainties of the hereafter by devising a narrative of one's own. This I shall classify as a metanarrative of authorship. The most interesting of such metanarratives is that by William B. Hunter, who, in the very act of challenging the Miltonic authorship of the theological treatise, resorts to Phillips's account as a way of supplementing it with a tale of how the *De Doctrina Christiana* must have come into being in its earliest incarnation. It is through Hunter's metanarrative that we encounter the "true author" of the *De Doctrina Christiana*. As we shall see, the true author is allegedly one of Milton's own students, that is, one of his amanuenses. Hunter arrives at this ascription by rereading the word "dictation" ("The next work after this, was the writing from his own dictation, some part, from time to time, of a Tractate"). Although readers have assumed from this statement that Milton was using his students as scribes for his own treatise, in fact, what Milton was having them do was to produce not his own work but *their* work, their individual tractates. For Hunter, the word "dictation" here means not simply transcribing what is spoken but issuing an "authoritative direction."[45]

The idea is of interest to the reading I offer, because it extends the procuratorial role of the students to what might be considered outright authorship. Although I find Hunter's reading a bit tendentious, I share his desire to liberate Milton's students from the kind of "secretarial" role associated with the function of scribes. So liberated, these students (in Hunter's view) become authors to themselves.[46] He accordingly concludes that the *De Doctrina Christiana* began with Milton's "dictation" or direction to his students to compile their own religious digest or florilegium from the writings of the "ablest of Divines, who had written of that Subject; *Amesius, Wollebius,* & c.," supported by a gathering of pertinent biblical proof texts. For Hunter, this would represent something of the ur-text, later altered by a process of textual emendation. It is from this vantage point that Hunter invents a nameless author (a sort of Miltonic alter ego), who travels abroad to complete his education and, during his journey, assimilates the radical doctrines of continental authorities. These views, the "author" incorporates into his text.

After his journey, he returns home faithfully to England and to his "old teacher." With him, the radicalized author carries his "now much-elaborated schoolboy exercise," which is none other than a version of the theological treatise that has come down to us. The copy of the treatise that the author delivers to his teacher remains in Milton's possession until his death. Who this author is remains a matter of conjecture. "We can conclude," Hunter surmises, "that something happened to him: he died or left England, perhaps as a persona non grata" some time possibly after the Restoration. No doubt but that "the unknown author had been an esteemed friend of Milton" who "for some reason could no longer work on his great projected religious treatise." As an act of homage to this author, "Milton carefully preserved his manuscript and dictated over the years a considerable number of what he regarded as minor improvements." Milton may also have planned to publish the work "for which he no doubt assumed full responsibility."[47]

I recount Hunter's narrative of authorship not because I agree with it but because it calls into question the automatic association of author and work while fashioning a kind of phantom author who moves from one station to the next but who never really comes fully into being. For all practical purposes, he is transparent, void of personality, either exiled or dead. I like the fact that Hunter has him on the run, fleeing England, perhaps in disgrace: an adventuresome rogue of a fellow whose radical proclivities got him into trouble after the Restoration. It is all a fiction, of course, but it is a fiction with a purpose: that of interrogating what the Miltonic faithful are determined to see as the inevitable fate of the *De Doctrina Christiana*. This is a fate that imbues the theological treatise with a canonical legitimacy, one that brooks no possibility of unwarranted interventions by rogues that might threaten the good name of the one to whom it owes its true and indisputable authorship.

There is clearly more than a modicum of mischief in what Hunter has wrought, and one senses that he is aware of it. Nonetheless, his invention of a new, nameless author is refreshing in its willingness to entertain its own world of possibilities, ones (consciously or not) in keeping with the notion of the author as a construction, as that which is nameless and indeed ultimately deprived not only of identity but of life itself in the production of the text. By fashioning his own version of the author, Hunter has located the space left empty by the author's disappearance and (almost playfully) has filled the space with his own daring projection, his own construction of authorship. In short, he has invented a narrative of authorship to counter all other narratives that have been construed by the Miltonic faithful as entirely consistent with what is known about Milton's life and work. It is the nature of these narratives that will engage us here.

<h1 style="text-align:center">III</h1>

The narratives of authorship that the Miltonic faithful have fashioned are firmly grounded in the discovery and transmission of the manuscript called the *De Doctrina Christiana*. The story of the unearthing (bringing that which is "post-humus" to light) of the manuscript assumes the form of what I would call the romance. In its broadest terms, this is a mode in which the quest for truth is finally realized through a plot that exalts a hero able to make all things right. As the nearest of all narratives to that of wish fulfillment, the romance provides that closure which delights in the alleviation of all doubt and uncertainty of any sort. The romance portrays an ideal world enhanced by tales of adventure, discovery, and reclamation. Crucial to this world is an emphasis upon rank, title, and the power of destiny to reward the hero in his quest.[48] The ironies implicit in the application of this mode to the circumstances surrounding the discovery of the theological treatise will become evident as the narrative unfolds.

The courageous hero of the narrative is a librarian, one Robert Lemon, Sr., whose exalted title, that of Deputy Keeper of His Majesty's State Papers, is sufficiently daunting to ward off any who might question the veracity of his endeavors and to bestow an aura of authority to any task he elects to undertake.[49] Begun in 1818, the task at issue was that of systematically arranging for the Crown such critical documents as the royal letters, Irish and Scottish correspondence, and the Gunpowder Plot papers. These, as well as other documents, fell under Lemon's purview as Deputy Keeper. Laboring assiduously on this noble undertaking, Lemon made a remarkable discovery in November of 1823. As he worked his way methodically to the Middle Treasury Gallery in Whitehall, he came across two manuscripts buried in a large cupboard (or "press"), itself seated "at the bottom of one of the Presses at the end of the main room" of the Old State Paper Office. One was what has come to be known as the *De Doctrina Christiana* and, the second, what has come to be known as the Skinner Transcript of Milton's Letters of State.[50]

Lemon himself has provided invaluable accounts of his discovery.[51] These are significant not only for what they say about the circumstances of the discovery but also for the way in which the presumption of authenticity is already present in Lemon's own assessment of what he has discovered. In the case of the theological treatise, the quest (and I invoke this term deliberately) for the author is immediately realized by a perusal of the manuscript. As a result of that perusal, the Deputy Keeper of His Majesty's State Papers triumphs in the knowledge that the holy grail has been secured. The name of "Milton" is the key to the otherwise-hidden treasure. Thus, in an account titled "Milton's Posthumous Work" (January 1824), Lemon begins guardedly with what he acknowledges is essentially a presumption: "this valuable manuscript is *presumed to be* the long lost, posthumous, Theological Work of Milton" (italics mine). It doesn't take long, however, for the tone of cautious reserve to give way to one of complete assurance, as Lemon's "presumed to be" is transformed into a "most certainly is." Delighted with the import of his discovery, Lemon is careful to describe his first encounter with the manuscript as a "hidden" document: "wrapped in two or three sheets of printed paper," apparently proof sheets, the document is one that might never have come to light had Lemon not retrieved it. Alas, this document (given its importance) has not received the care it deserves, for "the outside cover," Lemon observes, is "a piece of torn, dirty, brown paper."[52] The document was obviously "cast off," and it is now up to Lemon to reclaim it for posterity. In this tale of discovery and reclamation, Lemon defies the gods: through his efforts, a long-lost work will be made available to the world. One is immediately taken with the sense of adventure and delight with which Lemon treats his quest. The accuracy of his account (and therefore the correctness of his conclusions) is attested by an appended affadavit, signed by Lemon's colleague Charles Lechmere and Lemon's son Robert.[53] Subsequent accounts by Lemon confirm the wholeness of the document, which Lemon declares "perfect, and complete in all its parts": "not a sentence, or even a single word has been discovered to be deficient."[54]

As the narrative of discovery broadens, it moves from the confines of the Old State Paper Office to the highest reaches of government. What in Lemon begins as "presumption" and culminates in certainty is heralded by the very powers of the state. Thus, the narrative unfolds in a manner that asserts not only the authenticity of the document but the towering status of its author as the national poet. In the context of the romance of authorship that plays itself out here, the two (authenticity and status) go hand in hand. Accordingly, we are told that Parliament itself took up the cause as an issue of national significance. There is no hint of presumption (to use Lemon's word) in the Parliamentary proceedings. Addressing the issue of the document's authenticity (as if that were even necessary), Parliament immediately declared that "this was the undoubted work of the immortal Milton." As such, "there was no question whatever as to the genuineness of the work," one, we recall, to which Parliament ascribed the title of the second book: *De Dei Cultu*.

No matter: for Parliament both author and title are a given. When those in high public office so decide, who is to challenge them? They derive their confidence from no less an authority than George IV himself. For him the fact of the work's authenticity was never in doubt. Convinced that the document is not just the real thing but that it should be made officially available "to the public," he authorized the placement of the document into "competent hands" for eventual publication both in the Latin and in English translation.[55] Clearly, this was one work in which the highest powers of the kingdom had a personal stake. As such, the treatise assumed a privileged status from the time of its discovery to the point of its publication. Short of having been authorized by forces beyond the ken of mortal beings, the document was issued, as it were, from the top down. King and Parliament had an investment in this work: its dissemination amounted to the realization of a cause, one in the name of "the immortal Milton." Once author and work coalesced in one unified whole, there was no separating them.

Every romance requires a scribe, and in this case it is the Reverend Charles R. Sumner, a trusted servant of the kingdom. As we know, his were the "competent hands" into which the trust of King and Parliament was placed. A young clergyman on the rise to an eventual bishopric, Sumner would be best able to edit and translate the work. Because of his background, moreover, he would be best equipped to deal with the theological intricacies of the treatise. More than that, his clerical station would bestow upon a work already blessed by regal authority a kind of ecclesiastical recognition. Church and state, then, conspired to make public the putative document of one whose reputation as iconoclast and rebel was now conceived as the "immortal Milton," the very source of nationalistic fervor. That old rebel and champion of the regicides had come in from the cold. Only in the world of romance might such an event be realized. As the event bore fruit, the genre of romance assumes an almost hagiographical resonance. Thus, according to Charles Sumner's son George, his father worked tirelessly on the manuscript night after night for months on end, "until three or four o'clock in the morning with a wet bandage on his forehead, and green tea by his side to ward off sleep."[56] His was an act of homage and sacrifice both to the state and to the poet-of-poets, who was brought to the fore as the true author of the long-lost work now made available to the public for the first time. With its emphasis upon suffering and self-sacrifice, the narrative of high adventure assumes a martyr-like quality, a willingness to suffer for truth's sake so that Milton's name might receive all the credit it is due.

The binding tie between the treatise and Milton was even further strengthened through the intercession of the young poet and fellow of Trinity College, Cambridge, William Sidney Walker, who as "resident on the spot," not only revised and corrected the proof sheets but altered the translation (without Sumner's approval) so that the results were more nearly in keeping with the language of Milton's own writings. As an "enthusiastic admirer of Milton," Walker was determined to honor the poet by having all his works cohere. Any doubts about the true canonicity of the theological treatise would thereby be entirely dispelled by such an act of homage (YP 6:4–5). To encounter the *De Doctrina Christiana* through what is commonly known as the Sumner translation, then, is already problematical because of the deliberate accretions imposed on the text by William Sidney Walker as an act of homage to the master. It is impossible to read the "Sumner" translation (that is, Sumner "improved" by Walker) without encountering a Miltonic overlay produced by the transposition of canonical utterances onto a work that may or may not accord with the particular phrasing that the translator or translators have elected to adopt. In response to this act of "forging" utterances, William B. Hunter astutely speaks of the "echo chamber" of Walker.[57] It is an echo chamber in which Walker as a kind of ventriloquist makes Milton speak. Whose voice does one hear in the translation: Sumner's, Walker's, Milton's? With Walker as scribe of scribes, the romance of authorship comes full circle: no strings are left untied, closure is the order of the day, harmony prevails.

Two quarto editions arose from Sumner's labors, the Latin text and the English translation, each edition published separately by Cambridge University Press in 1825. Whereas the title page of the Latin edition appeared as *Joannis Miltoni Angli De Doctrina Christiana Libri Duo Posthumi, quos ex schedis manuscriptis deprompsit, et typis mandari primus curavit Carolus Ricardus Sumner, A. M. , Bibliotechæ Regiæ Praefectus*, the title page of the English edition appeared as *A Treatise On Christian Doctrine, Compiled from the Holy Scriptures Alone; By John Milton, Translated From the original by Charles R. Sumner, M. A. , Librarian And Historiographer To His Majesty, And Prebendary Of Canterbury*.[58] Sumptuously produced, both editions contain elaborate dedications to King George IV. The Latin edition speaks of having been published as the result of royal order or authority, a view expressed by the English edition as well: "In obedience to Your Majesty's gracious command, I have executed a Translation of the recently discovered theological treatise of Milton, which I have now the honour of laying most humbly at Your Majesty's feet." The dedications bespeak their "official" standing and royal authority.

As such, the first published editions (Latin and English) are as much the vehicles of power as they are sources of scholarly authority. Having been accorded the imprimatur of the King himself, they serve to challenge any who might dare call their standing into question. In keeping with the romance elements that grace the narratives of discovery and reclamation, the royal publication of the theological treatise represents the act of bearing forth the holy grail with all its powers to an expectant public. Such in brief are the events through which the theological treatise of John Milton was made known to the world. The quality of romance that distinguishes these events is as much a part of the culture of attribution and authentication as the bibliographic and thematic characteristics of the manuscript itself. The romance quality in particular militates against any attempt by the "disaffected" to call into question the authorship of a work that both Crown and Church have officially deemed canonical. To engage in such an expression of disaffection would represent a violation of both regal and ecclesiastical protocol. No one wants to be held guilty of sedition or of sacrilege.

Unless one's name is Thomas Burgess, Bishop of Salisbury. It is well known that these offenses are just what that scoundrel perpetrated by calling into question the canonicity of the *De Doctrina Christiana* shortly after the publication in 1825.[59] In a series of discourses delivered before the Anniversary Meetings of the Royal Society of Literature (in 1826, 1827, and 1828), Burgess sought desperately to explode the romance of authorship and thereby to challenge "the establishment" that had so enthusiastically endorsed the notion of the *De Doctrina Christiana* as an indisputable part of the Miltonic canon. Burgess's efforts resulted in an ambitious work that collected his discourses in a single volume *Milton Not the Author of the Lately-Discovered Arian Work "De Doctrina Christiana"* (1829).[60]

Important in its own right, the work suggests the extent to which the investment in the canonicity of the *De Doctrina Christiana* by those in power effectively silenced anyone who might call their conclusions into question. This is certainly what Burgess attempted to do and for his efforts was silenced. Not only did he issue no more attacks on the canonicity of the treatise; according to William B. Hunter, his enforced silence is made evident by the absence of his 1829 book from any English library. More astonishing still is the absence of the book from the library of the Royal Society of Literature, the founder and first president of which was Burgess himself.[61] In response to this unusual circumstance, Hunter perceives the trace of royal censorship. Burgess's "attacks on the authenticity of the treatise," Hunter says, "must certainly have embarrassed the royal sponsor," that is, George IV, who was beset at the time by political problems of his own. "An agent of the king easily and silently stopped further discussion of the issue of Milton's authorship by threatening to cut off the monarch's support of the Society."[62]

In an excellent study of Burgess and Milton, James Ogden maintains that Hunter possibly goes too far in his "conspiracy theory," but even Ogden allows that the disappearance of Burgess's book is "remarkable" and finally concedes that there is indeed something about the whole affair that smacks of conspiracy.[63] I find Hunter's conspiracy theory entirely credible. Credible or not, the narrative that Hunter proposes moves the genre of romance (tinged at times with elements of hagiography) into a new realm, that of intrigue. The stakes are high indeed when the question of authorship (specifically of the Miltonic sort) arises. In the world of Milton scholarship that exists today, there is no George IV on hand to silence the seditious William B. Hunter, who will no doubt continue to have his say indefinitely. On the other hand, the forces (represented by some of the most respected Miltonists in the field) that have solemnly leagued themselves against Hunter (and his allies) are such that any but the most courageous, if not foolhardy, would persist in calling into question what the heirs of George IV have set his seal upon.

For our purposes, Burgess is interesting in his determination to erase any possibility of Miltonic authorship not only by arguing that the theology of the *De Doctrina Christiana* (particularly, its Arianism) is inimical to the views (especially those of the Trinitarian sort) that Milton held throughout his career, but by making the treatise wholly "other" in its provenance. Rather than the work of the great English poet, the theological treatise becomes the work of a foreigner: it was "probably written by some Dutch or German Theologian," Burgess observes slightingly. There is really nothing "English" about the work, which more nearly reflects the disposition of "foreigners" than the concerns of those who are natives of English soil. In a note, Burgess names a host of foreigners such as Beza, Bucer, Calvin, Camero, Cappellus, Erasmus, Gomarus, and Junius to suggest that their "alien" sensibilities are more nearly in keeping with the heterodox outlook of the *De Doctrina Christiana*.[64] In short, Burgess renders the treatise and its authorship "alien" for the purpose of dismissing any possibility of a verifiable English provenance.

This kind of "alienation" is in keeping with Burgess's portrayal of Milton as an author whose native sensibility would hardly be receptive to all that the treatise with its heterodoxies represents. Having launched this argument to erase the possibility of a Miltonic authorship and replaced that authorship with a non-English "other," Burgess moves into the realm of the personal. There, he emphasizes the dire infirmities that Milton suffered, notably his blindness, as a way of maintaining that the very work itself (with its encyclopedic amassing of proof-texts to support a multitude of arguments) would have been alien to Milton. Such a work would have represented a Herculean labor to a sighted author, but to a blind author (even of Milton's stature) a work of this nature and magnitude would have been next to impossible. This is especially true because of the extent to which Milton was obliged to rely upon amanuenses who were often less than dependable. Accordingly, Burgess contends that "the Dictation of so large a work as this Latin Treatise by a blind man, required the most constant and attentive assistance of a competent amanuensis. But Milton had no such assistance."[65]

Burgess invokes Milton's August 15, 1666, letter to Peter Heimbach, Councillor to the Elector of Brandenburg, to support the idea of the difficulties involved in depending upon inept amanuenses.[66] In his letter, Milton "desires his friend to excuse the errors of writing and punctuation, and to impute them to the ignorance of the boy, wholly unacquainted with Latin, who wrote it from his dictation; and complains of the misery of dictating to him letter by letter, what he had to say." Burgess concludes that "if a single short epistle was a work of such irksome difficulty, what must we think of the practicability of dictating to casual and incompetent amanuenses a treatise of seven hundred pages in quarto, full of the most minute citations of chapter and verse."[67] The rendering of both the author as alien and the work as alien in this manner prompts Burgess to erase any possibility of Miltonic authorship. It is no doubt one of the great ironies that when Maurice Kelley sought to categorize the various amanuenses responsible for the text of the *De Doctrina Christiana*, he assigned to this unknown boy (whom Kelley labels Amanuensis B) an entire series of emendations made with a heavy hand and a coarse quill (CM 6:30).[68] No concerns with the possibility of alienation here: it is this very boy who for Kelley played a major role in the revisions of a manuscript that the good bishop would just as soon have remained buried in the Middle Treasury Gallery in Whitehall.

IV

Moving from the various narratives that constitute the question of authorship, we must examine in greater detail the question of text. The two questions, of course, are intimately related: in fact, they overlap. They, in turn, give rise to further questions. For this purpose, we need to return to the Sumner editions (which are really the composite versions of Sumner/Walker) of both the Latin and the English produced from the Lemon copy found in the Middle Treasury Gallery in Whitehall. From there, we shall return to the copy of the "original" now held at the Public Record Office (SP 9/61). Doing so will lead to the crucial question of what does the authorship of the theological treatise mean in the context of the transmission of texts from one version to the next and from one generation to the next. That is, to what extent is it possible to assume that the act of reading the document known as the *De Doctrina Christiana* (as published in 1825) is tantamount to reading the PRO manuscript referenced as SP 9/61, and to what extent is it possible to assume that the act of reading the SP 9/61 is tantamount to reading the text that an author known as John Milton produced? These issues are made even more problematical by the fact of Milton's blindness.

It is clear that the publication of Charles R. Sumner's two editions of the

De Doctrina Christiana in 1825 represented an event of great proportions. Francis E. Mineka has provided a detailed account of the flurry of activity recorded in the critical reception that surrounded the event from the out-set.[69] Beyond its immediate reception, however, it is not clear how central the document (either in its Latin dress or in its English dress) proved to be in the determination of the intricacies of its author's theological views. I sense that the two editions led a divided life, one in which the commerce between the Latin and the English was slight. My inclination is to suggest that if the *De Doctrina Christiana* was read at all, it was considered essentially in its En-glish dress. It is worthy to note that Milton's great biographer David Masson observed in 1880 that although the treatise had been some "fifty years before the world," it nonetheless "seems to have found few real readers."[70]

The two editions (Latin and English) were united only in the early twentieth century with the publication of the Columbia University Press edition of the *De Doctrina Christiana* in *The Works of John Milton* (1931–38). In that edition, the Latin text and the English translation of Charles R. Sumner appeared side-by-side on facing pages for the first time.[71] By pub-lishing the theological treatise in that format, the editors of the treatise (James Holly Hanford and Waldo Hilary Dunn) were in effect suggesting the primacy of the Latin over the English. The English was to be seen for what it is, a supplement to the Latin "original." This venerable edition might be said to have set the standard as an *editio princeps* until the publication of the most recent translation of the *De Doctrina Christiana* by John Carey (with Maurice Kelley as editor) as a volume in theYale University Press edition of the *Complete Prose Works of John Milton* (1953–82). Unlike the Columbia edition, the Yale edition unfortunately looked backward to the nineteenth-century practice of excluding the Latin. With the publication of the Yale edition, the *De Doctrina Christiana* came to have a split identity yet once more. Given the sense of authority that the Yale edition has assumed in Milton studies, the Carey translation would appear to possess its own place of privilege, one that the Sumner translation initially enjoyed (and, it might be argued, continues to enjoy to this day).

In their own way, both the Sumner translation and the Carey translation might well be looked upon as "authored texts." This is no small point, for as all translators know, they veritably assume the responsibility of authorship in the act of attempting to transmute the meanings and nuances of one lan-guage into those of another, an act that is essentially impossible. The question of authorship very much resides in the way translators take upon themselves the authority to render the sense of the text as they see it. As such, translators are both interpreters and authors. It is their language through which we hear (at a distance) the echo of the voice they seek to utter in their own words. In the newly rendered text, the voices of the translators are accordingly always before us. As much as they might attempt to erase themselves in the act of presencing the author whose text is to be rendered anew, the translators re-create that text in their own image. As a matter of necessity, that image will be the result of the translators' own predilections and habits of mind, which in turn are the products of the milieu in which the translators practice their art. The result is that the Sumner translation, on the one hand, and the Carey translation, on the other, are largely two different works. Each may portray itself as the *De Doctrina Christiana* in English form, but both in style and in format just about the only thing that unites them is the title, and even that (as it is delineated in the heading to Book I) differs significantly from Sumner to Carey.[72]

Moreover, the determination to make the work as a whole conform to the Miltonic outlook became part of the agenda of the act of translation from the very outset. We recall that, under the influence of the Milton enthusiast William Sidney Walker, the Sumner text was emended to make certain that the final translation was in keeping with the stylistic practices of the poet. Whether in the Sumner translation or in the Carey translation, the text, presents us with two choices of authorship, each quite independent of the Latin text. In our consideration of that text, we might well be tempted (and I would argue are in fact tempted) either to move from the Carey translation to the Sumner translation before finally arriving at the Latin "original" or, what is also likely, not to bother with the "outdated" Sumner translation (and certainly not with the Latin) at all. Under these circumstances, the Latin text is either viewed at two removes (first through the eyes of Carey and second through the eyes of Sumner) or erased entirely.

But even those who scrupulously insist on bypassing both Sumner and Carey in an attempt to deal with the "original" Latin (which constitutes, after all, the printed embodiment of the manuscript itself) must face this perplex-ing question: To what extent is it possible to assume that the Latin document known as the *De Doctrina Christiana* is consonant with the PRO manuscript referenced as SP 9/61? In their "Prefatory Note" to the Columbia University Press edition of the *De Doctrina Christiana*, James Holly Hanford and Waldo Hilary Dunn make perfectly clear just how vexed that question is. In his transcription of the manuscript for the press, Sumner solemnly declared (in Latin, the official language of attestation) that he "followed his scribal origi-nals with minute fidelity [ne puncto quidem mutato, et litteris maiusculis fideliter servatis]." As Hanford and Dunn observe, that statement is "wide of the truth." Their own collation of the manuscript for the press demonstrates that, despite Sumner's best intentions, "there are in each printed page of his text perhaps a dozen variations from the original." Although these variations are for the most part on the order of "spelling, punctuation, and capitalization," Hanford and Dunn cite significant instances in which Sumner has "silently supplied, corrected, and even rearranged biblical references, broken or combined paragraphs, and adopted small emendations." Moreover, there are even "misreadings of the manuscript, and an occasional misprint."[73] One need only glance at the section titled "Notes on the Latin Text" in the Columbia edition (CM 17:432–78) to realize the extent to which Sumner's text and the source text (SP 9/61) differ. Although the table of additions, corrections, and insertions in this section tends to conflate the SP 9/61 manuscript with the Sumner emendations, the editors have assembled some forty-five pages of alterations to highlight the uncertain state of both the SP 9/61 and the Sumner text. Addressing the differences between the two texts, one senses the daunting range of scribal variants that engaged the editors as they made their way through the manuscript.[74]

Then there is the issue of the manuscript itself, the so-called SP 9/61. How is one to understand the question of authorship in an encounter with this as the "original" or base text? Are we finally here on surer ground? Hardly. To determine the extent of the uncertainties that surround the manuscript, one need only recall Kelley's own description of it in his Introduction to the Yale *Prose*. Totalling 745 pages (at times incorrectly numbered), the manuscript is no longer in its original binding, as the result of having been "repaired and rebound" in the 1930s. Two primary "hands" have been identified as those responsible for the transmission of the text as it has come down to us. As indicated, the first is that of Daniel Skinner, whose "hand" is said to have been responsible for pages 1–196, 308, 571–74, and "numerous recopied passages and corrections elsewhere in the manuscript"; the second, that of one Jeremie Picard, whose "hand" is said to have been responsible for pages 197–308a, 309–548, 553–71, and 575–735. In addition to these major hands, one finds "here and there" (through pages 198–733 of the manuscript) the hands of an as-yet "undertermined number of anonymous revisers."

Loath simply to leave the hands of these revisers as disembodied extensions of unnamed beings, Kelley assigns them names in the form of alphabetical designations (a common practice). But this mode of identification raises as many questions as it answers, in part, because it gives the impression of conclusiveness when there is only uncertainty. Having identified "four major strata of revisions," Kelley proceeds to explain his methodology as follows: The strata of revisions, he asserts, "I assign to Amanuensis A, B, M, and N, though the M entries may be the work of two scribes." We are already in hot water, for M may hide the faces (or hands) of more than one scribe. The uncertainties mount. "Of the twenty-six remaining entries," Kelley con tinues guardedly, "I assign—but not always with complete certainty—nine to Amanuensis C, four to Amanuensis O, and two to Amanuensis R." The "may be" of M gives way to the uncertainty of C, O, and R." But there is more: "The eleven entries thus left, which I call Later Hands, show no conclusive resemblance to one another or to the other hands in the manuscript, and could possibly represent eleven different scribes; but since several of the entries are printed, we are probably dealing with a lesser number of scribes, and perhaps even with some that we have already noticed, who on occasion shifted from script to print" (YP 6:11–14).[75] Although the account gives rise to more questions than it answers, it is just the sort of jockeying that one must engage in to make sense of what Kelley calls the complex "strata" of the revisions.[76] To be sure, Kelley might commence with the assurance of two identities (or at least two names, those of Daniel Skinner and Jeremie Picard, respectively), but from there, as much as he attempts to keep the uncertainties of the manuscript in check, he must willy-nilly conclude with the indeterminacy that arises from the frank admission of an inability even to assign letters to all those hands.

In a consideration of the manuscript itself, we might find it enlightening to engage specific alterations that emerged as the result of the intervention of the amanuenses. A case in point is what survives in the manuscript as two versions of the same text, one, that of Jeremie Picard (SP 9/61, 307A) and, the other, that of Daniel Skinner (SP 9/61, 308).[77] Because both versions are present on sequential pages of the manuscript, the transition from the Picard text to the Skinner metatext is instructive. To assess the nature of that transition and the uncertainties that arise from it, we shall take into account pages 307 and 307A of the Picard (Figures 1 and 2, respectively) and 308 of the Skinner (Figure 4).[78] The transition from Picard to Skinner is not a simple one, for pages 307A and 308 are unaccountably separated by a blank page (Figure 3), numbered 156 [sic]. Even assuming that the blank page functions as a marker of some sort to divide Skinner from Picard, it is not clear whose hand is responsible for the pagination of the blank page or why the page is numbered 156. But this is only the beginning. A glance at the multiple deletions and interlineations that mark the Picard text and the transcription rendered in the Skinner version reveals just how vexed and uncertain the issue of transcription can become.

Although many examples could be cited, I shall confine myself at the outset to one, the term *duntaxat* ("alone," "only," "merely").[79] Addressing text and metatext, one can readily see that the term is clearly evident in the Skinner transcription, which has as a heading *Israelitis duntaxat* (SP 9/61, 308; Fig. 4). Unless one examined the manuscript version of the Picard text, one would be unaware of the uncertainties that attend this phrase. In the

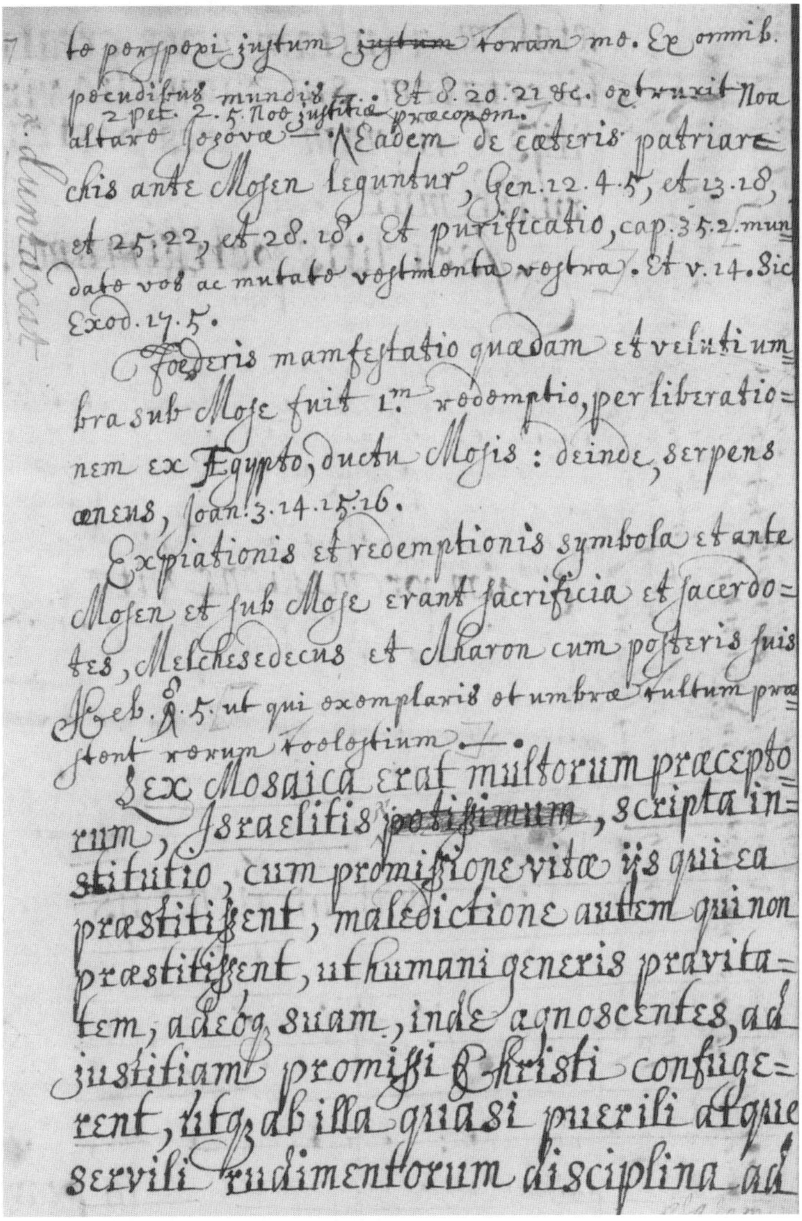
te perspexi justum ~~justum~~ coram me. Ex omnib.
pecudibus mundis ... Et 8.20.21 &c. extruxit Noa
2 Pet. 2.5. Noe justitiae praeconem.
altare Jehovae. Eadem de caeteris patriar-
chis ante Mosen leguntur, Gen.12.4.5, et 13.18,
et 25.22, et 28.18. Et purificatio, cap.35.2. mun-
date vos ac mutate vestimenta vestra. Et v.14. Sic
Exod.17.5.
Foederis manifestatio quaedam et veluti um-
bra sub Mose fuit 1.m redemptio, per liberatio-
nem ex Aegypto, ductu Mosis: deinde, serpens
aeneus, Joan.3.14.15.16.
Expiationis et redemptionis symbola et ante
Mosen et sub Mose erant sacrificia et sacerdo-
tes, Melchisedecus et Aaron cum posteris suis
Heb. 8.5. ut qui exemplaris et umbrae cultum prae-
stent rerum coelestium.
Lex Mosaica erat multorum praecepto-
rum, Israelitis ~~potissimum~~, scripta institutio, cum promissione vitae iis qui ea
praestitissent, maledictione autem qui non
praestitissent, ut humani generis pravitatem, adeoque suam, inde agnoscentes, ad
justitiam promissi Christi confuge-
rent, itque ab illa quasi puerili atque
servili rudimentorum disciplina ad
x. duntaxat

Figure 1. *De Doctrina Christiana* (Press mark 9/61, 307).

Figure 2. *De Doctrina Christiana* (Press mark 9/61, 307A).

Figure 3. *De Doctrina Christiana* (Press mark 9/61, 156).

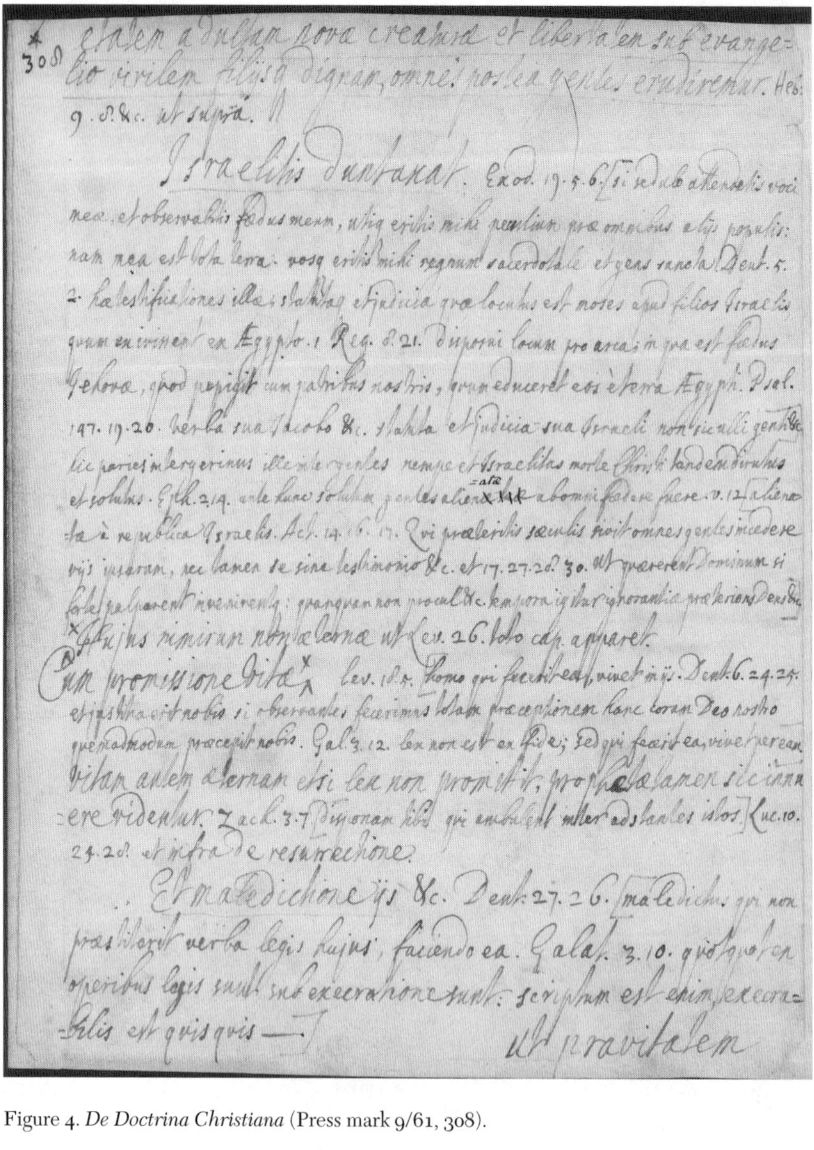
308 etatem adultam nova creatura et libertatem sub evange=
lio virilem filijsq dignam, omnes postea gentes erudiremur. Heb:
9. 8. &c. ut supra.
Israelitis duntaxat. Exod. 19. 5. 6. [si seduló attenderitis voci
meæ, et observabitis fœdus meum, utiq eritis mihi peculium præ omnibus alijs populis:
nam mea est tota terra. vosq eritis mihi regnum sacerdotale et gens sancta] Deut. 5.
2. testificationes illæ, statutaq et judicia quæ locutus est Moses apud filios Israelis
quum exirent ex Ægypto. 1 Reg. 8. 21. disposui locum pro arca, in qua est fœdus
Jehovæ, quod pepigit cum patribus nostris, quum educeret eos è terra Ægypti. Psal.
147. 19. 20. verba sua Jacobo &c. statuta et judicia sua Israeli non sic ulli genti &c.
hic paries intergerinus ille inter gentes nempe et Israelitas morte Christi tandem dirutus
et solutus. Eph. 2. 14. ante hunc solutum gentes alienatæ ab omni fœdere fuere. v. 12. [aliena=
=ti à republica Israelis. Act. 14. 16. 17. Qui præteritis sæculis sivit omnes gentes incedere
vijs ipsarum, nec tamen se sine testimonio &c. et 17. 27. 28. 30. ut quærerent Dominum si
forte palparent inveniren[t]q: quanquam non procul &c. tempora igitur ignorantiæ præteriens Deus &c.
× ejus nimirum non æterna ut Lev. 26. toto cap. apparet.
Cum promissione vitæ × Lev. 18. 5. homo qui fecerit ea, vivet in ijs. Deut. 6. 24. 25.
et justitia erit nobis si observantes fecerimus totam præceptionem hanc coram Deo nostro
quemadmodum præcepit nobis. Gal. 3. 12. lex non est ex fide; sed qui fecerit ea, vivet per ea.
vitam autem æternam etsi lex non promittit, prophetæ tamen sic innu=
=ere videntur. Zach. 3. 7. [disponam tibi qui ambulent inter adstantes istos] Luc. 10.
25. 28. et infra de resurrectione.
Et maledictione ijs &c. Deut. 27. 26. [maledictus qui non
præstiterit verba legis hujus, faciendo ea. Galat. 3. 10. quotquot ex
operibus legis sunt, sub execratione sunt: scriptum est enim, execra=
=bilis est quisquis —]
ut pravitatem

Figure 4. *De Doctrina Christiana* (Press mark 9/61, 308).

Picard text, the author appears to have struggled with the phrase, for, although *Israelitis* is written clearly enough, the word *potissimum* ("chiefly," "principally," "above all") originally following it is crossed out (not only on page 307, but on page 307A as well; Figs. 1 and 2). Did Picard cross out the word at the instruction of the author? Did the version (or versions?) of the text that Picard putatively copied (or recopied) likewise contain the deletion? Once the decision had been made to substitute *duntaxat* for *potissimum*, how certain is it that *duntaxat* (Fig. 1) and *Duntaxat* (Fig. 2) were not themselves in a state of flux during the process of revision? Finally, what is the purpose of the substitution? That is, what changes in meaning are generated? Answers to these questions are difficult to come by.

In the first instance of what was to have been a phrase beginning with "Israelitis" in the Picard text (SP 9/61, 307; Fig. 1), the deleted word, as indicated, is "potissimum," but, although there is sufficient room above the deleted word to insert another word, none appears in its place, despite the obvious presence of a caret between *Israelitis* and *potissimum*. To make matters more difficult, a substitution is nowhere to be found in the margin of the entire paragraph in which *Israelitis potissimum* occurs. To locate the substitution, one must proceed to the top of the page in the left margin where *duntaxat* (preceded by a caret) is indeed to be found. There is no doubt, of course, where the marginal word belongs in the body of the text, but the reason for the placement of the word in the upper left-hand margin of the page is at least open to question. The situation becomes even more vexed in the treatment of the phrase *Israelitis potissimum* on page 307A (Fig. 2). Although it is clear that the word *Duntaxat* (this time, with a capital D) is inserted above the deleted word *potissimum*, the insertion does not appear to be in the same hand as that which inscribed *duntaxat* on the preceding page (307). One can simply not assume a clear chronology and provenance in the process of correction, insertion, and substitution.

Kelley would have us believe otherwise. In his "Revisions in the Manuscript of Milton's *De Doctrina Christiana*" in the Yale edition, he asserts that for page 307, "DUNTAXAT SUBSTITUTED FOR POTISSIMUM DELETED M," and for page 307A (which Kelley unaccountably numbers 308a), "DUNTAXAT SUBSTITUTED MARGIN FOR POTISSIMUM DELETED M / THIS REVISION LATER DELETED AND RECOPIED IN TEXT SKINNER" (YP 6:822). This statement raises more questions than it answers, for (as noted) not only is there no page numbered 308a in the manuscript, but it assumes first that *duntaxat* (307) and *Duntaxat* (307A) are in the same hand (they are not), and, outside of noting the deletion of *potissimum* in the text of 307A, it does not take account of the deletion of *duntaxat* in the margin or the capitalization of *Duntaxat* above the caret in the text. In his analysis of the deletions, Kelley even goes so far as to identify the source as that Janus-faced fellow "M." All this is essentially speculation. What appears so clearly in the recopied version of Skinner is certainly problematical in Picard. The nature of the Picard text is such that in many instances one simply doesn't know what to make of the interlineations, marginalia, deletions, and substitutions. Even Kelley allows that it would "require the eyes of Lynceus and the ants of Psyche" (YP 6:809) to provide a truly accurate account of what is happening in the Picard text.[80]

Who bears the responsibility for the interlineations, marginalia, and the like? That is, who is ultimately the author? Finally, what does the change from *potissimum* to *duntaxat* imply? In both the Sumner translation (for the CM) and the Carey translation (for the YP), the phrase is handled as follows: "INTENDED FOR THE ISRAELITES ALONE" (CM 16:103, 105; YP 6:517). But surely the author sought to make a fine distinction between that which is intended for the Israelites "alone" *(duntaxat)* and that which is intended for the Israelites "chiefly" *(potissimum)*. That which is intended for the Israelites is the *Lex Mosaica*, a phenomenon that in the mind of the author exists on a plane more nearly in keeping with the lowly and restrictive connotations of *duntaxat* than on the more nearly exalted and exclusive connotations of *potissimum*.

This is all conjecture, to be sure, but the semantic implications (complications) of the substitution need to be taken into account (and acknowledged) in any attempt to do the text justice. It would be comforting to know the answers to the questions raised by the substitutions and the manner in which they appear as interlineations and the like. But given the uncertainties that surround both the text and its production, the attempt to resolve all such questions ultimately gives rise to more questions than it answers. The question of authorship is implicated in all attempts to clarify the mysteries surrounding the text and its alterations. All that is available to us are the amanuenses (whether in the form of Picard and the alphabetical "hands" or in the form of Skinner), and the questions that their presence raises serves only to complicate matters even further.[81] As indicated by the long marginal passages on page 307A of the SP 9/61, the questions raised by the *potissimum/duntaxat* alterations only begin to suggest the complexities and uncertainties that surround the text. Once again, one is prompted to ask the fundamental questions relating to authorship, those having to do with the relationship between author and scribe, how one is to understand the meaning of the text transcribed, by what authority the amanuenses consider themselves authorized to alter the text (either in the "original" or in translation), what constitutes the "original" text, how it was composed, and a whole series of corresponding questions.

In light of these uncertainties, one wonders about the way in which each of those responsible for transcribing the text fulfilled the role of the amanu-ensis.[82] That role is already implicit in the very etymology of the term "aman-uensis": "(servus) a manu," or "slave at handwriting."[83] If the role of the amanuensis were confined solely to that of *servus*, there might not be as many unexplained issues to consider, but, as we have seen, the amanuensis is not only a *servus;* he is also an *emendator* (either through his own initiative or through the initiative of the author). It is in the scribe's assumption of the role of the *emendator a manu* that questions arise, for one's natural inclination is to ask at what point the *emendator* assumes the role of *auctor*. At what point, that is, are the changes wrought in a text the responsibility of the individual who is transcribing the text in the capacity as a scribe? In an illuminating essay on the texts of Milton's works, John T. Shawcross observes that the "intervening hands" of scribes (as well as compositors, in the case of texts that were published) did indeed alter Miltonic texts for various reasons.[84] In other words, the scribe was most definitely an *emendator a manu,* one whose intervening hands most assuredly played a part in the shaping of a work. This may appear to be a given, but it bears repetition at every point.

In the case of the *De Doctrina Christiana* manuscript, then, we must consider the possibility that on various occasions a group of unidentified amanuenses emended the text they were enlisted to transcribe. Uncertainties that underscore the production and transmission of the manuscript prompt us, moreover, to question precisely what it meant to be an amanuensis, what distinguishes an individual who transcribes directly from dictation as opposed to one who copies earlier drafts, and how we are finally to determine the circumstances under which the act of transcription occurs. Especially in the attempt to come to terms with Milton's works and to engage matters of canonicity, questions of this sort assume paramount importance. They have a crucial bearing not only on the nature of Miltonic texts but on the question of authorship. Both questions are inextricably bound together in the form of a subtle knot.

These questions become even more vexed if the so-called author of the document suffers from a debilitating condition such as blindness. In his biography of Milton, John Toland observes of the composition of *Paradise Lost* that the poet "by reason of his blindness" was "obliged to write by whatsoever hand came next, ten, or twenty, or thirty Verses at a time; and consequently must trust the judgment of others at least for the Pointing and Orthography."[85] It is this notion of trusting the judgment of others (a trust, I suggest, that extends to matters well beyond those of "Pointing and Orthog-raphy") that is so germane to an understanding of how a text such as the *De Doctrina Christiana* was produced. The task not only of composing the text (itself replete with a multitude of proof-texts) but of reviewing the outcome of the transcriptions and of implementing the revisions becomes that much more onerous if one is afflicted with blindness. It is a task that would "require sinews almost equall to those which Homer gave Ulysses," and even then one is put to the expense of trusting the judgment of others who become of necessity one's hands and one's eyes.

It seems that those (like Thomas Burgess and William B. Hunter) who have called the idea of the Miltonic authorship into question have been the most vocal in their awareness of the difficulties that attend the affliction of blindness and of the role of the amanuensis in the production of the text.[86] Those determined to assert with full confidence the canonicity (and with it, the sole authorship) of the text are dismissive of any argument that would use blindness as a reason to raise the question of authorship in the first place. If the role of the amanuensis is addressed at all, its function is one that in no way compromises a belief in the power of the author to enjoy complete control over the production of the text. For true believers, the heroics of authorship (or what I have designated the romance of authorship) thus assume renewed significance. In their adherence to a belief in canonicity, the Miltonic faithful embrace a view of authorship that conceives the One True Author as imbued with almost superhuman strength and fortitude. (One might suggest that it is a view that Milton himself fostered throughout his career.)

Blindness is not so much a liability as an asset. It is a condition through which the author transforms himself into a figure of both faith and perseverance. Some thirty-five years after the first publication of the theological treatise, Samuel Leigh Sotheby addressed the issue of the blind author by requesting "many distinguished Antiquarians, Literary Men, and kind Friends" to blindfold themselves so that they might re-create the conditions under which Milton himself produced his great works. Sotheby's intention was to demonstrate "that any body, *totally blind*," is still able to produce an entire range of works of complexity.[87] Given Milton's divinely inspired writings, there was no question in Sotheby's mind about the provenance of the *De Doctrina Christiana* and the ability of Milton to author such a work. Blindness simply intensified the aura of glory with which Milton as author of the treatise was imbued.

Responding to the text of the theological treatise, those inclined to adopt the view of the One True Author are similarly inclined to endorse the notion that the treatise is whole and finished as it stands. Such a notion, we recall, is already evident in Robert Lemon's statement that the manuscript he discovered is "perfect, and complete in all its parts." Well before the current debate about authorship, Gordon Campbell argued persuasively that the treatise is essentially "unfinished."[88] In response to Campbell, Maurice Kelley staunchly asserted that despite all the deletions and interlineations discernible throughout the text (at least in the Picard version), the treatise is essentially "complete."[89] It would also be reassuring if this were the case. In its present state, however, the text prohibits this kind of assurance. Instead, the treatise must be seen for what it is, that is, a "working manuscript," a work in progress.[90] Campbell et al. argue that the physical state of the manuscript supports this conclusion. That many of the pages contain large gaps between the lines, for example, suggests that the text has been deliberately "set out to admit interlinear additions and accretions." Moreover, the large left margins on these pages would appear to provide for running notations. As we have seen, this is a manuscript that has been subjected at various times to the process of revision. "Beneath the seeming finalities of the text," as represented by the transcription of Daniel Skinner or by the printed editions (which would lead one to believe that the work is "finished"), one finds "an altogether more problematic and unstable manuscript." According to Campbell et al., one must be sensitive at all times to the "two principal components" that constitute the text. Each of these components exists in a complex relationship with the other. The first component might well be an ur-text of some sort reflected in Picard's fair copy of a theological treatise (or possibly treatises) composed at an earlier time. This ur-text is visible in the Picard text that Skinner has not recopied. The second component, in turn, is reflected in all the various "accretions, most surely visible in unascribed marginalia" and interlineations. It is not clear what here is Miltonic or non-Miltonic in origin or to what extent the ur-text may be "a Miltonic synthesis of a multiplicity of sources."[91]

This is a view that conceives the *textus receptus* as the product of copying and recopying earlier documents. The copy that has come down to us thereby becomes a stage in the process of transmission, a process that was never able to attain full or complete fruition. What results is the *De Doctrina Christiana* manuscript in its unfinished state. Interesting as this estimate is, the distinctions between text and ur-text as "visible" components within the manuscript itself must be viewed as the product of healthy speculation, as a reading between the lines or an interpretive "interlineation" of its own sort. What you think you see is not always what you get. I am inclined to problematize the situation even further and suggest that, although this is a manuscript that might lead one to construct a theory of ur-texts, the "strata" (to adopt Kelley's designation) upon which the manuscript is founded are not so readily discernible as Campbell et al. would have us believe.

Whatever one makes of these strata, Campbell et al. are surely correct in their description of the manuscript as a "palimpsest."[92] According to the OED, the word is derived from the Latin *palimpsestus* through a Greek root meaning "scraped again" or a "parchment whence writing has been erased."

Already in use in the seventeenth century, it has come to mean "a parchment or other writing-material written upon twice, the original writing having been erased or rubbed out to make place for the second." As such, it is "a manuscript in which a later writing is written over an effaced earlier writing." In the introduction to the fine collection of essays titled *Palimpsest*, George Bornstein observes that "although we tend to think of major works as fixed or stable, a surprising number of them display upon examination a palimpsestic quality." So the Bible itself existed in multiple versions in pre-Christian antiquity and has been transmitted through numerous translations, each claiming its own authority.[93]

Encountering the ongoing debates over the authorship of the *De Doctrina* among contemporary Miltonists, biblical authorities would immediately recognize the terrain, for the redactionists and practitioners of the so-called "documentary hypothesis" in biblical criticism have approached the text of Scriptures from corresponding points of view for generations.[94] Thus, Ralph G. Williams observes that whereas the Bible "has been the site of the most energetic efforts in our tradition" to establish a "secure text," the texts themselves "continually complicate or resist such efforts." With their "absorption of sources extant or lost," their "complex reworking of earlier material," their implicit "references to amanuenses and to variant authorial versions," and their "involvement in parallel textual traditions," these texts constitute "the most extraordinary symphony (or is it allophony?) of voices."[95]

Well before the documentary hypothesis found its way into biblical criticism, the author of the *De Doctrina Christiana* revealed an intimate knowledge of the palimpsestic quality of both the Hebrew Scriptures and the New Testament. He was well aware of the existence of textual variants and the extent to which the transmission of the manuscripts themselves gave rise to their own problems in the establishment of textual authority. So in the chapter titled *De Scriptura Sacra* (I. xxx), the author does not hesitate to address the fact of the instability of the biblical text brought about by the uncertain transmission of the codices and manuscripts that have been passed down to his own time. With that idea in mind, he acknowledges the physical "corruptions" to which the biblical text has been liable from the very outset: "The external scripture, particularly the New Testament, has often been liable to corruption [saepe corrumpi potuit] and is, in fact, corrupt [et corrupta est]."

The bald statement *et corrupta est* makes clear how willing the author of the treatise is to engage the text on its own terms. He is not afraid to declare that this unfortunate situation has come about because the text has been "committed to the care of various untrustworthy authorities, has been collected together from an assortment of divergent manuscripts, and has survived in a medley of transcripts and editions." No one knows more than the author of the treatise the pitfalls and shortcomings that arise through the attempt to impose order on the chaos of manuscript culture. The uncertainties that surround the *textus receptus*, moreover, are compounded by the absence of any ur-text. So we are informed that "we possess no autograph copy: no exemplar [autographum exemplar] which we can rely on as more trustworthy than the others" (YP 6:587–89; CM 16:274–77; SP9/61, 395–97). In his discussion of Scriptures, the author of the *De Doctrina Christiana* might just as well be referring to his own theological treatise as to the sacred text that serves as the basis of doctrinal belief.

I believe the time has come to approach the *De Doctrina Christiana* in the spirit that the author of the theological treatise approaches the Scriptures, that is, as a text that "has often been liable to corruption [saepe corrumpi potuit] and is, in fact, corrupt [et corrupta est]." What this means is implicit in the term "corrupt" *(corruptus)*, which, with its ties to *corrumpere*, suggests the rather violent idea of breaking to pieces, of bursting, and of destroying.[96] As applied to the theological treatise, corruptus and corrumpere imply the inherent instability of the text, the danger that it might well self-destruct. To a great extent, the *De Doctrina Christiana* shares this characteristic with those codices that constitute the Scriptures themselves, specifically the New Testament. With the *textus receptus* of the theological treatise before us, we are bound to iterate that we too "possess no autograph copy: no exemplar [autographum exemplar]," and, thus, in the strictest sense, neither "text" nor "author." All that we do possess is a collection of "hands," or, if you will, the voices of the amanuenses whose hands have left their mark on the text. To be sure, we have names for two of the individuals to whom the hands (and voices) belong: Jeremie Picard and Daniel Skinner. Beyond that, we have a lot of letters (A, B, C, M, N, O, R). The precise roles of Picard and Skinner in the act of transcription, however, are finally a matter of conjecture.

The prevailing belief concerning those roles is delineated by Maurice Kelley, who speaks with a conviction born of the need to affirm the existence both of text and author and thereby to counteract the perils of a work that keeps threatening to self-destruct. "Though Picard's hand does not appear until the second section of the manuscript, pp. 197–735," Kelley observes, "he must nevertheless be considered the first scribe in the document because all other hands in the manuscript appear in the margins or between the lines of his writing." "Conversely," Kelley says, "though the first section of the manuscript, pp. 1–196, is in Skinner's hand, he must be considered the last scribe in the document because whenever his hand appears in conjunction with another, his writing is always marginal or interlinear, recopying the work of another scribe."[97] This appears to make splendid sense, except that it is all

finally (and necessarily) the logic of conjecture, a logic founded on the crite-
rion of internal evidence that arises from an examination of the work itself.[98]
As we have seen in our discussion of the recopied pages (text and metatext)
already present in the manuscript, such evidence has much to say for it. But it
still does not take into account all those other hands, where they come from,
and why they are there.

The more we move into the maze of the text, the more we are caught in
its web. The relationship between text and metatext has still not been fully
established, and will not be so until further evidence is available. In the act of
venturing any conclusions about the provenance of a work as a whole, one
must have recourse to a host of corroborative evidence based on indisputable
matters of fact. A crucial determinant would be the discovery of the first
portion of the manuscript, presumably in the hand of Jeremie Picard, but this
too, of course, is ultimately a matter of conjecture, no doubt a most reasonable conjecture but conjecture nonetheless. Assuming (for the sake of argument) that the first portion of the manuscript is indeed in Picard's hand, we
have no way of telling what this portion of the manuscript contained in the
form of its own interlineations and marginalia. Nor is it certain whether or in
what form the versions that predate the Picard text existed and (assuming
that they did) how one is to understand the nature of *their* provenance.

In the consideration of the provenance of the *De Doctrina Christiana*,
we must acknowledge finally that conjecture is the order of the day, but even
conjecture is instructive insofar as it establishes a context for sensitizing us to
the mystery of the text itself. From the very point at which the manuscript
was discovered, those who sought to strip back the layers of its composition
ventured the names of individuals who might have been responsible for
transcribing the text in its various forms. It is useful to trace the genealogy of
attribution in order to arrive at a greater sense of where we stand as we move
from the foundational moments of the discovery of the text to what transpires
at the present. Robert Lemon's attributions are germane in the construction
of that genealogy. In his examination of the newly discovered manuscript,
Lemon was certain that he recognized the hands of Milton's nephew Edward
Phillips and two of Milton's own daughters, Mary and Deborah. For Lemon,
the first part of the manuscript (which he calls "a fair, corrected copy" of an
original now lost?) is clearly that of Mary, whose writing is distinguished by a
"small beautiful Italian hand." The remainder of the manuscript, in turn,
appears in the "small, strong, upright character" of Edward Phillips. Moreover, the various interlineations and marginal notations, along with "small
pieces of writing pasted in," fall for Lemon under the stewardship not just of
Mary but of Milton's youngest daughter, Deborah.[99]

The production of the manuscript was, it seems, kept all in the family. In

Lemon's discourse, one becomes especially aware of what might be called the gendering of hands that produced the manuscript: the male, with his "small, strong, upright character," finds its correspondence in the female, with her "small beautiful Italian hand." Somehow, the construction of the hands as male and female is consistent with the personality of that male author who was so widely known at one time as the Lady of Christ's College. Embedded in the very hands through which the manuscript was produced is an implicit gender classification that is a mark of the author to whom the work itself is attributed. In his "Preliminary Observations" to his translation of the *De Doctrina Christiana*, Charles R. Sumner not only reiterates the views expressed by Lemon but emphasizes even further the importance of recognizing the presence of what he calls the "female hand," one that must be acknowledged, despite all the misogynist claims that have been leveled at the "paternal conduct of Milton."[100] The construction of identity through attribution, then, reconceives the text as the product of an author whose amanuenses become an extension of his own personality.

V

What then of Jeremie Picard and Daniel Skinner? They have their stories, too, stories that serve not to dispel the anxieties associated with our palimpsest but to intensify them. As the two primary "hands" through which we owe the transmission of the *De Doctrina Christiana*, Picard and Skinner exist in a murky world of uncertainty, innuendo, and supposition. As William B. Hunter observes, Picard is a shadowy figure, one about whom we know relatively little.[101] It is clear that (in addition to the pages that bear his stamp in the *De Doctrina Christiana*) there are various documents that Picard transcribed for Milton, including entries in the flyleaf of Milton's family Bible, in the Commonplace Book, and the text of "Methought I saw my late espoused saint," among others.[102] The period of his association with Milton is customarily dated between 1658 and 1660, but there is evidence that Picard was employed by the government in the mid-1650s. John T. Shawcross remarks that it is possible Milton employed him at that time, or even possibly earlier.[103] In any case, the period 1657 (or 1658) to 1660 might well have been the time that Picard worked on the manuscript of the *De Doctrina Christiana*.[104] After the Restoration, we possess no record of a relationship between Picard and Milton. In response to the post-Restoration silence, Gordon Campbell et al. raise the prospect of intrigue to explain the lack of evidence. Adopting the adage that "absence of evidence is not evidence of absence," Campbell et al. offer the following conjecture. With the onset of the Restoration, "Milton may well have stopped working on the manuscript" for a variety of reasons, including "the need to secure his sensitive papers in a clandestine location." Not only the state papers but the treatise might well have been seized had Milton's study been searched. The state papers would have been confiscated and the treatise subjected to charges of heresy.[105]

However one responds to the views of Campbell et al., they raise challenging issues in their conjectures concerning the post-Reformation silence surrounding both the association of Picard and Milton and the disposition of Milton's papers. But all is conjecture nonetheless. One must keep on inventing narratives to explain the absence of concrete evidence. In the context of these narratives the figure of Jeremie Picard is hedged round with conjecture and uncertainty. Who is Picard, anyway? Aside from having been identified as one of the two primary sources of the transcription of the *De Doctrina Christiana*, Picard has left us little information about the basic circumstances of his life. Is it possible that Picard was really a "Mr. Packer," one of Milton's students (or "Scholar"), to whom Aubrey refers (in a marginal notation affixed to his "Minutes")?[106] We simply don't know. What happened to Picard after the Restoration? Once again, we don't know.

On the other hand, there is yet another story (a strange one indeed) that serves to underscore the uncertainties surrounding this mysterious figure who was apparently of such importance to Milton.[107] In a German travel book published in 1724, the author, one Aulus Apronius (i.e., Adam Ebert), recounted his experiences in England in 1678. Part of his account is a description of the New Bethlehem Hospital (the London Hospital for the Insane, Bedlam) and its inmates. The hospital, he writes, is a low, long, red, building, filled with "melancholy people." Among them, he found the secretary of "the well-known Milton." The so-called secretary "ate nothing but the straw of the bed on which he was lying. But when he noticed a stranger, he pointed miserably with his finger at his forehead in order to show that he lacked reason. It puzzled the traveler that a fool knew that he was a fool. Once he had smashed a window; also he had not been willing to rest until he had been brought glue so that he could patch the holes with the paper which he had been reading."[108] According to admission books for Bethlehem, this individual was one "Jeremiah Piskard."[109]

In light of this reference, Hunter supplements his earlier metanarrative of authorship through which he had traced the authorship of the theological treatise to one of Milton's former students. As a result of Elton's findings, Hunter is now able to name this student. It is none other than Jeremie Picard (or Piskard or Packer), who went abroad, "where he developed new and eccentric religious ideas that he entered in his manuscript." During the mid- or-late 1650s, he returned to "his old teacher in England," where he assumed the role of amanuensis. In that capacity, he shared with his mentor "his now elaborated, recopied, and treasured if heterodox treatise." During the next decade, however, he suffered misfortune. Either he died or left the country as a *persona non grata* (to use Hunter's earlier phrase), or he experienced a mental breakdown and was unable to complete his great work. This was the treatise that came to be known as the *De Doctrina Christiana*, which remained in Milton's care. Thus supplementing his earlier metanarrative with this tale of recognition, Hunter concludes with what is no doubt an ironic flourish: "The former teacher," Hunter remarks, "could have occasionally visited him [Piscard/Picard] at his current appropriate address, the London Hospital for the Insane, Bedlam."[110]

Both Ebert's account and Hunter's supplement to his own earlier metanarrative are fascinating in what they suggest about the question of authorship. Ebert's account moves the discussion into the realm of madness. That perhaps is finally the most appropriate place for a discourse that has no end among those who find themselves lost in wandering mazes of uncertainty. Along with the "melancholy people" of Ebert, these seekers after the "author" might find themselves consigned to a new site of production: that low, long, red building occupied by Milton's amanuensis. The irony of such a reading is not lost on Hunter, who views the London Hospital for the Insane as precisely the place where one Jeremie/Jeremiah Picard/Piskard/Packer of multiple identities resides. According to this reading, the romance of authorship assumes a new bearing, one imbued with an ironic self-awareness that underlies the quest for the "author."

It is a self-awareness that all who are determined to discover the exact provenance of the theological treatise would do well to possess. Is the man of multiple identities in some sense the alter ego of one whose name has been "forged" on a work that he may or may not have "authored"? (This is a name, we recall, that is there and not there: now you see it; now you don't.) Does the man with the disappearing name visit the man of multiple identities in Bedlam from time to time? Perhaps so, but we shall not know for certain until we have definitive evidence that will establish the true identity of Jeremie/Jeremiah Picard/Piskard/Packer and what he was up to both before and after the Restoration. For the time being, we must allow him to reside in Bedlam, where he is accompanied by the melancholy people who are his compatriots and where he is visited on occasion by one through whom the debate over authorship engages us now and no doubt shall continue to engage us for years to come.

This leaves us the fascinating figure known as Daniel Skinner.[111] He is the one who transcribed (recopied?) the first 196 pages (along with additional pages) of the palimpsest we call the *De Doctrina Christiana*. He is also the one who transcribed the Letters of State, which, like the theological treatise, is now preserved in the Public Record Office. Although we know more about Daniel Skinner than we do about Jeremie Picard, the nature of Skinner's relationship with Milton, as well as his role in the transmission of the theological treatise, is far from certain.[112] In fact, it is tantalizingly obscure, and with that obscurity arise questions about how reliable his transcription is, questions that have already been addressed earlier in this study. I now wish to complicate matters even further by suggesting the extent to which the Milton/Skinner relationship is itself finally a conundrum, one that renders the Skinnerian presence in the theological treatise all the more unsettling.

The beautiful, lucid hand of Daniel Skinner that marks the portion of the theological treatise he is said to have recopied masks, it would seem, a condition of uncertainty and even tumult reflected in our attempt to understand the nature of Skinner's identity and the putative relationship Skinner cultivated with John Milton. The prevailing tendency is to produce narratives around Skinner based primarily upon his own self-estimates, delineated principally in his letters, and upon the estimates of those with whom he has corresponded or has had dealings. These documents render Skinner ultimately elusive. There is the "good" Daniel Skinner and the "bad" Daniel Skinner. The good Daniel Skinner is the figure that he seeks to project in his letters; the bad Daniel Skinner is the figure that emerges as one penetrates beneath the young man's rhetoric of self-representation.

In his biography of Milton, William Riley Parker generally opts for the good Daniel Skinner. Thus, Parker records that Skinner (born about 1651) came of good stock as the son of "a prosperous London merchant" who was "possibly a relative of Milton's friend and former student, Cyriack Skinner." Although the suggestion of a relationship between the families of Daniel Skinner and Cyriack Skinner might serve to enhance the portrait of Daniel, Parker admits that he has no evidence to justify his claim. Nonetheless, the possibility of such a tie (no matter how remote) places Daniel in a privileged position, one that reinforces the narrative of a young man in a quest for the knowledge and counsel that the old, blind man might provide. Parker accordingly creates a scenario in which Milton aided Skinner in preparation for admission to the university, in this case, Trinity College, Cambridge, where Skinner did matriculate in the 1670s. Building upon what amounts to a narrative of "bonding," Parker observes that Skinner "made himself especially useful to his teacher." Possessed of native intelligence and strong scribal abilities, the young man no doubt proved himself to be "an almost ideal amanuensis." Now that the narrative of bonding and nurturing has Skinner ensconced in Milton's good graces, Parker is able to proceed to the crucial issue at hand—the transcription of the theological treatise, among Milton's other papers. "Intent upon getting his papers in shape for publication," Parker conjectures, the blind author had his protégé produce "clear transcripts" of works earlier written by various hands and now in need of editing and "perhaps final revision."[113]

The narrative even enables the biographer to draw some chronological conclusions. Thus, although there is no record of when this process of transcription was begun, Parker still conjectures that it "seems likely" to have been some time before 1670. We now have a narrative of authorship and transcription that allows for dating. More to the point, the narrative allows for the establishment of an enduring relationship. It is clear to Parker that Milton came to trust his young friend without reservation, so much so that Milton "bequeathed" to Skinner as an "affectionate legacy" the manuscripts not only of the Letters of State but of the theological treatise, among other works. "The elderly Milton was much drawn to bright young men," Parker benignly observes, but to none was he drawn more fondly than this one. Parker sees in the Milton-Skinner relationship the bond of father and son that the great man never really had the opportunity to enjoy. It appears that father and son shared a tacit understanding that Skinner would arrange for the publication of the letters and the treatise abroad, "making what he could out of them for his pains."[114] The papers represented an inheritance of sorts in payment for all that the son had performed as a service to his surrogate father.

What such a reading of the "good" Daniel Skinner does is to eliminate any possibility of uncertainty in the paternal bequest of one's treasures to the wholly loving and responsible son, an individual who will behave solely in the father's best interest. The narrative that arises from this reading is hermetically sealed: nothing can threaten its standing as a story of filial obedience. There are no unprofitable servants here. Under these circumstances, one is entirely certain of the circumstances underlying not only the relationship between father and son but the nature of authorship and the transmission of the author's work for generations to come. The responsibility for that transmission has been securely placed in the hands of one in whom the author has complete confidence. Recopying the author's work for posterity, the scribe fulfills the father-son relationship admirably.

The implications of the narrative are those that conceive author, work, and transmitter as heir in the most ideal, indeed, in the most romantic, of terms. Those who fashion and believe in such a narrative are certain that the plot has a beginning, middle, and end in which all possible questions are resolved and all potential loose ends are tied up." Parker himself, however, is aware of the difficulties associated with Daniel Skinner. Acknowledging in his account of Skinner's behavior that the young man's character was not above reproach, Parker nonetheless adheres to the "good" Daniel Skinner, a view reflected in Parker's own rhetorical question: "Who will now pass judgment on this 'very pretty young man'?"[115] The answer, of course, is just about everyone committed to the notion of the "bad" Skinner. It is this notion that sheds light on how Skinner is conceived by those who inclined to call into question the narrative of nurturing and support fostered in Parker's account.

According to this contrary dispensation, Skinner is conceived not as the faithful servant or protégé of the "great man," but as the kind of untrustworthy opportunist who behaves in a totally reprehensible manner. Once the circumstances of this behavior are considered, they call into question the terms of any narrative that seeks to foster a benign reading of Skinner's behavior. In his assessment of that behavior, Maurice Kelley, for example, calls into question the idea that Skinner either acted as Milton's amanuensis or had established any sort of meaningful bond with Milton during the time that Skinner and Milton were presumably acquainted. For Kelley, all the speculation about a nurturing relationship is simply that, mere speculation. Moreover, Kelley argues that there is no concrete evidence to substantiate the claim that Milton actually bequeathed his writings to Skinner at all. Rather, it appears that shortly after Milton's death, Skinner simply "helped himself to Milton's papers with little, if any, 'By your leave'" (YP 6:37). Kelley's view derives much of its authority from a letter discovered among the papers of Sir Henry Coventry, Sir Joseph Williamson's predecessor as Secretary of State for the Northern Department and, since 1674, his counterpart in the Southern Department. (The letter is now in the collection of the Marquis of Bath at Longleat.[116]) It must be stated at the outset, however, that the authority this letter enjoys is very difficult to ascertain, because the document itself is neither dated, addressed, nor signed. It appears to have been written (at some point between 1676 and 1677?) by an anonymous informant concerning the events following Milton's death. By his own admission, the informant allows that his information is based on second-hand knowledge. Nonetheless, he writes: "I am informed that since the death of Mr. Milton his Books have byn lookt over by one Mr. Skinner a scholar and a bold young man who has cull'd out what he thought fitt, & amongst the rest he has taken a manuscript of Mr. Milton's written on the Civil & Ecclesiastical Government of the Kingdom."[117] It is unclear what is implied by the reference to a manuscript on the civil and ecclesiastical government, but, whatever is implied, it is quite clear that the author of the unsigned letter views Skinner as suspect in his proceedings, indeed, as one who took the opportunity (without approval) to make off with whatever came to hand.[118]

The portrait that emerges here is one of Skinner as an opportunist who filched whatever he could get his hands on for the purpose of his own gain. In their study of the provenance of the *De Doctrina Christiana*, Campbell et al. are even more direct in their estimate of Skinner. For them, Skinner was essentially "a tomb-robber who somehow secured access to papers, perhaps too carelessly regarded by Milton's widow."[119] Kelley concludes that Skinner's "manifest untrustworthiness" is such that we are *not* at liberty to assume that he "worked on the Picard manuscript at Milton's direction and that he received it from Milton as a legacy." This means that whatever Skinner did with the documents he filched was undertaken after Milton's death and not necessarily as the result of Milton's directive (YP 6:36–37).[120]

What we know of Skinner's activities once the documents were in his possession appears to confirm a reading of the "bad" Skinner. Those activities amount to something like a drama of a wayward youth ambitious to make his mark in the world but frustrated at every turn. One cannot help but think of Skinner as a rogue embarked upon adventures ultimately doomed to failure. The details of his adventures (already the subject of much discussion) need not concern us here.[121] Suffice it to say that this unscrupulous "bold" young man set himself two goals, neither of which bore fruit. First, he sought to get the theological treatise and the Letters of State published by the Dutch printer Daniel Elzevier (Elzevir); second, he sought to secure an appointment in the English embassy at Nimeguen, in the Netherlands. Although Skinner enjoyed the support of Samuel Pepys, the young man found his efforts for advancement effectively sabotaged by Sir Joseph Williamson, Secretary of State.[122] Skinner may well have filched the documents of the dead Milton, but Sir Joseph made certain that the papers of what he called "that late villain Milton" would not be allowed to infect an unsuspecting public. In keeping with Sir Joseph's view, Daniel Elzevier hypocritically protested that he too would have nothing to do with so suspect a figure as John Milton. (As Parker observed some time ago, Elzevier's protestations rang hollow, given the printer's record of having advertised seven Milton editions for sale in 1674.) The whole matter of Skinner's aspirations and the surreptitious activities of Sir Joseph and others to thwart those aspirations amounted to what Parker calls a series of double crosses that ultimately resulted in a betrayal of the memory of Milton himself as a result of the way in which his papers were handled after his death.[123]

As recorded in his correspondence with Samuel Pepys in 1676, Skinner's story is a tale of bad faith and indeed betrayal on all sides.[124] The letters clearly bespeak a frustrated individual whose principles are easily compromised. Among these letters, that which Skinner sent to Pepys from Rotterdam on 9/19 November 1676 will serve as an example of the extent to which Skinner was willing to manipulate Pepys in order to further his own ends.[125]

With all the rhetorical force that poor Skinner (in need of cash and bereft of his hopes for preferment) has at his disposal, he first attempts to explain to Pepys why he has not yet repaid a loan that Pepys had tendered him some time earlier. The extravagance with which Skinner praises Pepys ("Thus methoughts I hugg'd my self a long time with the hopes of soe good and great a Patron") reeks of a sycophantic extravagance that is meant not only to flatter and appease Pepys (who wanted to be repaid) but to play upon Pepys's sympathy by suggesting the dire straits in which Skinner found himself (unrelieved by his own father, who as a successful merchant was certainly in a position to advance his son the money he needed).

As the letter unfolds, Skinner does not hesitate to engage in an act of self-aggrandizement by reminding Pepys that Milton had bequeathed his papers to the young man: "Your worship may please to remember I once acquainted you with my having the works of Milton which he left behind him to me." Assuming that Skinner actually filched the papers, we would certainly be correct in charging Skinner with what amounts to an outright lie. If Skinner does indeed lie about how the papers came into his possession, his statement of "bequeathal" might well signal his desire to believe in the story he has created in his own defense. One senses an element of self-delusion here. Lies beget lies that are compounded by additional lies. Thus, in his letter to Pepys, Skinner offers what amounts to a false account of his dealings with Daniel Elsevier and Sir Joseph Williamson. No doubt to mollify Pepys even further, Skinner assures his "patron" that he has nullified his agreement with Elsevier and is now in possession of the papers. These assertions are simply not true.[126] Once again, Skinner fabricates a narrative to suit his own ends. Having dug himself into a pit thus far, he proceeds to dig himself in even further. He maintains that he is "soe farr from ever procuring a line of Milton printed," that he is prepared to consign his copies and all his other papers "to the fire."

Here, he distances himself from Milton as far as possible. Although Skinner "happen'd to be acquainted with Milton in his lifetime," the young man protests that he was never in the least "tainted" by any of Milton's "principles." Skinner is so free of such taint that he does not hesitate to declare his unrivaled and everlasting loyalty to king, church, and country. The correspondence that follows Skinner's letter suggests that Pepys was more than able to see through the young man's blandishments. In fact, Skinner's letter does little more than exacerbate Pepys's suspicions and apprehensions. Skinner, Pepys charges in his letter of 17 November 1676, is guilty of something tantamount to a "crime" from which he must be absolved. In short, Pepys is not to be taken in by the falsifications of which the young man has proven himself guilty.[127] This is the bad Skinner, a young man whose short-comings must be seen to outweigh whatever virtues the good Skinner might be able to claim. At the heart of this struggle between the good and the bad Skinner (and the narratives that portray this struggle) lies the fate of the papers that Skinner putatively filched in his quest for self-aggrandizement.

If the qualities that distinguish the bad Skinner are accurate, then this was a decidedly self-serving individual capable of theft and more than willing to lie about his activities in order to save his skin. More egregious still, this record of shortcomings was exacerbated by a whole complex of double crosses for which Skinner, although not the only guilty party, was nonetheless an all-too-willing participant. On balance, one must conclude that the bad Skinner finally outdoes the good. When we think of Skinner we are reminded not simply of youthful extravagance but of the subterfuge that sacri-ficed any sense of confidence he might have otherwise enjoyed. "Who will now pass judgment on this 'very pretty young man'?" Skinner, it would seem, passed judgment on himself. Given the uncertainties that surround Skinner and his activities, one might well be hesitant to stand by his transcription as a scrupulous witness of an earlier text , which itself is no doubt a copy of ear-lier texts.

Who was ultimately responsible for these earlier texts? Where is his signature to be found? The answer is not to be had. The very notion that the Skinner text is a copy of an earlier version is itself finally a supposition, for the absent text is precisely that: absent. We are understandably inclined to be-lieve that the Skinner text is a recopying of an earlier Picard version, but we ultimately do not know. Assuming that it is indeed a recopying, how trust-worthy can it be? Given what we know of Skinner's character, we would be justified in concluding that we are dealing with a highly untrustworthy and potentially duplicitous copyist at best. In his edition of the Letters of State for the Yale University Press edition of Milton's prose works, J. Max Patrick observes that the texts recopied by Skinner for that undertaking are "unreli-able." As they are recorded in the Columbia edition, the variants demon-strate that Skinner "frequently tampered with the wording to 'improve it'" (YP 5:472).

One might well surmise that what is true of the Letters of State is no less true of the *De Doctrina Christiana*, and, in fact, our earlier glance at the variants that do exist reveals that there are indeed discrepancies. The situa-tion once again prompts us to recall what the author of the theological trea-tise says in the chapter titled *De Scriptura Sacra* (I.xxx) about the New Testament: this is a document that had been committed to the care of "way-ward and uncertain guardians [*custodibus tam incertis tamque lubricis*]" through whose "bad offices" it has been transmitted in a state that is essentially "corrupt" (YP 6:589; CM 16:278; SP 9/61, 397). It is the term *lubricis* that is particularly telling. Implying that which is "slippery," "smooth," and "deceitful," it goes far to suggest how the "bad" Skinner might well have conducted himself in his transcription of substantive portions of the theological treatise.

However one might be inclined to interpret the unfolding narrative of Daniel Skinner, one point is clear. He provides no greater assurances than does Jeremie Picard of how much trust we should place in the integrity of the text of the so-called *De Doctrina Christiana* as it presently stands. Those whom we generally recognize as the two major "hands" in the transcribing/ recopying of the theological treatise do not offer much hope for the possibility that the notion of either author or text rests on solid ground. That man of many identities (Jeremie/Jeremiah Picard/Piskard/Packer) still remains a shadowy figure lodged among the poor melancholy souls who have taken up residence in the London Hospital for the Insane. The young fellow who represents himself as Milton's protégé may or may not have occupied that privileged position. Even if he had been that fortunate, he so violated whatever relationship he might have had with his mentor that it little matters what the nature of the relationship was. Like the shadowy Picard, Skinner presents us with a conundrum as baffling as can be.

What is certain is that the narratives through which the roles of Picard and Skinner are inscribed render the question of authorship all-the-more problematical. If the *De Doctrina Christiana* is a palimpsest upon which many layers of writing have been effaced by other layers, it is also a work that has given rise to multiple narratives through which the lives of those who have left their mark on it are inscribed. These, in a sense, are its authors as much as the individual we would like to call the One True Author is the source of its begetting. Whereas the Miltonic faithful are never in doubt about the identity of the One True Author, those of us who are unwilling to subscribe categorically to this belief remain open to the uncertainties, indeed, the mysteries, that the text encodes. For this is finally a posthumous text, one born after the death of its father, a belated text, unearthed (perhaps like Milton's own body) by those determined to claim its canonicity by virtue of a signature (and perhaps even a title) "forged" on an otherwise anonymous document. Name and title appear and disappear at will, are written and rewritten, in the multiple narratives through which a work called the *De Doctrina Christiana* has been proclaimed beyond the shadow of a doubt the most precious possession of one John Milton Englishman.

University of Illinois, Chicago

NOTES

I take this opportunity to extend my heartfelt thanks to Professors William B. Hunter, John T. Shawcross, and Stanley Fish for their astute and careful reading of the manuscript and for their wise and judicious suggestions. I also wish to thank the Institute for the Humanities at the University of Illinois at Chicago, which awarded me a fellowship for the 2000–01 academic year to work on Milton's theology. My colleagues at the Institute and its superb director Mary Beth Rose provided the kind of intellectual stimulation necessary to advance my project. Throughout my discussion of the *De Doctrina Christiana*, I take into account the manuscript itself, now housed at the Public Record Office (PRO), Kew, Richmond, Surrey, under the press mark SP 9/61, which I cite by page number. The four images of pages of the manuscript reproduced here are published by permission of the PRO. In addition to examining the manuscript at the PRO, I also had at my personal disposal both a microfilm and a photocopy of the original. For their good offices in placing the manuscript at my disposal, I thank the staff of the PRO, and I am especially grateful to Ian Malcolm, Microfilm Officer, PRO, for his invaluable assistance in securing the microfilm of the manuscript for me. My examination of the manuscript has been aided by the sharp eye of my wife Roslyn C. Lieb. Finally, I thank John Malcolm Cullars, Bibliographer for the Humanities, Richard J. Daley Library, University of Illinois at Chicago, for providing photocopies of the microfilm.

1. See Hunter's "Visitation Unimplor'd": Milton and the Authorship of "*De Doctrina Christiana*" (Pittsburgh, 1998). Among the several studies that constitute the debate from its early stages up to the present, see William B. Hunter, "The Provenance of the *Christian Doctrine*," *SEL* 32 (1992): 129–42, and in the same issue "Forum: Milton's *Christian Doctrine*," with responses by Barbara K. Lewalski (143–54), John T. Shawcross (155–62), and a counterresponse by William B. Hunter (163–66). Adding his own voice is Gordon Campbell, "The Authorship of *De Doctrina Christiana*," *MQ* 26 (1992): 129–30. Continuing the debate, see Hunter, "The Provenance of the *Christian Doctrine*: Addenda from the Bishop of Salisbury," *SEL* 33 (1993): 191–207; "Forum II: Milton's *Christian Doctrine*," appeared in *SEL* 34 (1994) along with essays by Maurice Kelley, "The Provenance of John Milton's *Christian Doctrine*: A Reply to William B. Hunter" (153–64); Christopher Hill, "Professor William B. Hunter, Bishop Burgess, and John Milton" (165–94); and William B. Hunter, "Animadversions upon the Remonstrants' Defenses against Burgess and Hunter" (195–203). In an attempt to make sense of the debate and to provide a full and unbiased account of the issues, Gordon Campbell, Thomas N. Corns, John K. Hale, David I. Holmes, and Fiona J. Tweedie combined forces to produce the immensely helpful "The Provenance of *De Doctrina Christiana*," *MQ* 31 (1997): 67–117, hereafter referred to as Campbell et al. Among articles that continue to appear are Paul R. Sellin, "The Reference to John Milton's *Tetrachordon* in *De Doctrina Christiana*," *SEL* 37 (1997): 137–49; Barbara K. Lewalski, "Milton and the *De Doctrina Christiana*: Evidences of Authorship, *Milton Studies* 36, ed. Albert C. Labriola (Pittsburgh: 1998), 203–28."Responses" and "Further Responses" were issued by William B. Hunter and Paul R. Sellin, respectively, in *MQ* 33 (1999): 31–37. See also Stephen N. Fallon, "Milton's Arminianism and the Authorship of *De Doctrina Christiana*," *Texas Studies in Literature and Language* 41 (1999): 103–27; William B. Hunter, "*De Doctrina Christiana*: Nunc Quo Vadis," *MQ* 34 (2000): 97–101; and Paul R. Sellin, " 'If Not Milton, Who Did Write the DDC?': The Amyrauldian Connection," *Living Texts: Interpreting Milton*, ed. Kristin A. Pruitt and Charles W. Durham (Selinsgrove, Pa., 2000), 237–63. In keeping with her earlier arguments on behalf of a Miltonic authorship, Barbara K. Lewalski reasserts that point of view in her new work, *The Life of John Milton: A Critical Biography* (Oxford, 2000), 415–19.

2. References in my text to the Latin of the *De Doctrina Christiana* are to *The Works of John Milton*, 18 vols. in 21, ed. Frank Allen Patterson et al. (New York, 1931–38), hereafter

designated CM and cited parenthetically by volume and page number. References to translations of the *De Doctrina Christiana*, as well as to Milton's prose works in general, are to either the CM or the *Complete Prose Works of John Milton*, 8 vols. in 10, ed. Don M. Wolfe et al. (New Haven, 1953–82), hereafter designated YP and cited parenthetically by volume and page number.

3. In an illuminating essay, "Milton and 'Of Christian Doctrine': Doubts, Definitions, Connotations, and Milton," in *Explorations in Renaissance Culture*, ed. Tita French Baumlin (Springfield, Mo., 2001), John T. Shawcross seeks to move the discussion of the authorship of the *De Doctrina Christiana* in a similar direction. He demonstrates that even those writings by Milton acknowledged as canonical pose complex questions of what it means to be an author. Thus, the *Artis Logicae Plenior Institutio ad Petri Rami Methodum Concinnata* (1672) not only replicates almost verbatim the *Dialecticae Libri duo* of the French philosopher and educational reformer Peter Ramus (fleshed out by the commentary of George Downame, Bishop of Derry, among other commentators), but appends an abridged version of Downame's own *Praxis Logicae Analytica*, along with an abridged and greatly edited *Life of Peter Ramus* by the Swiss Ramist scholar Johann Thomas Freigius (Freige). Despite the multiplicity of "authors" represented by these documents, the *Artis Logicae* is conceived as the work of one author, John Milton. As Walter J. Ong wisely observes, the *Artis Logicae* is "presented so that the work of Ramus, Milton, Downame, and the other commentators form one continuous text" (YP 8:144). Corresponding instances appear in such works as the *Accedence Commenc't Grammar* (1669), the *History of Britain* (1670), and *A Brief History of Muscovia* (1682). Either published during Milton's own lifetime or issued posthumously, these works make problematic the whole idea of authorship.

4. On the efficacy of internal, as opposed to external, evidence see Ephim G. Fogel, "Salmons in Both, or Some Caveats for Canonical Scholars," *Evidence for Authorship: Essays on Problems of Attribution*, ed. David V. Erdman and Ephim G. Fogel (New York, 1966). In an encounter with either internal or external evidence, "an experienced scholar will surely be intelligently skeptical about both types and will bring to bear upon *all* attributions a stringent analysis" (71). Such an outlook is one that should ideally underscore any discussion of the provenance of the *De Doctrina Christiana*.

5. See, for example, both the Columbia edition (Latin original and English translation) and the Yale edition (English translation) for the printed forms (CM 14:2, 3, 16, 17; YP 6:117, 125). The practice of typesetting the name and the initials in these forms can be traced to the original editions.

6. For the two appearances of the name in the manuscript, see SP 9/61, 1, 7. For the initials, see SP 9/61, 5. The initials are circled in the manuscript.

7. Campbell et al., "The Provenance of *De Doctrina Christiana*," 92–93. Campbell et al. surmise that Milton's name "may have been added in the nineteenth century."

8. Even before the debate over authorship began, the editors of the Columbia edition of Milton's works asserted (without elaboration) that "IOANNES MILTONVS ANGLUS" and the initials "I.M." are "evidently added in a later hand" (CM 17:432). Maurice Kelley, the editor of the treatise for the Yale *Prose*, summarily dismisses such a finding as not at all evident (YP 6:117 n. 1). For Kelley, the "hand" is contemporary with Milton, rather than "later." (The editors of the Columbia edition neglect to specify what they mean by "later.") Interestingly, the Latin form of the name that appears in the treatise ("IOANNES MILTONVS") is uncharacteristic of the forms that Milton adopted. As Kelley himself observes, the form that Milton customarily preferred was "Miltonius," not "Miltonus" ("A Review of Four Entries on the Milton Mss. in *A Milton Encyclopedia*," *MQ* 20 [1986]: 32; cited by Campbell et al., "The Provenance of *De Doctrina Christiana*," 93).

9. As William B. Hunter observes, "it is evident from examination of the original pages of *DDC* that they bore no author's name at all," nor do we have any true idea of who was responsible for the signatures themselves. "Their purpose, however, is obvious: to identify the author of an otherwise quite anonymous manuscript" ("Visitation Unimplor'd," 45–46). In short, the very presence of signatures and initials (by a signatory who is himself anonymous) serves only to compound the mystery. The signature becomes a mark not of identification but of occlusion, if not subterfuge.

10. In the Columbia University Press edition, this is rendered *John Milton An Englishman His Christian Doctrine Compiled From the Holy Scriptures Alone In Two Posthumous Books* (CM 14:17).

11. So the *OED* (under "posthumous," s.v.), citing Drummond of Hawthornden (1619): "He [Ben Jonson] was posthumous, being born a month after his father's death." For the Latin etymology, see *A Latin Dictionary*, comp. Charlton T. Lewis and Charles Short (Oxford, 1879), s.v.

12. See Lewis and Short's *A Latin Dictionary*, s.v.

13. See my discussion of the disinterment in *Milton and the Culture of Violence* (Ithaca, N.Y., 1994), 3–10.

14. John Milton, *A Treatise of Christian Doctrine, Compiled From the Holy Scriptures Alone*, trans. Charles R. Sumner (Cambridge, 1925), x. The heading to the first book of the treatise in this edition emphasizes its posthumous state: *A Posthumous Treatise On Christian Doctrine Compiled From Holy Scriptures Alone: In Two Books By John Milton.* Sumner's "Preliminary Observations" reappears in the Bohn edition of *The Prose Works of John Milton*, 5 vols. (London, 1848–53), vol. 4, xi. Incorporating Sumner's translation, the Columbia edition also includes *Posthumous* in the title as a heading to the first book (CM 14:17).

15. My own examination of the manuscript convinces me that, whereas there might be a punctuation mark after *duo*, it is not particularly evident. At the very least, it has been written over by the "p" in *posthumi*. In any case, there certainly is a period after *posthumi*. None of this provides clear evidence of the provenance of *posthumi* in the production and copying of the manuscript.

16. *Visitation Unimplor'd*, 44–45. I am not convinced that this is the case.

17. In an e-mail to me of March 21, 2001, John T. Shawcross maintains that "*posthumi* is given in [Daniel] Skinner's hand as is the rest of the title."

18. See Joseph Moody McDill, *Milton and the Pattern of Calvinism* (1938; reprinted Folcroft, Pa., 1969), 401.

19. Maurice Kelley, "The Recovery, Printing, and Reception of Milton's *Christian Doctrine*," *HLQ* 31 (1967): 35, 37 n. 9; and William B. Hunter, " '*De Doctrina Christiana*': Nunc Quo Vadis," 98. It was so named by William Sidney Walker, who, as will be discussed, aided in the translation of the treatise.

20. I discuss this matter in more detail below.

21. See SP 9/61, 7, 462. For the title of the second book, CM has *De Dei Cultu*, but the preposition *De* does not appear in the title heading of the manuscript, nor does *De* appear in the heading of the first chapter of the second book, which has *Bonis operibus*, not *De Bonis Operibus*, as mistakenly transcribed in the CM. The CM also misleadingly reprints the author/title designation as it appears as a heading of the first book of the manuscript but it is totally absent from the second book: *IOANNIS MILTONI ANGLI De Doctrina Christiana . . .* (17:2).

22. In *Caput primum* of the second book, the phrase *Dei cultu* becomes *cultu Dei* by way of an insertion (SP 9/61, 462).

23. All this discussion of posthumous authorship might lead one to recall Roland Barthes's views concerning the so-called "death of the author," but the arguments that Barthes mounts are based on premises alien to the kinds of issues that engage us here. Whereas Barthes's outlook is

tied to the commonplace post-Nietzschean philosophy concerning the death of God, notions of authorship that pertain to such a work as the *De Doctrina Christiana* are based on assumptions fully at odds with the "death-of-God"/"death-of-author" controversy. Stanley Fish has prompted me to see the modes of thought grounded in the *De Doctrina Christiana*, on the one hand, and the theories of Barthes, on the other, as alien. See Barthes's "The Death of the Author," in *Image Music Text*, ed. and trans. by Stephen Heath (New York, 1977), 142–48. Of interest in the same volume is Barthes's "From Work to Text," 155–64. Likewise of interest is Michel Foucault, "What Is an Author?," *Textual Strategies*, ed. Josue Harari (Ithaca, 1979), 145–50, and passim.

24. The issue of Miltonic authorship in general is one that has increasingly engaged scholars over the past several years. Most recently, see *Milton Studies* 38, ed. Albert C. Labriola and Michael Lieb (Pittsburgh, 2000). Of particular interest in this collection is Joseph Wittreich's illuminating essay " 'Reading' Milton: The Death (and Survival) of the Author," 10–46. While arguing on behalf of a multi-authored presence of Milton in his works, Wittreich nonetheless is confirmed in his belief that the *De Doctrina Christiana* is, in a sense, the exclusive product of one author, John Milton (41–43).

25. Sonnet 7, in *The Complete Poetry of John Milton*, ed. John T. Shawcross (Garden City, 1971), 10. All references to Milton's poetry in my text are to this edition.

26. *Lycidas*, 82–83.

27. Compare the discussion of Holy Scriptures in book I, chapter 30, of the *De Doctrina Christiana*, a chapter I address later in this essay. In that chapter, the author speaks in particular of the authority of Scriptures (the text of which is uncertain) giving way to the Spirit of God within us.

28. My translation. Whereas YP 6:121 has "my dearest and best possession," CM 14:9 has "my best and richest possession."

29. See Arthur Sewell, *A Study in Milton's Christian Doctrine* (London, 1939), 1–3; Maurice Kelley, *This Great Argument: A Study of Milton's "De Doctrina Christiana" as a Gloss upon "Paradise Lost"* (Princeton, 1941), 26–32; Introduction to YP 6:15–22. For William Riley Parker, the entire theological treatise is the product of a three-year period (May 1655–May 1658) rather than a work produced in stages. See Parker's *Milton: A Biography*, 2d ed. rev., ed. Gordon Campbell, 2 vols. (Oxford, 1996), vol. 2, 1052,

30. See Hunter's discussion of Milton's *"Index Theologicus"* (CM 18:227), drawn from several cross references in the Commonplace Book (*Visitation Unimplor'd*, 2–3). In his entry on the *Index Theologicus* in *A Milton Encyclopedia* (vol. 4, 103), Hunter calls into question the assumption that the *De Doctrina Christiana* owes its provenance to the *Index*.

31. Questions surrounding both the stages and the dates of composition are noted in John M. Steadman's thorough and balanced treatment of the *De Doctrina Christiana* in *A Milton Encyclopedia*, vol. 2, 112, and passim. From the time of its publication in 1825, the *De Doctrina Christiana* has raised various questions regarding a date (or dates) of composition. Steadman summarizes as follows: (1) before 1641, (2) 1643–45, (3) 1655–58, (4) 1658–60, and (5) 1660 or later. As Steadman observes, "one, two, or even three stages of composition" are possible. In a letter to me of March 27, 2001, John T. Shawcross invokes Allan H. Gilbert's *On the Composition of "Paradise Lost," a Study of the Ordering and Insertion of Material* (Chapel Hill, 1947) as an exemplary source of information on how Milton's works were composed. "If Gilbert is generally right about how *PL* was put together from sections written earlier," we might well consider the possibility that some of the sections of the *De Doctrina Christiana* were correspondingly "written earlier and separately and then put together in organized fashion." In any case, any consideration of the dates of composition must be undertaken in the context of the debate over authorship. See also James Holly Hanford, "The Date of Milton's *De Doctrina Christiana*," *Studies in Philology* 17 (1920): 308–18.

32. In *The Early Lives of Milton*, ed. Helen Darbishire (New York, 1965), 9, 29, 31, 47, 61, 192, 269.

33. See John T. Shawcross's entry on Milton's biographers in *A Milton Encyclopedia*, vol. 1, 165–67, for a detailed discussion of the authority each of the lives enjoys.

34. At least this is the conclusion drawn by William B. Hunter, who focuses on the last three to establish a context for the emergence of the *De Doctrina Christiana* (*Visitation Unimplor'd*, 19–25).

35. As an altogether accurate source of biographical information concerning his uncle, Phillips is, to be sure, not above reproach. He errs, for example, in his account of the dates of his uncle's birth and death. Phillips's biography precedes the letters in *Letters of State, Written by Mr. John Milton, To most of the Sovereign Princes and Republicks of Europe. From the Year 1649. Till the Year 1659* (London, 1694). Appended to Phillips's life of his uncle, in turn, is a "Catalogue of his [Milton's] Works, never before Printed." The catalogue is instructive as much for what it omits as for what it includes. Under the heading of the "Opera Latina," the catalogue makes no mention of the "perfect System of Divinity" discussed in the life itself. No doubt, there is no reference to the *De Doctrina Christiana* because it had not been published in Milton's lifetime. Likewise omitted is "Mr. John Milton's Character of the Long Parliament" (1681). The catalogue also excludes any reference to *Of Education*, which was most certainly published during Milton's lifetime. I mention these discrepancies because the catalogue is germane to the Columbia University Press edition of *The Works of John Milton*, the editors of which compiled a list of the "Prose Works Erroneously Ascribed To Milton" based upon the works not mentioned in Phillips's catalogue. The editors reasoned as follows: Any work *not* mentioned by Phillips in his catalogue must be deemed suspect, because "there is no doubt that Phillips enjoyed his [Milton's] confidence and published his own list at a time when prejudice no longer made any concealment necessary" (CM 18:693–39).

36. Milton's nephew Edward Phillips (1630–96?), the elder of the two sons of Edward and Anne Milton Phillips, studied with his uncle from about 1640 to 1646. Edward's younger brother John Phillips (1631–1706?) was the first to be under his uncle's care as resident in Milton's household and the last to depart. Whereas Edward Phillips was with his uncle until at least 1646, John remained until autumn 1652. See John T. Shawcross's entry on Milton as tutor in *A Milton Encyclopedia*, vol. 8, 96–98.

37. "The Life of Mr. John Milton," *Early Lives*, 60.

38. See *OED*, s.v.

39. "The Life of Mr. John Milton," *Early Lives*, 61.

40. "The Life of Mr. John Milton," *Early Lives*, 61. The extent to which the *De Doctrina Christiana* is "collected" out of William Ames and John Wolleb is perhaps debatable. For an account of Wolleb's influence, see Maurice Kelley, "Milton's Debt to Wolleb's *Compendium Theologiae Christianae*," *PMLA*, 50 (1935): 116–18.

41. "The Life of Mr. John Milton," *Early Lives*, 61.

42. The ten-to-fifteen years of age reference is to Phillips's own account ("The Life of Mr. John Milton," *Early Lives*, 60). The reference to the bow and the sinews of Ulysses is to *Of Education* (YP 2:415). In Milton's educational tract, this latter reference, of course, is specifically to teachers, but it applies equally well to students. The age range that Milton projects in *Of Education* is between twelve and twenty-one years. Edward Phillips's idealized account of what he and his brother John experienced under the tutelage of their uncle must be seen in the context of John Aubrey's observations concerning Mary Powell's having "often-times heard his [Milton's] Nephews cry, and beaten" ("Minutes of the Life of John Milton," *Early Lives*, 14).

43. Dobranski, *Milton, Authorship, and the Book Trade* (Cambridge, 1999), 6.

44. "The Life of Mr. John Milton," *Early Lives*, 61.

45. *"Visitation Unimplor'd,"* 30. For Hunter's reading of "dictation," see *OED*, s.v. "Dictation" in Hunter's sense appears in the *OED* under definition 2.

46. The phrase derives from *Paradise Lost* 3:122.

47. *"Visitation Unimplor'd,"* 30–33. For the sake of argument, Paul Sellin suggests other possibilities for authorship, "based upon the tenable assumption that Milton was hostile to the treatise or an enemy of the author" responsible for producing it ("If Not Milton," 237).

48. I draw here upon Northrop Frye's analysis of romance in the *Anatomy of Criticism: Four Essays* (Princeton, 1957), 186–87, which remains a classic in its field.

49. See the account of Lemon in the *Dictionary of National Biography*, ed. Leslie Stephen and Sidney Lee, vol. 11, 910–11 (hereinafter designated as *DNB*). Interestingly enough, Gordon Campbell views Lemon as anything but a "hero." Campbell calls Lemon an "ambitious and unscrupulous man," who "forged Milton's name on the manuscript of the theological treatise" ("The Authorship of *De Doctrina Christiana,*" *MQ* 26 [1992]: 129–30). It is unclear what evidence Campbell enlists to support this conclusion. On the other hand, Lemon, it appears, was a close friend of that old forger John Payne Collier (Hunter [citing Campbell], *Visitation Unimplor'd*, 47).

50. Kelley, Introduction to the *Christian Doctrine* (YP 6:3–4). Like the manuscript of the *De Doctrina Christiana* (SP 9/61), the Letters of State (SP 9/194) are preserved in the Public Record Office. The collection of transcriptions of Milton's Letters of State was written in the same hand (that of Daniel Skinner) as that which transcribed the first part of the *De Doctrina Christiana*. In support of the canonicity of the *De Doctrina Christiana*, scholars all-too-often cite the Skinner transcription of the Letters of State. As John T. Shawcross wisely observes, this fact alone is insufficient to assume evidence of authorship of the theological treatise (*John Milton: The Self and the World* [Lexington, Ky., 1993], 279). Skinner had attempted to arrange for the publication of the Letters of State, but before such arrangements could be made, the first edition of the *Literae Pseudo-Senatus Anglicani Cromwellii* (Amsterdam, 1676) appeared. For an account of the circumstances surrounding its publication, see Shawcross, "A Survey of Milton's Prose Works," *Achievements of the Left Hand: Essays on the Prose of John Milton*, ed. Michael Lieb and John T. Shawcross (Amherst, 1974), 347–60.

51. As Kelley notes (Introduction to *Christian Doctrine* [YP 6:3]), there are three manuscript reports of Lemon's discovery. These are found attached at the end of SP 9/61. My references are to the manuscript of the first report.

52. "Milton's Posthumous Work" (January 1824, 1). Kelley observes that "the treatise was wrapped in proof sheets of an Elsevier Horace" and, along with the Letters of State, wrapped in a dark paper envelope addressed "To Mr. Skinner, Mercht." (YP 6:3). In his first report, Lemon concludes mistakenly that the Skinner referred to here is Cyriack Skinner, Milton's student, friend, and amanuensis.

53. The announcement of Lemon's discovery appeared in *The Literary Gazette* (January 17, 1824, 41), reprinted in *The Times* (January 21, 1824, 2e). See Kelley, Introduction to *Christian Doctrine* (YP 6:3–4).

54. I refer to Lemon's "Account of the Posthumous Theological Work of Milton, recently discovered by Mr. Lemon, Sen. Deputy Keeper of His Majesty's State Papers" (January, 1824, 6), appended to SP 9/61.

55. *The Parliamentary Debates*, n.s. 10 (London, 1824), cols. 1465–66; cited by Kelley in YP 6:3–4.

56. George Henry Sumner, *Life of Charles Richard Sumner, D.D.* (London, 1876), 97, cited by Kelley, Introduction to *Christian Doctrine* (YP 6:4–5).

57. Hunter, *"De Doctrina Christiana: Nunc Quo Vadis,"* 98–99. Walker speaks of his attempt to render the treatise more "Miltonic" by virtue of the alterations he has incorporated

into the text. In what amounts to a "forging" of utterances, Walker provided hundreds of "parallels" between the theological treatise and individual statements in Milton's works. The problems inherent in such an act of phrasing in accord with canonical works by Milton are reflected not only in the Sumner translation but in the Carey translation as well. See also Kelley, "The Recovery, Printing, and Reception of Milton's *Christian Doctrine*," 37 n. 9.

58. For a detailed list of subsequent editions (Latin and English), see Kelley, YP: 6,vii–viii. Extremely helpful in this regard is Albert J. Th. Eisenring, *Milton's "De Doctrina Christiana": An Historical Introduction and Critical Analysis* (Fribourg, 1946), 16–18. For a discussion of the omission of "Posthumous" ("*posthumi*") from the title page of the translations but the inclusion of the term as part of the title heading to the first book in the Sumner translations, see above.

59. See the account of Burgess in the *DNB*, vol. 3, 313–14.

60. The full title of Burgess's work is *Milton Not the Author of the Lately Discovered Arian Work "De Doctrina Christiana." Three Discourses, Delivered at the Anniversary Meetings of the Royal Society of Literature In the Years 1826, 1827, and 1828. To Which is Added, Milton Contrasted With Milton, and With the Scriptures* (London, 1829). This is a very rare volume indeed. Like Hunter, I have secured a copy that for some reason found its way to the Public Library of Cincinnati and Hamilton County, Ohio. I express here my appreciation to the Cincinnati Public Library for microfilming the book and sending me the microfilm, along with a hard copy. I have deposited a copy of the hard copy (along with the microfilm) in the Library of the University of Illinois at Chicago. In "The Provenance of the *Christian Doctrine*: Addenda," Hunter notes that in 1826, Burgess republished Milton's final prose tract *Of True Religion*, with a detailed introduction (*Protestant Union. A Treatise of True Religion, Heresy, Schism, and Toleration. To which is affixed a preface on Milton's Religious Principles and Unimpeachable Sincerity* [London, 1826]), arguing against the canonicity of the *De Doctrina Christiana* (191).

61. Hunter, "The Provenance of the *Christian Doctrine*: Addenda," 191; and "Animadversions upon the Remonstrants' Defenses against Burgess and Hunter," 101–102. In "Bishop Burgess and John Milton," *Bibliographical and Contextual Studies* (Lampeter, 1997), 79–98, James Ogden makes clear that Burgess's commentary, along with other early editions and commentaries, is in the collections of the Founders' Library, University of Wales.

62. "Animadversions," 202.

63. "Bishop Burgess and John Milton," 93–94.

64. Burgess, *Milton not the Author*, 66. Many (if not most) of Burgess's arguments reappear in various ways in Hunter's own arguments against canonicity.

65. Burgess, 66.

66. For the letter to Heimbach, see YP 8:3–4; CM 12:113–15.

67. Burgess, 67–68.

68. See Kelley's discussion of this boy in *This Great Argument*, 51–53, 248.

69. Francis E. Mineka, "The Critical Reception of Milton's *De Doctrina Christiana*," *University of Texas Studies in English*, 22 (1943): 115–47. See also Maurice Kelley, "The Recovery, Printing, and Reception of Milton's *Christian Doctrine*," 35–41.

70. *The Life of John Milton*, 6 vols. (1880; reprinted Gloucester, Mass., 1965), vol. 6, 817.

71. In 1827, the Latin of Sumner's text was reprinted in one volume by E. Fleischer, Braunschweig. As indicated, the Bohn edition of *The Prose Works of John Milton* (1883–84) has the Sumner translation "revised and corrected."

72. Whereas Sumner has JOHN MILTON AN ENGLISHMAN HIS CHRISTIAN DOCTRINE COMPILED FROM THE HOLY SCRIPTURES ALONE IN TWO POSTHUMOUS BOOKS, Carey has THE ENGLISHMAN JOHN MILTON'S TWO BOOKS OF INVESTIGATIONS INTO CHRISTIAN DOCTRINE DRAWN FROM THE SACRED SCRIPTURES ALONE.

73. The editors gloss over their own illuminating textual criticism by refusing to take account of the implications of what they have observed. They conclude with this rather bland observation: "As a whole, however, his [Sumner's] text is remarkably correct in all essentials" (CM 17:428). One can't have it both ways. As Hanford and Dunn themselves acknowledge in their careful perusal of the text, misreadings, emendations, corrections, rearrangements, and combinations abound. In an attempt to address this situation, the editors maintain that their edition of the manuscript is "a compromise between a complete reproduction of the original, which would in any case be possible only in a facsimile, and a reduction of the text to some such consistency as might have been given it if a seventeenth century printer had set it, and Milton with his own eyes corrected the proof" (CM 17:427–28). In fact, a facsimile edition is finally in the works, a project that, given the advanced state of Milton studies, should have been undertaken generations ago.

74. Among the many instances that might be cited, Book 1, Chapter 27 ("*De Renovatione, Ubi Et De Vocatione*") is a case in point. In addition to changes in script (and therefore movements from one scribe to the next), entire passages appear in the SP 9/61 version that are not present in the Sumner text. Thus, after a paragraph on "The Calling of Man [*Vocatio*]" in the SP 9/61, a paragraph suddenly appears, only to be deleted by one of the scribes. Even without the block deletion (along with a marginal comment) that this paragraph sustains, it reveals internal deletions, insertions, and corrections of its own. Elaborating what has gone before and raising distinctions (with appropriate proof texts) between external and internal vocation (SP 9/61, 222–23), this passage has a dialogic quality of assertion and counterassertion. None of this is present in the Sumner text (either the Latin or the English) or in the Carey text, for that matter. All three texts (including the Latin) read as if the "original" were one continuous document, void of problems and uncertainties. Whether one focuses on the specific text alluded to here or on the document as a whole, there is no sense that fissures of any sort destabilize the text at various points. An entire subterranean world of text and metatext is eliminated in the cause of surface calm. Again, to what extent is it possible to assume that the Latin document known as the *De Doctrina Christiana* is consonant with the PRO manuscript referenced as SP 9/61? The answer is that such an assumption is beset by a multitude of problems, if not perils. Even those who address the Latin text of the *De Doctrina Christiana* should be wary of assuming that they are encountering anything like the "original." The result is that, even bypassing the Sumner and Carey translations, the Sumner edition of the Latin is in a very real sense "authored" by Sumner, whose work has been in various ways "improved upon" by Sumner's own silent collaborator William Sidney Walker. These all complicate the meaning of authorship in the ongoing debate over the question of who authored the *De Doctrina Christiana*.

75. In *This Great Argument*, Maurice Kelley addresses the issue of amanuenses and the presence of multiple "hands" (40–45; 218–51). In the case of Daniel Skinner, one is understandably prompted to ask why he elected to conclude his copying at page 196 and then resume his copying with pages 308, 571–74, etc. Although there is a long insertion in the hand Amanuensis A (SP 9/61, 549–52), Kelley fails to address its significance.

76. In the unpublished "Selected Papers of Maurice Kelley, 1935–1971" (housed at Princeton), one finds the letter of J. Milton French (to whom Kelley had sent a copy of his book *This Great Argument*). Although French praises the work, he raises interesting questions about Kelley's designations of the amanuenses: "May I raise a few questions about points that bothered me slightly to which you can probably return easy answers. Why do you call your amanuenses A, B, M, N, and O? Why not A, B, C, D, E, and F?" Why indeed?

77. For some reason that I cannot fathom, Kelley refers to page 307A (clearly numbered in the text) as 308a. He attempts to justify this substitution as follows: "page 308 is Skinner's copy of the page by Picard *numbered in these notes 308a*" (my italics). The qualifier "numbered in these

notes" is simply confusing. As if to elaborate, Kelley continues, "page 308a is the original Picard version that Skinner recopied to form page 308" (YP 6: 822). Not only is Picard's transcription actually numbered 307A, but it, in turn, is followed by a blank page (curiously numbered 156). This page is then followed by a page numbered 308, which is the recopied 307A. Both the pagination and the text of 308 are clearly in Skinner's hand. To make matters even more complicated, the pagination is such that below 307A is the number 4; above the 308, in turn, is likewise the number 4. (The practice of alternate numbering is followed elsewhere in the manuscript.) What accounts for the presence of the subscript and superscript is entirely uncertain. As John T. Shawcross notes, the pagination throughout the manuscript is not original with Picard: it might have originated with Skinner. The oddly numbered pages (made evident in the pagination 156 mentioned above) occur frequently. Shawcross speculates that they might be later notations inserted "to accord with the printed edition (?)" or to "indicate pages in the copy sent to the printer" (March 27, 2001, letter to the author).

    78. This is book 1, chapter 26: 6:517–18 in the YP; and 16:102–105 in the CM.

    79. According to Lewis and Short's *A Latin Dictionary*, s.v., the preferred form is *dumtaxat*. The term *Duntaxat* appears as part of the full title of the *De Doctrina Christiana*.

    80. The son of Aphareus and Arene, and the grandson of Perseus, Lynceus was gifted with "preternaturally keen sight." He was even able to see things underground (entry by James Hunter in the *Encyclopedia Mythica*, www.pantheon.org/mythical/articles/lynceus.html).

    81. Shawcross offers the very wise suggestion that the nature and textual "positioning" of the emendations, interlineations, and marginalia within the manuscript should be examined with an eye to the possibility that they may "fall into a pattern." Some, he suggests, may be "corrections," whereas others may represent an actual change (or clarification) of an idea. What is implied by such concerns is that the various "authors" of the text may include a number of "Miltons" over time. In short, the nature and positioning of emendations, interlineations, and the like, themselves have a bearing on the question of authorship (March 27, 2001, letter).

    82. For an illuminating discussion of Milton's amanuenses, see John T. Shawcross's entry "Amanuenses," in *A Milton Encyclopedia*, vol. 1, 41–43. Shawcross notes the presence of scribal emendations in various texts by Milton. See also Shawcross's "Notes on Milton's Amanuenses," *JEGP* 58 (1959): 29–38. The problems attendant upon securing dependable amanuenses are addressed by the early biographers. See, for example, the description by Jonathan Richardson, Sr., of the blind author faced with the task of "perpetually Asking One Friend or Another who Visited him to Write a Quantity of Verses he had ready in his Mind" (*Early Lives*, 289).

    83. See the entries for *amanuensis* and *servus* in Lewis and Short's *A Latin Dictionary*, s.v. For *amenuensis*, I take the form (*servus*) *a manu*, as cited in the *OED*, s.v.

    84. In *The Riverside Milton*, ed. Roy Flannagan (Boston, 1998), xix. Fascinating in this regard is Shawcross's discussion of Milton's Sonnet 11 ("I did but prompt the age"). A comparison of the transcription in Milton's hand with a copy of an unidentified scribe (in the Trinity College manuscript) makes clear the extent to which the Miltonic text has been altered by the amanuensis (xxvii, n. 6).

    85. *Early Lives*, 178. For a detailed discussion of the scribal alterations to which the first book (in the surviving manuscript) of *Paradise Lost* was subjected, see *The Manuscript of Milton's Paradise Lost Book I*, ed. Helen Darbishire (Oxford, 1931), esp. xviii–xix. Darbishire observes that although Milton might well have closely supervised the transcription of his epic, more than one of his amanuenses, "with the manuscript in hand, introduced an alteration where he thought it necessary, without Milton's authority" (xxii–xxiii). In "Orthography and the Text of *Paradise Lost*," John T. Shawcross raises a crucial question about the nature of the Miltonic text that is consistent with the one I have raised (in a decidedly different context) about the *De Doctrina Christiana*: "Can we be certain that the received texts" are the ones that Milton sought

to produce? "The problems of a blind man apparently dictating his work to a number of people of varying abilities cannot lead to assurance that the received texts are even near perfect" (*Language and Style in Milton: A Symposium in Honor of the Tercentenary of "Paradise Lost,"* ed. Ronald David Emma and John T. Shawcross [New York, 1967], 120).

86. See Burgess, *Milton not the Author*, 23, 27–29; Hunter, *Visitation Unimplor'd*, 98.

87. *Ramblings in the Elucidation of the Autograph of Milton* (London, 1861), 141.

88. *"De Doctrina Christiana*: Its Structural Principles and Its Unfinished State," *Milton Studies* 9, ed. James Simmonds (Pittsburgh, 1976), 243–60.

89. "On the State of Milton's *De Doctrina Christiana*," *ELN* 27 (1989): 43–48. Kelley attempts, unsuccessfully, I think, to distinguish between that which is "complete" and that which is "finished." Whereas the designation "complete" is "limited to content," the designation "finished" is limited to "presentation of content." Having ventured this distinction, Kelley then observes that because the terms "Finis" and "Totivs Operis Finis" appear at the end of the manuscript, Milton himself considered his treatise "complete" (46–47). See SP 9/61, 735. Cf. YP 6:807; and CM 17:420, 421.

90. Campbell et al., "The Provenance of *De Doctrina Christiana*," 93.

91. Ibid., 93–95.

92. Ibid., 95

93. *Palimpsest: Editorial Theory in the Humanities*, ed. George Bornstein and Ralph G. Williams (Ann Arbor, 1993), 1–2.

94. Julius Wellhausen (1844–1918) may have inaugurated his own version of the "higher criticism" or "documentary hypothesis" in the late nineteenth century, but the idea of finding various strata in the biblical text is much older. The idea of distinguishing the various amanuenses (A, B, M, N, etc.) in the *De Doctrina Christiana* is reminiscent of the references to the JEDP texts in the Hebrew Scriptures. For the biblical text, see David Noel Freedman, "Editing the Editors: Translation and Elucidation of the Text of the Bible," *Palimpsest*, 232.

95. "I Shall Be Spoken: Textual Boundaries, Authors, and Intent," *Palimpsest*, 48.

96. See the entries for *corruptus* and *corrumpere* in Lewis and Short's *A Latin Dictionary*, s.v.

97. "Considerations Touching the Right Editing of John Milton's *De Doctrina Christiana*," in *Editing Seventeenth-Century Prose*, ed. D. I. B. Smith (Toronto, 1972), 32.

98. William B. Hunter concurs in this logic but does so guardedly: "Thus it is a safe assumption that Hand Two [Picard] originally wrote out the entire work and that Hand One [Skinner] copied from it" the pages attributed to Skinner (*Visitation Unimplor'd*, 35). It is Hunter's cautious use of the word "assumption" that one should heed in drawing conclusions about the issue of provenance. If there is anything Hunter has taught us, it is to be wary of coming to hasty conclusions.

99. "Account of the Posthumous Theological Work of Milton" (January, 1824, 4–6).

100. *A Treatise of Christian Doctrine*, trans. Charles R. Sumner (Cambridge, 1825), xv–xvi.

101. *"Visitation Unimplor'd,"* 37.

102. Campbell et al., "The Provenance of *De Doctrina Christiana*," 90.

103. See Shawcross's entry "Amanuenses" in *A Milton Encyclopedia*, I, 42–43.

104. Campbell et al., "The Provenance of *De Doctrina Christiana*," 90.

105. Ibid., 91.

106. Shawcross, "Amanuenses," *A Milton Encyclopedia*, I, 43. For Aubrey, see his "Minutes of the Life of John Milton," *Early Lives*, 9.

107. The story is recounted in William Elton's "New Light on Milton's Amanuensis," *HLQ*, 26 (1963): 383–84.

108. *Auli Apronii vermehrte Reise-beschreibung von Franco Porto der Chur-Brandenburg durch Teutschland, Holland und England*, 69. Cited by Elton, 383.

109. Elton has "Pickard," but Campbell et al. correct the reference, which is "Piskard." Although the record book covers the period 1683–1701 rather than the earlier period of 1678, Elton suggests that Pickard [Piskard], that is, Picard, might have been institutionalized both in 1687 and in 1700.

110. Hunter, "Responses," 36.

111. For references, see John T. Shawcross, comp., *Milton: A Bibliography for the Years 1624–1700* (Binghamton, 1984), s.v.

112. The fullest account of Skinner, with citations from the primary sources, is to be found in Campbell et al., 67–93.

113. Parker, *Milton: A Biography*, vol. 1, 610–11.

114. Parker, *Milton: A Biography*, vol. 2, 1130–31 n. 17. The justification for much of Parker's narrative springs from Aubrey, who refers to "Mr. Skinner" as Milton's "disciple." This for Parker is the individual that Aubrey subsequently identifies as "Mr. Skinner, a merchant's son, in Mark Lane." For pertinent documents, see J. Milton French, *The Life Records of John Milton*, 5 vols. (New Brunswick, 1954), vol. 5, 69–70, and passim.

115. Parker, *Milton: A Biography*, vol. 1, 611.

116. Campbell et al., 73.

117. Cited in YP 6:37.

118. It is interesting to note that J. Milton French, " 'That Late Villain Milton'," *PMLA* 55 (1940): 103, actually views the informant's statement as support for Skinner's self-representation as the put-upon scholar to whom was bequeathed the essential writings we discuss here.

119. "The Provenance of *De Doctrina Christiana*," 91. See Parker: "Milton's widow [Elizabeth Minshull] told Aubrey 'she gave all his papers to his nephew' [Edward Phillips]." (*Milton: A Biography*, vol 2, 1167, n. 89). See Darbishire, ed. *Early Lives*, 4.

120. Kelley cites other instances of Skinner's "manifest untrustworthiness," that is, his propensity to lie as a means of furthering his own ends. See, for example, Kelley's discussion of Skinner's lying to Samuel Pepys, an individual who supported Skinner in his time of need (YP 6:37, n. 7).

121. In addition to Campbell et al., 67–93, see French, " 'That Late Villain Milton'," 102–15, with Maurice Kelley's "Addendum: The Later Career of Daniel Skinner," 116–18; Parker, *Milton: A Biography*, vol. 1, 610–11. See also H. Scherpbier, *Milton in Holland: A Study of the Literary Relations of England and Holland before 1730* (1933; Folcroft, Pa., 1969).

122. For an account of Williamson, see *DNB*, vol. 21, 473–78. John Evelyn describes Sir Joseph as a grasping and "subtle" individual (474).

123. In *Milton: A Biography*, vol. 2, 1131–32, n. 22, Parker details all the double crosses of which Skinner was guilty. Having perpetrated a series of double crosses, Skinner, in the end, "double-crossed Milton" through his disavowal of Milton's teachings and the betrayal of his memory. Skinner was not, however, the only double-crosser. As Parker points out, Elzevier too was nothing more than "a glib liar and double-crosser."

124. Campbell et al. suggest that Pepys was willing to accommodate Skinner in part because Pepys was at the time having an affair with Skinner's sister Mary (70), a reason that, although cynical, has much to recommend it. Nonetheless, one suspects Pepys also took a natural liking to the young man.

125. Samuel Pepys, *Letters and the Second Diary of Samuel Pepys*, ed. R. G. Howarth (London, 1933), 57–65.

126. Keeping hold of the papers, Elsevier ultimately returned them to Skinner's father,

who, in turn, placed them in the hands of Sir Joseph Williamson. Once in possession of the papers, Sir Joseph promptly had them deposited (still in their wrapper) in Whitehall, where they were not discovered until 1823. (See Elsevier's letters of February and March 1677 to Skinner's father, as cited in Campbell et al., 85–86, and the comments on the disposition of the papers [87].)

　　127. Pepys, *Letters and the Second Diary of Samuel Pepys*, 57–65.